RJ
506
A9
A924
1991

AUTISM: STRATEGIES FOR CHANGE

AUTISM
Strategies for Change

A COMPREHENSIVE APPROACH TO
THE EDUCATION AND TREATMENT
OF CHILDREN WITH AUTISM AND
RELATED DISORDERS

*Edited by Gerald Groden, Ph.D.
and M. Grace Baron, Ph.D.*

Foreword by ROBERT BOWLES
President, National Society for Children and Adults with Autism

Gardner Press, New York & London

Copyright © 1991 by Gardner Press, Inc.
All rights reserved. No part of this book may be reproduced in any form, by photostat, microfilm, retrieval system or any means now known or later devised, without written permission of the publisher.

GARDNER PRESS, INC.
19 UNION SQUARE WEST
NEW YORK, NEW YORK 10003

ALL FOREIGN ORDERS EXCEPT CANADA AND SOUTH AMERICA TO:

EUROSPAN/GARDNER
3 HENRIETTA STREET
COVENT GARDEN
LONDON, ENGLAND WC2E 8LU

Library of Congress Cataloging-in-Publication Data

Autism : strategies for change.

  Includes bibliographies and index.
  1. Autism—Treatment. 2. Autistic children—
Rehabilitation. 3. Behavioral assessment of children.
4. Autistic children—Education. I. Groden, Gerald.
II. Baron, M. Grace. [DNLM: 1. Autism—in infancy &
childhood. 2. Autism—therapy. 3. Education, Special.
WM 203.5 A9385]
RJ506.A9A924 1987   618.92'8982   87-8682
ISBN 0-89876-135-2, Clothbound
ISBN 0-89876-184-0, Tradepaper

Design by Raymond Solomon

Printed in the United States of America

Foreword

AUTISM: Strategies for Change is an apt title, as it delineates important problems and then clearly puts forth both time-proven and innovative methods for their resolution—many of the latter were developed by the authors of this volume. Clinicians, parents, and students of autism who are, or want to be, advocates for change will find in this book a blueprint, and much detail, on how to bring change about. This applies at the level of program planning and management as well as of clinical or education practice.

The Center from which this book originates has been a leader in the field in ensuring that all necessary services—including psychological, educational, developmental, communication, psychiatric and medical assistance, and physical and occupational therapy—are provided in a flexible manner so that the "whole" child or young adult is helped to develop to his or her maximum potential and family stability and integrity are maximized.

The model presented is admirable in many respects. It emphasizes the importance of children and young adult learning procedures to manage their own behaviors instead of being externally controlled, thus acquiring the tools to *help themselves* in difficult times. This emphasis on self-control makes this a unique volume in clinical practice with persons who have autism and an important addition to the growing literature on *positive* programs. I am also happy to see an emphasis on working intensively with families to enhance children's home behaviors and functioning, which too often has been a neglected area. The book also rightly underscores the fact that autism is still poorly understood, and so an ideal model of services must include research, and the development of new procedures—behavioral, developmental, and medical—if real progress is to be made.

I commend the authors for bringing these activities to our attention. Both professionals and parents can learn from the material presented herein to help make this a better world for our children and young adults. I hope they will apply what they learn, and will use it as a foundation for the development of even more effective approaches.

Robert Bowles
President
National Society for Children
and Adults with Autism

Preface

Adequate programs for children and young adults with autism and related disorders still do not exist in many communities. These individuals in the past either received no services or were inappropriately placed with persons with other types of problems, and consequently failed to progress. All too often the result has been wasted lives, grief to families, and finally incarceration in state hospitals. In the past, where programs did exist, they were often based on disparate and inappropriate theories. For example, an early theory guiding services to these children was psychoanalysis. Recently, as our understanding of autism has improved, new approaches have been developed that are more appropriate to the needs of this population.

This volume presents the philosophy of a *full-service, real-life* approach to services for these persons, assessment and treatment strategies for many of the disciplines involved, and systems that integrate disciplinary activities. The book was written by professionals actively engaged in providing treatment and educational services to these children and young adults. Although the services and strategies presented exist in a particular setting, the Groden Center, they are applicable in any setting, i.e., public schools or private schools or centers, which has available to it the services of the necessary disciplines.

The book is intended for those who are currently, or expect in the future, to be working with children and young adults with autism or related disorders. Specifically it should be of interest to advanced undergraduates, graduate students, and professionals in the fields of severe developmental disabilities, behavioral disorders, and other severe handicapping conditions. This volume also is intended to be helpful to parents of children with these problems who have some familiarity with the literature in this field. Because it reflects innovative thinking and procedures based upon current knowledge and practices in the field, readers in the area of education, as well as those in clinically oriented programs, should find it of interest.

Finally, to be concise, he or his, etc., is used through the text to indicate he or she, etc.

This book is warmly dedicated to the children and young adults whom we have had the privilege of helping, to their families who have worked so hard with us to improve their childrens' opportunities and who have expended so much effort in the support and development of our programs when that support was so badly needed. This book is also dedicated to the staff of the Groden Center, at all levels, who throughout the years have demonstrated their dedication to, and deep concern for, children and young adults with autism and similar disorders. Finally, appreciation is expressed to state and local agencies, as well as individuals, who have provided the necessary support to make these programs possible.

Acknowledgments

We want to express our gratitude to Patricia Wisocki, Ph.D., who encouraged us to begin this book, and to other members of the Groden Center's Professional Advisory Board, including Gary LaVigna, Ph.D., Beth Sulzer-Azaroff, Ph.D., Anne Donnellan, Ph.D., J. Gregory Olley, Ph.D., Marty Pollack, Ph.D., Ellen Reese, M.A. and Paul Weisberg, Ph.D., who supported our efforts to not only provide quality services but also to communicate about them to others in the field.

Our colleagues and co-contributors, June Groden, Joseph Cautela and Dale Domingue, deserve special mention for their very helpful suggestions throughout.

An edited volume relies heavily on the skills and the forbearance of a secretarial staff. We thank our secretaries, Jean Murphy, Lucy Ferreira and Kathleen Leeming, for their competence and good will, and Sharon Zarrella for her contributions to the organization of the final manuscript.

The editors also wish to express appreciation to their parents who have always served as a source of inspiration and encouragement.

Table of Contents

Foreword — v

Preface — vii

Acknowledgments — ix

Contributors — xvii

1 Introduction — 1

    Description of A Child with Autism by a Mother
    Autism
        Description
        Etiology
        Behavior Therapy
        Current Issues
        Program Overview
        Chapter Descriptions
        References

2 Behavioral Assessment Procedures for the Evaluation of Children with Autism — 21

    Problem Definition
    Establishment of Treatment Goals
        Specificity
        Workability
        Relevance

Establishing Priorities Among Behavioral Domains
Present Performance Level: Baseline Assessment
Antecedent and Consequent Events
Behavioral Observation
   Frequency Measures
   Interval Recordings
A Contextual Example
Home Visit
A Sample Behavior Evaluation
   Behavioral Evaluation Format
Events Found to Be Reinforcing
Events Found to Be Aversive
Curriculum Domains
   Independent Living Skills
   Social Interaction
   Idiosyncratic Problem Behaviors
Summary
A Final Comment
References

3 Behavioral Programming: Expanding our Clinical Repertoire   49

The Current Behavioral Repertoire
Basics of Behavioral Programming
   Choice of Intervention
The Expanded Behavioral Repertoire: Self-Control Procedures
   Relaxation Training
   Covert Conditioning
Conclusions
References

4 Intellectual Functioning and Assessment   75

Intellectual Functioning
   Level of Functioning
   Pattern of Functioning
   Specific Cognitive Deficits
Intellectual Assessment
   Choices of Instruments
   Dealing with Behavioral and Attentional Deficits
Utilization of Assessment Results

      A Behavioral Sample
      Basis for Discussion with Parents
      Individualized Program Planning and Evaluation
   References

5 Teaching Communication to Children with Severe Language Impairment   99

   Purpose of Chapter
   A Developmental-Ecological-Behavioral Model
      Principle I
      Principle II
      Principle III
      Principle IV
      Principle V
      Principle VI
   Evaluating Language Disorders in Children with Autism
      Referral
      History
      Behavioral Observations (Communication Emphasis)
      Content
      Comprehension
      Production
      Alternate Forms of Communication
      Other Considerations
   Treating Language Disorders in Children with Autism
      Setting Goals
      Reevaluation to Note Progress
      Effectiveness of Treatment
   Specific Treatment Contexts
      Language in Play
      Communication in Daily Routines
   Summary
   References

6 Medical Evaluation and Management of the Child with Autism   135

   Medical History
      Family History
      Preconception and Gestation
      Perinatal Period

Neonatal Period
Early Development Data
Pediatric Evaluation
  Initial Observations
  Anthropometric Data
  General Physical Examination
  Neurologic Examination
  Behavioral Data
Laboratory Investigations
  Electroencephalogram
  Biochemical Evaluation
Treatment
  Drug Treatments
  Vitamin/Metabolic Therapies
  General Health Care
Conclusions
References

7 Parent and Family Involvement   151

   Literature Survey of Behavioral Parent Training
     Childhood Problems
     Content
     Individual versus Group Training
     Settings
     Techniques
     Parent Cooperation
     Autism
   A Model for Maximizing Family Competence
     Goals of the Model
     Elements of the Model
   Conclusions
   References

8 Teaching for Performance: A Guide for Preparing
   Clinicians and Teachers of the Severely Handicapped   179

       Personnel Preparation: Current Status
       Teaching for Performance Model: A Conceptual Base
         The Field/Service Setting
         The Trainee
         The Program Philosophy

Personnel Instruction Program (PIP)
Description
Application
Summary
References

9 A Systems Approach for Educators and Clinicians Working with Persons with Autism: Putting It All Together — 203

Assessment
  Comparison of Functional and Traditional Assessment
  Sources of Data for Functional Assessment
  Summary of Assessment
Plan Development
  The Spectrum: A Model for Integrating Personalized Plans
  Designation of Plan Components
  Summary
Implementation
  Relationship Between Planners and Implementors
  Environmental Design
  Scheduling Concerns
  Intervention Strategies
  Documentation Procedures
Ongoing Data Analysis
  Analysis and Review Procedures
  Considerations in Program Change
  Summary of Ongoing Data Analysis
Chapter Summary
References

Index — 237

Contributors

M. Grace Baron, Ph.D.
Associate Professor of Psychology
Director of E. W. Amen Nursery School
Wheaton College
Norton, Mass.

Joseph R. Cautela, Ph.D.
Professor of Psychology
Behavior Therapy Institute
Sudbury, Mass.

Marie Chesnick, M.Ed.
Boston Children's Hospital

Dale Domingue, M.S.
The Groden Center
Providence, R.I.

Gerald Groden, Ph.D.
Director
The Groden Center
Providence, R.I.
Adjunct, Associate Professor
 of Psychology
University of Rhode Island
Kingston, R.I.

June Groden, Ph.D.
Director
The Groden Center
Providence, R.I.
Adjunct, Assistant Professor
 of Psychology
University of Rhode Island
Kingston, R.I.

Leesa Mann, M.A.
Child Development Center
 of Rhode Island Hospital
Providence, R.I.

Anne Pentecost, M.Ed.
The Groden Center
Providence, R.I.

Siegfried Pueschel, M.D.
Medical Director
Child Development Center
 of Rhode Island Hospital
Associate Professor of Pediatrics
Brown University Program
 in Medicine
Providence, R.I.

Susan E. Stevenson, M.Ed.
The Groden Center
Providence, R.I.

Suzanne Swope, Ed.D.
Professor of Language
 and Communication
Emerson College
Boston, Mass.

Patricia Wisocki, Ph.D.
Professor of Psychology
University of Massachusetts
Amherst, Mass.

CHAPTER

1

Introduction

Gerald Groden, Ph.D.
Grace Baron, Ph.D.

Description of a Child with Autism by a
   Mother
Autism
   Description
   Etiology
   Behavior Therapy

Current Issues
Program Overview
Chapter Descriptions
References

DESCRIPTION OF A CHILD WITH AUTISM BY A MOTHER

"We start with an image—a tiny, golden child on hands and knees, circling round and round a spot on the floor in mysterious, self-absorbed delight. She does not look up, though she is smiling and laughing; she does not call our attention to the mysterious object of her pleasure. She does not see us at all. She and the spot are all there is, and though she is eighteen months old, an age for touching, tasting, pointing, pushing, exploring, she is doing none of these. She does not walk, or crawl up stairs, or pull herself to her feet to reach for objects. She doesn't want any objects. Instead, she circles her spot. Or she sits, a long chain in her hand, snaking it up and down, up and down, watching it coil, for twenty minutes, half an hour—until someone comes, moves her or feeds her or gives her another toy, or perhaps a book." (Clairborne-Park, 1982).

AUTISM

Description

AUTISM AS A DISTINCT DEVELOPMENtal problem was first brought to the general attention of professionals in 1943 by L. Kanner, a psychiatrist at Johns Hopkins University (Kanner, 1943). He described a group of children who did not relate to others, evidenced a delay in speech development and did not use what speech they did develop for communicative purposes, engaged in repetitive behavior, showed distress upon change, possessed good rote memory, and were relatively normal in physical appearance—and the term he applied to these children was "infantile autism." He used the word infantile because of his observation that autistic abnormalities had already been present in these children in infancy. He chose the word autistic because of the children's apparent lack of interest in relating to others. Following Kanner's paper, other reports appeared that described such children (Despert, 1951; Van Krevelen & Kuipers, 1962; Bosch, 1970; Bakwin, 1954). Careful review of the literature also reveals accounts of autistic-like children even prior to Kanner's paper (Darr & Worden, 1951; Vaillant, 1962), although the problem was not called by that name. Since Kanner first described infantile autism and up to the present, there have been confusion and a lack of agreement concerning the children to whom the term applies. It is not unusual for writers to use the terms autism; childhood schizophrenia, a psychosis of childhood often characterized by a greater degree of language facility as well as delusions and hallucinations; and childhood psychosis, a term including all types of severe childhood psychopathology, interchangeably (Laufer & Gair, 1969). As Rutter (1978) has pointed out, the fact that Kanner chose the term autistic was unfortunate as it had been employed much earlier by Bleuler (1950) to refer to the withdrawal into fantasy displayed by schizophrenic persons and so implied a rich fantasy life, and also because it suggested a relationship to adult schizophrenia.

Subsequent investigators have attempted to reduce the confusion by carefully studying these children and describing their distinctive characteristics. In an attempt at parsimony, Eisenberg and Kanner (1956) reduced the essential symptoms of autism to two: extreme aloneness and preoccupation with the preservation of sameness. In an attempt to clarify the distinct features of the disorder further, Rutter (1966) and Rutter and Lockyer (1967) compared children diagnosed as autistic with those with other emotional or behavioral disorders to determine which characteristics were present in all, or nearly all, children with autism, and which were present only occasionally. Three symptoms emerged that appeared to be uniquely related to autism: (1) failure to develop social relationships; (2) language retardation with impaired comprehension, including echolalia and pronominal reversal, and (3) ritualistic or compulsive behaviors. Other characteristics sometimes seen in the autistic groups were repetitive movements, especially of the hands and fingers; a short attention span; self-injury; delayed bowel control; and the smelling of objects.

Ornitz and Ritvo (1968) have emphasized perceptual disturbances as the primary symptom of autism, stating that these children show either hyper- or hypo-responsiveness, or that their degree of responsiveness alternates between these two extremes. Rendle-Short (1969) lists 14 symptoms of autism, and states that seven of these must be present for the diagnosis to be made. Rutter (1978) has suggested a multiaxial approach to the classification of autism in which the behavioral syndrome, the intellectual level, the physical status, and the psychosocial situation are described on separate, independent axes, as all these variables could have a bearing on whether or not the term autism should be used.

In recognition of the problem, the National Society for Children and Adults with Autism (1978), with the assistance of its professional advisory board (many of whose members have been in the forefront of research in the field), has proposed a definition of autism. The society defines it as a behavioral syndrome, the essential features of which are typically manifested before 30 months of age and include disturbances of (1) developmental rates and/or sequences; (2) responses to sensory stimuli; (3) speech, language, and cognitive capacities; and (4) capacities to relate to people, events, and objects. It should be noted that according to this definition, all of the stated characteristics must be present for the diagnosis to be applicable. Behaviors that may accompany the syndrome, but are not necessarily a part of it, include lability of mood, lack of appreciation of real dangers, self-injurious behaviors, and stereotypic and repetitive movements of limbs or the entire body. The society's list of four necessary characteristics is compatible with Kanner's initial behavioral descriptions (good rote memory can be covered in item 1), and also with Eisenberg and Kanner's two essential features. Eisenberg and Kanner's "preoccupation with the preservation of sameness" and Rutter's "ritualistic or compulsive behaviors" can be covered by item 4, disturbance of "capacities to relate to people, events, and objects." Ornitz and Ritvo's emphasis on pathological responsiveness is also included. The American Psychiatric Association's *Diagnostic and Statistical Manual of Mental Disorders* (1980) now includes autism as a pervasive developmental disorder specifically to recognize the distortions in autism in multiple, basic psychological functions. Recently the syndrome of autism has been related to that of the learning disabled (Shea and Mesibov, 1985). Almost certainly, further research will affect this definition. Readers interested in reviewing historically important writings on descriptions of children with autism are referred to Donnellan's book, *Classic Readings in Autism* (1985).

Etiology

The role of parents and family factors in the etiology and maintenance of this disorder has been a subject of controversy. Although Kanner described the parents of these children in such a way that might have led others to view them as the cause of their children's disorders, he did not suggest a causal relationship himself. In his classic 1943 paper, he notes:

One other fact stands out prominently. In the whole group, there are very few really warmhearted fathers and mothers. For the most part, the parents, grandparents, and collaterals are persons strongly preoccupied with abstractions of a scientific or artistic nature and limited in genuine interest in people. . . . The question arises whether or not or to what extent this fact has contributed to the condition of the children. The children's aloneness from the beginning of life makes it difficult to attribute the whole picture exclusively to the type of the early parental relations with our patients. We must, then, assume that these children have come into the world with innate inability to form the usual, biologically provided affective contact with people just as other children come into the world with innate physical or intellectual handicaps.

Other investigators and clinicians (Ferster, 1961; Garcia & Sarvis, 1964; Ward, 1970) did make the causal leap, an assumption that later was referred to by Kanner as "cherchez la mère." Bettleheim (1967), who directed the well-known Orthogenic School in Chicago, stressed the critical importance of parental rejection in the etiology of autism and advocated separation from the rejecting parent during therapy. According to Lovaas and colleagues (1978): p. 387

From this point of view, autism is seen as a defense against a parental environment that is singularly cold and potentially destructive. This presumed parental psychopathology, combined with the child's conviction that he is threatened with total destruction by insensitive and irrational powers, causes the child to withdraw into his inner autistic world. Angry parental rejection of the child is seen as the cause behind the child's failure to form normal relationships toward people; as a result, he never moved on developmentally to relate (cathect) to the external world. His peculiar behaviors are viewed as manifestations (symptoms) of this combined effect of fear of his parents' anger toward him and the correlated failure of ego development. For example, the autistic child's excessive preoccupation with rotating and spinning both himself and other objects is seen as symptomatic of the inescapable, vicious circle he is caught in—a cycle of longing and fear, of wanting and needing so much from other people and, at the same time, of being mortally afraid to let that longing be known, either to the other people or to himself. Insistence on sameness is thought to be an expression of a feeling of helplessness about influencing the external environment and is thus an attempt to reaffirm a limited hold on an otherwise fluctuating and frightening world. Self-destructive behaviors are often considered to reflect the child's attempts to injure his mother because she had hurt him. When he hurts himself, he is retaliating on his own terms.

These psychogenic hypotheses, however, were generally based on uncontrolled observations, and results of systematic investigation of them and therapies stemming from them were largely negative (Rutter, 1968; Rutter & Bartak, 1971). In 1964 Rimland published his highly influential book, *Infantile Autism*, which thoroughly reviewed the existing literature and postulated a neurobiological basis for the disorder. At present, most professionals who have a knowledge of these children favor a physiological basis for the syndrome, "with at least several physical and/or genetic bases" (Ritvo & Freeman, 1984; Morgan, 1986). With the increasing acceptance of a physiological basis, psychotherapy has gradually given way to more structured approaches. These approaches have provided a more systematic and ordered environment for learning, and have been reported to produce more positive gains (Schopler et al., 1971; Bartak & Rutter, 1973; Rutter & Bartak, 1971). In the study of Schopler and colleagues, the variables of attention, appropriate affect, relating, and nonpsychotic behavior were rated as the children alternated between relatively structured and unstructured environments. Structure means the extent to which an adult determined material to be worked with, the amount of time the child was to work, and the manner in which the child was to work. The results indicated that the children tended to react more favorably to the structured than the nonstructured setting.

BEHAVIOR THERAPY

The most promising approach to date has been that of behavior modification or behavior therapy, "a behavioral science technique which involves the application of principles derived from research in experimental psychology to alleviate human suffering and enhance human functioning. Unlike many other treatment methods, an intrinsic component of the behavioral technique is systematic, ongoing monitoring and evaluation of the effectiveness of treatment procedures. The goal of the behavioral approach is to improve self-control and independence by expanding an individual's skills and abilities in a wide variety of areas" (Brown et al., 1976).

Behavioral therapy has its roots in laboratory-based psychological studies of learning. After many years of careful research into such questions as how and under what conditions learning occurs, initiated by such eminent scientists as Pavlov (1927), Watson (1920), and Skinner (1938), generalized principles or laws that govern learning became evident. These principles highlighted the critical role of the antecedents and consequence of behavior, if that behavior is to be learned, and the differential effects of varying types of consequences. Important factors such as amount, timing, and scheduling of consequences also became evident. The body of knowledge specifying the role of consequences of behaviors in learning came to be known as operant learning or operant conditioning (Skinner, 1953). With this base of knowledge obtained in the laboratory, researchers began to assess the usefulness of the knowledge in helping persons with problems in schools, clinics, and institutions. They reasoned that these newly discovered laws might be effectively employed to assist persons to reduce or "unlearn" abnormal or maladaptive behaviors, and, in their place, to learn more normal or adaptive behaviors. Some of these landmark investigations were conducted by Skinner (1954), in his application of operant learning techniques to hospitalized psychotic adults; by Ferster and DeMyer (1962), who demonstrated that children with autism could show systematic learning in an environment in which stimuli and consequences were carefully related in accordance with learning theory principles to produce such learning; and by Baer and Sherman (1964), who showed that operant methods, including shaping, could be used effectively to teach these children to speak. Other important investigators included Wolfe et al. (1964), who showed that these same methods could reduce or eliminate behavior abnormalities in children with autism, and Lovaas and his colleagues, who attempted to increase social responsiveness in these children (Lovaas et al., 1965a), as well as decrease their self-injurious behaviors (Lovaas et al., 1965b).

Although the operant or consequence-based behavioral techniques were the first behavioral procedures to be used with children with autism, they represented only a portion of the available range of behavioral procedures. Wolpe (1958) pioneered the use of Pavlovian or classical conditioning-based behavioral procedures to eliminate fears and anxieties. One of these procedures, systematic desensitization, has been used widely and has spurred the development of many additional techniques based on respondent learning principles, including progressive relaxation and thought stopping (Groden & Cautela, 1981; LaVigna & Donnellan, 1985).

From these roots the field of behavior therapy has expanded its range to such problems as delinquency, sexual disorders, addictions, and neuroses (Bellack and colleagues, 1984). In addition, newer procedures, such as cognitive behavior therapy (Ellis, 1970; Beck, 1976; Meichenbaum, 1977), self-control therapies (Thoreson & Mahoney, 1974), and covert or imaginal procedures (Cautela & Kearney, 1986; Cautela & Baron, 1977), have also been developed.

Currently behavior therapy is broadly accepted as the most well-developed, reliable, and effective treatment intervention with persons who are autistic and severely behaviorally disordered. Its current development is marked by the following features:

1. The standard operant conditioning procedures—such as positive reinforcement, extinction, negative reinforcement, punishment—as well as more recent elaborations of these—such as self-control procedures—provide the clinician with a broad range of interventions. Behavior therapy has, in fact, evolved into a comprehensive set of tenets and procedures to be used with all populations for a wide variety of clinical problems. A number of reviews of behavioral procedures are available for the interested reader, including Foxx (1980); Groden & Cautela (1981); Kazdin (1984); Koegel et al., (1982); LaVigna & Donnellan-Walsh (1985); and Matson & DiLorenzo (1984).

2. There is a high degree of systematic research and related professional involvement in conferences, publications, and demonstration and service projects by behaviorally oriented clinicians and investigators.

3. There is increased collaboration by behavioral researchers and clinicians with medical, developmental, educational, and psychopharmacological colleagues in jointly addressing the issues of explanation and treatment in autism. Similarly, a growing awareness of human ecology has merged productively with a behavioral technology so that efforts at assessment and treatment can now be guided by an appreciation of each client's role in the "physical and contingency mileau" (Rogers-Warren & Warren, 1977) of his or her everyday life.

CURRENT ISSUES

An awareness of autism as a distinct developmental problem and the emergence of an effective and expansive behaviorally based technology present service providers and clinical researchers with support for further clarifying the nature of autism and its treatment. But it is apparent that the problems of children with autism and similar disorders and their families are complex and multifaceted. Designers and providers of services must be sensitive to this, and must create services that maximize the child's success in day-to-day functioning. Our early efforts and successes in understanding and intervening in the condition of autism must now meet a larger challenge: to organize what we know and what we can do in such a way as to provide the best possible services that we can to a child with autism. There are many issues that bear discussion relative to this; three of the most important are presented here.

Issue 1 Comprehensive, real-life, life span versus narrow, confined, age-limited services. Children with severe disabilities require comprehensive services, as well as the continuum of ever-changing, life-long services, if they and their families are going to achieve their full potential. While a day treatment, educational or vocational program may be the core intervention arrangement, services such as an extended day program, community or home-based respite services, family education and support, recreational activities, individual counseling, and time-limited or extended residential placement may be required at various times in a client's life. Providing only mandated services, offering services apart from and sometimes unrelated to real-life circumstances, or initiating and terminating services according to bureaucratically determined age levels can all limit the possible achievements of these children, and may even cause regression to levels already surpassed. The spectrum of services provided must be sensitive to the importance of each child developing to his full potential, to family needs, and to lifetime demands and opportunities. Otherwise we will have an imbalance in the child's development or the family system, which will have negating effects, ultimately harmful to the child. Providing stellar services to the behaviorally disordered child during the day, for example, while neglecting problems that the parent is having in coping with the child at home may result in a seriously dysfunctional family and eventual residential or institutional placement of the child.

Services must also be real life, in that they are related to real-life challenges and frequently occur in normal, real-life environments (Bronfenbrenner, 1974; Brown et al., 1976). Donnellan (1980) encourages service providers to ask themselves: "If this child is not taught this task, will someone have to do it for him?" This should always be kept in mind when planning curricula. Too often children can be seen performing tasks that no one would ever have to perform for him if he could not. Insisting on a variety of activities in real-life community settings helps to prevent artificiality of tasks, and also ensures that children learn relevant and necessary life skills, and that they learn them in a natural environment that encourages incidental learning and obviates the necessity for additional generalization training. Finally, children, service providers, and families are plagued by age-determined inclusionary/exclusionary requirements that prevent services when they should be offered and end them when they should be continued, and even extended. This can occur both because of the service provider's self-imposed restrictions and as a result of bureaucratic regulations. Chapters 2, 3, 8, and 9 will elaborate on several of these areas.

Issue 2   The child's role in the treatment program. Related to the critical issue of meeting a child's real-life needs is the question of the nature of the child's role in his own education and treatment program. Implicit in most decision-making and intervention procedures with children who are autistic or severely behaviorally disordered is the assumption that the child's role is a relatively *passive* one. He is assumed, at best, to be the "recipient" of our best technology and services. He or she is the person "for whom" individualized program plans are made, and "for whom" living and working arrangements are chosen. He is the person "about whom" data is taken, and he is the person "to whom" interventions are applied. The implicit (and thereby unexamined) assumption of external control results unfortunately in a child whose active participation and adaptation to real-life settings are limited by the availability of services and service providers.

A critical need, as we see it, in providing effective services is the elaboration of our existing intervention models to furnish our clients with skills in controlling and managing their own behaviors. Effective and complete service provision requires our clients not only to learn skills that are generalizable beyond the instructional setting, but also to learn to play as central a role as possible in managing their responses to the ever-changing requirement of real-life environments throughout their lives. What are the principles and procedures that will teach this new behavioral technology of client participation and self-control? Chapter 3 presents a rationale for expanding our current behavioral technology to include client involvement in learning self-controlling strategies for behavior changes. Two procedures, relaxation training and imagery-based covert conditioning procedures, are detailed.

Issue 3 Service responsibility. Who should be responsible for providing care, education, and treatment to persons with autism and other severe behavioral disorders? As Table 1-1 illustrates, this seemingly benign question about management of services has significant implications regarding *who* receives services, *who* oversees services, *what* services are received, and *where* and by *whom* the services are given.

Historically, service provision to children with disabilities, especially those with severe handicaps, has resided in the medical realm. Within this medical model, children were seen primarily as "patients." This model has received much scrutiny and criticism. One of the problems has been that while medical problems were well attended to, problems in other critical areas often were neglected. Thus we might have a child who was receiving excellent medical care but was not being taught critical social or self-care skills. Problems with this type of service delivery gradually led to the multidisciplinary team, in which specialists from many areas would evaluate the child and prescribe treatment. Again because of the continuation of traditional lines of funding, medical personnel played a dominant role. In the recent past, this model has become more flexible, sometimes with responsibility residing in the discipline that addressed the child's most difficult problems. Problems occurred with this model as well, however, as frequently there was an insufficient degree of integration of the various disciplines to provide a coordinated approach to the child's assessment and services (Favell et al., 1984). Also, the primary orientation was still usually medical. This led to a demand for coordination, and it is now more generally the case that such coordination among disciplines occurs. The term interdisciplinary gradually became preferable to multidisciplinary, implying that

Table 1-1
Comparison of Service Models

	Who Receives Services	Who Oversees Services?	What Services Are Given?	Where Are the Services Given?	By Whom Are Services Given?
Medical model	The child, according to diagnostic criteria	Physician or other designated specialist	Medical, diagnostic, treatment, and prevention services; referral to other services	Hospital or clinic	Multidisciplinary teams who give evaluations. Specialists—e.g., R.N., OT, PT, speech therapist—who provide services
Educational model	The child, according to the categories of testing and placement	Educational administrator	Academic and prevocational assessment and related services	School	Multidisciplinary teams who give evaluations. Educational specialists certified in MR, ED, etc. are the primary providers.
Whole-child model	The child, the child's family, and others, based on the child's program needs	Generalists with training in meeting multiple needs of the whole person throughout the person's life	A continuum of comprehensive services to meet the ever-changing needs of the whole child in such areas as: • Health • Education • Vocation • Recreation • Personal/social skills	Developmental centers for children who are normal or have special needs. These centers may be the site for services given, or may function to coordinate and monitor services provided elsewhere	A generalist, such as teacher-therapist prepared in a range of areas in human development. These persons may provide direct service or train and supervise others (e.g., parents) in the child's various environments.

such coordination and interdigitation did exist. More recently the term transdisciplinary has appeared, in which the fine line between disciplinary responsibilities is reduced and members take on some of the responsibilities that usually would be carried out by members of another discipline. Transdisciplinary has also come to mean that one member of the team would be able to carry out many of the recommendations of the other members of the team. The model has evolved so that this member may be a parent or another person in the natural community.

With the advent of Public Law 94:142, it appears that the pendulum is swinging in the direction of educational responsibility for the financing, and to some extent provision and monitoring, of comprehensive services for handicapped children. This trend is not without its problems. [1]The first is financial. Educational systems are suddenly being asked to fund comprehensive, complicated programs without the necessary financial resources. Schools are complaining that they cannot afford currently mandated services, or frequently they are supplying minimum services, with negative effects upon the children and their families.[1] Another problem is the inadequate preparation of educational personnel to undertake this complex responsibility. Although it appears that the responsibility is being transferred from medicine to education in the interest of sensitivity to the complex and multitudinous needs of children with handicaps, educational personnel are ostensibly no better equipped for this role than were physicians.

What is the answer? This is a most difficult question.[1] However, if federal legislation is intent, as it seems to be, on placing the responsibility for developmental programs for children with all conceivable disabilities under the jurisdiction of one system or authority, then that system or authority should be one that is sensitive to the needs of the *whole* child, no matter how many or what the disabilities may be, and unbiased in the provision of these services. One model for services might be child development centers; there are now schools throughout the country under the aegis of persons broadly trained in child development that would utilize the services of the various disciplines, such as psychology, education, physical therapy, and medicine. The degree to which these services are present could depend on the number of disabled children. The relative emphasis of a discipline in a particular center would depend upon the needs of that center. This alternative requires a conceptual shift from an educational to a developmental, or *whole-child,* model mode of services. Such a model could represent an ideal toward which we could be gradually moving, and which would guide interim practices. Perhaps one of the first practical steps would be to require broader training in human services for those who assume such positions as school principal.

These centers should also have basic and applied research components to reflect the fact that we do not know all there is to know about autism and about techniques to maximize the development of normal and disabled children, and that we view the development of improved treatment and educational methods as an integral part of efforts to enhance the lives of all children. Having research as a part of these centers would also help ensure the relevancy of applied research efforts to the developmental enterprise.

Perhaps the closest existing model to that which is proposed is Head Start. This program has evolved to provide a *wide* array of services, many of which had not been traditionally offered by schools, to meet the many needs of the child. Several years ago it was proposed that Head Start be absorbed into and run by the Department of Education. Zigler and others argued strenuously (and successfully) against this move, fearing that Head Start's broad focus might not be maintained. More specifically, in testimony before the U.S. Senate Committee on Governmental Affairs (1978), Zigler stated, "Head Start's inclusion in a Department of Education would jeopardize the program's unique status as a national laboratory for *all* children's services."

A national model, it is hoped, will evolve that places emphasis on the whole child, whether normal or disabled, and the family, and provides funding to reflect and support this synthesis. As will be seen, the model on which this volume is based is a major step in this direction.

PROGRAM OVERVIEW

The program—The Groden Center—that provides the setting for this book began services in the fall of 1976 for ten children. At present it serves over 75 children and young adults with autism and related disorders; they range in age from 18 months to 21 years. Dedicated to the whole-child model, the program's mission is to provide those services and activities most likely to enhance the lives of these persons and their families, both now and in the future (Groden and co-workers, 1984). These services and activities include:

1. An effective, comprehensive, multidisciplinary, real-life *continuum of services* for children with autism and related disorders and their families. A primary goal of the provision of these services is to enable these children to remain with their families in their community

and for the family units to lead life-styles as normal as possible. To this end the center initiates services as early as possible and provides an array of supportive services for parents. The center's Early Intervention Program, which serves families with children from infancy to three years of age (Groden et al., 1983a) is an example of early service initiation. The center's statewide Respite program, which provides trained respite workers to families on an as-needed basis (Groden et al., 1983b), is an example of supportive service provision.

The center's approach to the treatment and education of persons with autism and related disorders, as indicated earlier, is a coordinated one in which professionals repesenting different disciplines combine and share their skills to provide a comprehensive, unified program to help severely disordered persons overcome their disorders and to develop skills that will enable them to lead productive and dignified lives (Groden and Groden, in press).

The diversity of the staff reflects the complexity of the syndrome of autism. The staff, including consultants, represents the many disciplines necessary to understand and furnish effective services for these persons. Among these are psychology, special education, speech and language, medicine, psychiatry, social services, physical and occupational therapy, recreation, and art. The consultants are generally faculty members at institutions of higher learning both within and outside of Rhode Island. These institutions also are a source of graduate student interns and undergraduate trainees and volunteers who receive training at the center.

2. *Professional development* to contribute to the development of skills of the center's staff as well as other professionals who serve these populations. Activities to accomplish this goal include in-house staff training as well as numerous presentations at local and national meetings, and journal and book publications.

3. *Research* into the development of more effective methods of treating and educating these children and the prevention of these disorders. Innovative procedures for self-control, as developed in the program, such as relaxation and imagery procedures, have been presented at national conferences and in publications (Groden et al., 1984). In keeping with the program's commitment to interdisciplinary service and research, program staff, including its medical consultant, and program families are participating in a national multicenter study on the effects of fenfluramine on children with autism, which was coordinated through the University of California (Los Angeles) Neuropsychiatric Institute, and it has just completed a study on the role of the Fragile X chromosome in autism (Pueschel et al., 1985).

4. *Public awareness* to increase public understanding of these disorders and means of their alleviation. This is accomplished through presentations to lay groups, by newspaper and magazine articles, and by making the program accessible to persons in the community.

The Center's approach is characterized by three major perspectives: developmental, behavioral, and ecological. The developmental approach takes into consideration each child's developmental level in critical adaptive areas and promotes progress in these areas in accordance with the present knowledge of developmental principles. This approach emphasizes the fact that growth is organized and evolves through a series of stages, with earlier stages forming a basis for the development of later stages.

The treatment and educational approaches are behaviorally oriented, as it is this perspective that has the most solid scientific basis for use with this population. These behavioral methods, as indicated earlier, are based on principles of learning, task analysis, and continuous data recording and review.

The ecological perspective recognizes the need for understanding the reciprocal relationship between the children and their environment.

The following chapters will illustrate how the program's developmental, behavioral, and ecological approach is translated into principles and resultant services to benefit maximally the children and families being served.

The program components highlighted in this book (i.e., behavioral assessment and intervention, language and communication therapy, intellectual assessment, medical evaluation and management, family services, staff training and systems to guide program implementation) should serve to exemplify, but not limit, the range of services that can benefit a person with autism. Other program areas which are central to a comprehensive service spectrum, such as early intervention; curriculum options; social skills; integrated pre-school and elementary classrooms; vocational services, including supported on-site employment; family respite services; sibling support and training services; and community relations and advocacy could each merit a chapter of its own.

CHAPTER DESCRIPTIONS

Chapter 2 reviews approaches to assessment and characterizes the features of a behavioral assessment. It offers a guide for carrying out a behavioral assessment, particularly within the framework of a comprehensive assessment, educational, and treatment program. A section on assessment in the home environment, as well as a rationale for such an assessment, is included.

Chapter 3 on behavioral programming briefly summarizes the essentials of good behavioral programming with this population, and argues for an expansion of our clinical work with these clients to include a focus on self-control. It introduces two procedures (relaxation and covert conditioning) that can be used to teach self-control to persons with autism and severe behavior disorders.

Chapter 4, on intellectual functioning and assessment, provides a review of the literature on levels and patterns of cognitive functioning of these children, as well as suggestions for instrument selection and ways to achieve an adequate assessment in spite of behavioral and attentional difficulties. The chapter also discusses how an intellectual assessment can contribute to the planning, implementation, and evaluation of services for this population within a comprehensive education and treatment program.

Chapter 5, on teaching communication and language use to the severely handicapped, reflects recent developments in this field. Its practical emphasis provides a guide to language clinicians who work with similar populations. Finally, it presents a "third-party model" that expands the role of the language clinician from being involved in direct treatment to that of a catalyst for change.

Chapter 6 outlines elements of the medical assessment of children with autism and discusses the status of medical treatment. It presents the contributions that a medical assessment can provide as part of a total education and treatment program, and the ways in which the physician and other educational and treatment personnel can collaborate to assist these children.

The chapter on parent and family involvement, Chapter 7, presents a model that is sensitive to programming needs of the whole family, involves an integral evaluation component, and exemplifies the use of innovative procedures—for example, relaxation training in family counseling and imagery-based self-management techniques in working with family members.

Chapter 8 on personnel preparation presents a field-based model of personnel preparation that is adaptable to a variety of settings; encourages individualized instruction plans for each trainee; and is congruent with behavioral, ecological, and developmental principles. It can provide a working guide for similar programs as they design personnel preparation.

Finally, a systems theory approach to educational and treatment programs is used in Chapter 9, which details a method for integrating the planning, assessment, implementation, and evaluation of education and treatment programs with this population. This chapter also provides a guide to the intervention process, which highlights the role of many system variables that are essential to program effectiveness.

REFERENCES

American Psychiatric Association (1980). *Diagnostic and statistical manual of mental disorders* (3rd ed.). Washington, D.C.: Author.
Baer, D. M. & Sherman, J. A. (1964). Reinforcement control of generalized imitation in young children. *Journal of Experimental Child Psychology, 1,* 37–49.
Bakwin, H. (1954). Early infantile autism. *Journal of Pediatrics, 45,* 492–497.
Bartak, L. & Rutter, M. (1973). Special education treatment of autistic children: A comparative study. I. Design of study and characteristics of units. *Journal of Child Psychology and Psychiatry, 14,* 161–179.
Beck, A. T. (1976). *Cognitive therapy and the emotional disorders.* New York: International University Press.
Bellack, A. S., Hersen, M. & Kazdin, A. E. (1984). *International handbook of behavior modification and therapy.* New York: Plenum Press.
Bettelheim, B. (1967). *The empty fortress.* New York: Free Press.
Bleuler, E. (1950). *Dementia praecox order gruppe der schizophrenien* (J. Zinkin, translation) New York: Internation University Press. (Originally published in 1911.)
Bosch, G. (1970). Uber primaren autismus im kindesalter. Cited by G. Bosch in *Infantile autism.* New York: Springer-Verlag. (Originally published 1953.)
Bronfenbrenner, U. (1974). Developmental research, public policy, and the ecology of childhood. *Child Development 45* (1), 1–5.
Brown, L., Nietupski, I. & Hamre-Nietupski S. (1976). The criterion of ultimate functioning and public school services for severely handcapped students. In L. Brown, N. Certo, & T. Crowner, (Eds.) *Papers and programs related to public school services for secondary-age severely handicapped students.* Madison: Madison Metropolitan School District.
Brown, B. S., Wienckowski, L. A. & Stolz, S. B. (1976). *Behavior modification: Perspectives on a current issue.* Washington, D.C.: U.S. Government Printing Office.
Cautela, J. R. & Baron, M. G. (1977). Covert conditioning: A theoretical analysis. *Behavior Modification, 1* (3), 351–368.
Cautela, J. R. & Kearney, A. J. (1986). *The covert conditioning handbook.* New York: Springer.
Clairborne Park, C. (1982). *The siege: The first eight years of an autistic child with an epilogue 15 years later.* Boston: Little Brown.
Darr, G. C. & Worden, F. G. (1951). Case report twenty-eight years after an infantile autistic disorder. *American Journal of Orthopsychiatry, 21,* 559–570.
Despert, J. L. (1951). Some considerations relating to the genesis of autistic behavior in children. *American Journal of Orthopsychiatry, 21,* 335–350.

Donnellan, A. (Ed.) (1985). *Classic readings in autism.* New York: Teachers College Press.

Donnellan, A. (1980). An educational perspective of autism: Implications for curriculum development and personnel preparation. In B. Wilcox and A. Thompson (Eds.), *Critical issues in educating autistic children and youth.* Washington, D.C.: U.S. Department of Education, Office of Special Education, pp. 53–88.

Eisenberg, L. & Kanner, L. (1956). Early infantile autism 1943–55. *American Journal of Orthopsychiatry, 26,* 556–566.

Ellis, A. (1970). *The essence of rational psychotherapy: A comprehensive approach to treatment.* New York: Institute for Rational Living.

Ferster, C. B. (1961). Positive reinforcement and behavioral deficits of autistic children. *Child Development, 32,* 437–456.

Ferster, C. B. & DeMyer, M. K. (1962). A method for the experimental analysis of the behavior of autistic children. *American Journal of Orthopsychiatry, 32,* 89–98.

Foxx, R. M. (1980). *The highly disruptive client: Legal, clinical and administrative issues in developing and implementing behavior modification programs.* Workshop Presentation, Toledo, Ohio.

Garcia, B. & Sarvis, M. S. (1964). Evaluation and treatment planning for autistic children. *Archives of General Psychiatry, 10,* 530–541.

Groden, J. & Groden, G. (1987) Initiating and administering programs: Alternative settings. In D. J. Cohen and A. M. Donnellan, (Eds.) *Handbook of autism and disorders of atypical development.* New York: Wiley.

Groden, J., Groden, G., Baron, G. & Stevenson, S. E. (1984). Day Treatment Services for Children with Severe Behavior Disorders. In W. P. Christian, G. T. Hannah, and T. J. Glahn, (Eds.) *Programming effective human services: strategies for institutional change and client transition.* New York: Plenum Press.

Groden, G., Domingue, D., Chesnick, M., Groden, J. & Baron, G. (1983a). Early intervention with autistic children: A case presentation with pre-program, program and follow-up data. *Psychological Reports, 53,* 715–722.

Groden, G., Groden, J. & Goldenberg, A. (1982b). *Behaviorally oriented statewide respite program for families of autistic persons.* Presented at The American Association of Mental Deficiency Conference, May 31–June 4.

Groden, G. & Cautela, J. R. (1981). Behavior therapy: A survey of procedures for counselors. *The Personnel and Guidance Journal,* 175–180.

Kanner, L. (1943). Autistic disturbances of affective contact. *Nervous Child, 2,* 217–250.

Kazdin, A. E. (1984). *Behavior modification in applied settings* (3rd edition). Chicago: Dorsey Press.

Koegel, R. L., Rincover, A. & Egel, A. L. (1982). *Educating and understanding autistic children.* San Diego: College Hill.

Laufer, M. W. & Gair, D. S. (1969). Childhood schizophrenia. In L. Ballak and L. Loeb (Eds.), *The schizophrenic syndrome.* New York: Grune and Stratton.

LaVigna, G. & Donnellan, Walsh A. M. (1985). *Alternatives to punishment: Solving behavior problems with non-aversive strategies.* New York: Irvington Press.

Lovaas, O. I., Douglas, B. Y. & Newsom, C. D. (1978). Childhood psychosis: Behavioral Treatment. In B. B. Wolfman, J. Egan, and A. O. Ross, (Eds.) *Handbook of treatment of mental disorders in childhood and adolescence.* Englewood Cliffs, N.J.: Prentice-Hall.

Lovaas, O. I., Freitag, G., Gold, V. J. & Kassorla, I.C. (1965). Experimental studies in childhood schizophrenia: Analysis of self-destructive behavior. *Journal of Experimental Child Psychology*, 2, 67–84.

Lovaas, O. I., Schaeffer, B. & Simmons, J. Q. (1965a). Experimental studies in childhood schizophrenia: Building social behavior in autistic children by use of electric shock. *Journal of Experimental Research in Personality*, 1, 99–109.

Matson, J. L. & DiLorenzo, T. M. (1984). *Punishment and its alternatives: A new perspective for behavior modification*. New York: Springer Publishing.

Meichenbaum, D. H. (1977). *Cognitive behavior modification*. New York: Plenum.

Morgan, S. B. (1986). Early childhood autism: Changing perspectives. *Journal of Child and Adolescent Psychology*, 3 (1), 3–9.

National Society for Autistic Children (1978). Definition of the syndrome of autism. *Journal of Autism and Childhood Schizophrenia*, 8, 162–169.

Ornitz, E. M. & Ritvo, E. R. (1968). Perceptual inconstancy in early infantile autism. *Archives of General Psychiatry*, 18, 76–98.

Pavlov, I. P. (1927). *Conditioned reflexes: An investigation of the physiological activity of the cerebral cortex*. (Anrep, Ed.) (Six volumes.) London: Oxford University Press.

Pueschel, S., Herman, R. & Groden, G. (1985). Brief report. Screening children with autism for fragile X syndrome and phenylketonuria. Journal of Autism and Developmental Disorders, 15 (3), 335–338.

Rendle-Short, J. (1969). Infantile autism in Australia. *Medical Journal of Australia*, 2, 245–249.

Rimland, B. (1964). *Infantile autism*. New York: Appleton-Century-Crofts.

Ritvo, E. R. & Freeman, B. J. (1984). A medical model of autism: Etiology, pathology, and treatment. *Pediatric Annals*, 13(4), 298–305.

Rogers-Warren, A. & Warren, S. (1977). The developing ecobehavioral psychology. In Rogers-Warren & Warren, (Eds.). *Ecological perspectives in behavioral analysis*. Baltimore: University Park Press.

Rutter, M. (1978). Diagnosis and definition of childhood autism. *Journal of Autism and Childhood Schizophrenia*, 8, 139–161.

Rutter, M. (1968). Concepts of autism. *Journal of Child Psychology and Psychiatry*, 9, 1–25.

Rutter, M. (1966). Behavioral and cognitive characteristics of a series of psychotic children. In J. Wing (Ed.), *Early childhood autism*. Oxford: Pergamon.

Rutter, M. & Bartak, L. (1973). Special educational treatment of autistic children: A comparative study. Follow-up findings and implications for services. *Journal of Child Psychology and Psychiatry*, 14, 241–270.

Rutter, M. & Bartak, L. (1971). Causes of infantile autism: Some considerations from recent research. *Journal of Autism and Childhood Schizophrenia*, 1(1), 20–32.

Rutter, M. & Lockyer, L. (1967). A five to fifteen year follow-up study of infantile psychosis: Description of sample. *British Journal of Psychiatry*, 113, 1169–1182.

Schopler, E., Brehm, S., Kinsbourne, M. & Reichler, R. J. (1971). Effect of treatment structure on development in autistic children. *Archives of General Psychiatry*, 24, 415–421.

Shea, V. & Mesibov, G. B. (1985). Brief report: The relationship of learning disabilities and higher-level autism. *Journal of Autism and Developmental Disorders*, 15,4.

Skinner, B. F. (1938). *The behavior of organisms*. New York: Appelton-Century-Crofts.

Skinner, B. F. (1953). *Science and human behavior.* New York: Macmillan.
Skinner, B. F. (1954). A new method for the experimental analysis of behavior of psychotic patients. *Journal of Nervous and Mental Disease, 120,* 403–406.
Thoreson, E. R. & Mahoney, J. J. (1974). *Behavioral self-control.* New York: Holt, Rinehart & Winston.
Vaillant, G. E. (1962). John Haslam on early infantile autism. *American Journal of Psychiatry, 119,* 376.
Van Krevelen, D.A., & Kuipers, C. (1962). The psychopathology of autistic psychopathy. *Acta paedopsychiatrica, 29,* 22-31.
Ward, A. J. (1970). Early infantile autism. *Psychological Bulletin, 73*(5), 350–362.
Watson, J. B. (1920). *Behaviorism.* Chicago: The People's Institute.
Wolfe, M. M., Risley, T. R., & Mees, H. L. (1964). Application of operant conditioning procedures to the behavior problems of an autistic child. *Behavior Research and Therapy, 1,* 305–312.
Wolpe, J. (1958). *Psychotherapy by reciprocal inhibition.* Stanford, Calif.: Stanford University Press.
Zigler, E. (1978). Testimony to United States Senate Committee on Governmental Affairs, April 27.

CHAPTER

2

Behavioral Assessment Procedures for the Evaluation of Children with Autism

Patricia Wisocki, Ph.D.

Problem Definition
Establishment of Treatment Goals
　Specificity
　Workability
　Relevance
Establishing Priorities Among Behavioral Domains
Present Performance Level: Baseline Assessment
Antecedent and Consequent Events
Behavioral Observation
　Frequency Measures
　Interval Recordings
A Contextual Example

Home Visit
A Sample Behavioral Evaluation
　Behavioral Evaluation Format
Events Found to Be Reinforcing
Events Found to Be Aversive
Curriculum Domains
　Independent Living Skills
　Social Interaction
　Idiosyncratic Problem Behaviors
Summary
A Final Comment
References

VARIOUS THERAPEUTIC AND EDUCAtional endeavors take different approaches to assessment procedures. Some stress a search for the etiology or causes of a person's problem and use methods similar to those employed by a physician in tracking down the origins of a disease. For example, if a child displays poor motor control, delayed speech, or stereotypic hand movements, one might look for an internal cause, such as the malfunctioning of an important organ. When such a causal determination is made, medication or surgical intervention may be used to remedy the problem. Simply knowing the cause of a behavior pattern, however, does not necessarily ensure effective treatment. Retardation due to anoxia is an example of this point.

In still other cases, when the cause is known and corrected, the behavior pattern may not change because it has become independent of the original eliciting condition and is maintained by other environmental factors. This point is illustrated by the following example. A small boy was flying a large kite on a windy day. The wind shifted suddenly, lifted him off balance, and deposited him painfully on his knees. After receiving some consolation from his parents and siblings, he became fearful of the wind and refused to leave home if he could see the trees moving in even a light breeze. Knowledge of the cause of this fear was not enough to eliminate it. In fact in this case knowledge of the cause aroused such sympathy and "understanding" of the child's fears that it was detrimental to him. Removal of the fear was eventually brought about by a systematic desensitization to the effects of wind and some work with the family on realigning reinforcement contingencies.

A second approach to assessment is by symptomology, or classification, which consists of correlating a variety of behaviors within an individual and assigning that individual to a category. "Autistic" and "retarded" are examples of such a categorization. This method is convenient as a shorthand description of people with certain types of problems. It allows us to speak a common language and to get an initial impression of a person. It also is useful for facilitating social and administrative decisions about people by providing some basis for judging an individual's degree of deviation from a social or ethical norm. Often funding is dependent on classification systems. Thus in one year available money may be allotted for "autistic children," and in another year, the "developmentally disabled" may be funded.

Like assessment by etiology, assessment by classification has its limitations. Because the same label is used for a variety of behaviors, a common etiology is implied. The distinct differences inherent in an individual's life or problem area may be neglected. It is not possible for any two people to have arrived at the same spot down exactly the same path. Neither are any two people currently functioning in exactly the same way, under the same conditions, even if they share the same label. The environmental circumstances that created and maintain the problem, the genetic factors, and the learning histories are unique. A person's responsiveness to specific treatment methods may also be unique. Indeed, although labels may be helpful as brief descriptors of a range of behaviors, they are also potential sources of confusion or harm. It often happens, for instance, that an evaluator and a parent see different meanings in the same label. A child considered "aggressive," for example, might be physically or verbally abusive to self or others; might have frequent temper tantrums; or might throw things, break windows, tease animals, empty the kitchen cupboards of their contents, or scream for uninterrupted periods when reprimanded. Each of these behaviors requires different intervention strategies. Acceptance of the label without questioning it adds nothing to our knowledge of the child, nor to the treatment plan.

Labels may be harmful in two ways. Often a person who has been labeled with a categorical description is referred to by that label without considering current behaviors. Such a classification not only implies that the behavior is unchangeable, but makes it difficult for others to notice any behavioral change that occurs. For example, a child who struck out at other children and objects at the age of eight may carry the label of "aggressive" into adulthood, even if that behavior is never exhibited again. A child who is labeled "brain damaged" on the basis of either poor test performance or deficits in behaviors may be denied treatment because it is "a waste of time and energy." Thus the indiscriminant use of labels may lead to dehumanization of the individual or a permanent stigmatization of a person or group.

If a person uses a particular label as a self-description and comes to believe it, he may tailor his behavior to fit the label, rather than use the label as a descriptor for existing behaviors. For example, the person who considers himself retarded may avoid participation in activities that would disconfirm the label (e.g., "I can't do that because I'm retarded"). The label also may be used for secondary gain (e.g., "You owe this to me because I'm retarded").

The third approach to assessment is behavioral. A behavioral assessment focuses on those variables particularly relevant to treatment. The information elicited is specific and oriented to the explicit environmental and historical variables that control the observed behaviors. The assessment data are usually direct samples of behavior in specific situations, instead of indirect and generalized indicants of behavioral predispositions. Assessment continues throughout the course of treatment and the type of intervention employed is constantly revised. This interdependent relationship between assessment and intervention is a particular mark of the behavioral approach (Kanfer, 1972), and it necessitates a thorough understanding of assessment procedures and principles for anyone who acts as a change agent (Lanyon & Goldstein, 1971). Inadequate assessment or misinterpretation of assessment data may have serious consequences for the intervention strategy devised (Hayes, 1978).

It is the behavioral approach to evaluation that will be the main focus of this chapter. The following topics are covered: (1) a detailed description of the "nuts and bolts" of an initial behavioral evaluation; (2) a description of the way information is gathered within the context of the structured environment of a treatment center for children with autism over a four-week period; and (3) an example of an evaluation report written about a specific child.

PROBLEM DEFINITION

When a child is referred for treatment, the referring source rarely describes one isolated problem. Instead a child is usually spoken of in terms of labels that describe a series of events or a pattern of behaviors. For example, a child may be called "hyperactive" because he will not remain seated, pushes other children in line, stares into space instead of doing school work, and so forth. Another common way a child is described is in terms of the child's pattern of interaction with the referring source. For instance, a classroom teacher referring a child for treatment might complain about the fact that the child is "a handful," is always in trouble, and makes it difficult to teach the other children.

The first attempt at definition is accomplished by a careful reading of the reports from the child's previous placements. The behavioral evaluator examines the history of the behavioral difficulties to provide an estimate of the strength of the behavioral pattern. Further, the evaluator looks for indications of the level of cognitive functioning, and notes physical attributes, such as height, weight, the presence of medical problems and sensory deficits, medication history, and any personal assets or strengths the child may have. Eventually the behavioral evaluator must break down the descriptions into understandable units, by seeking answers to such questions as: What happens when the child does. . .? How often is "constantly destructive?" What did the parent do when . . . happened? What happened next? This is an attempt to *define operationally* the range of behavioral responses exhibited by a child. This process is useful not only for ascertaining the nature and extent of the complaint, but for hypothesizing about specific change procedures that may be incorporated into the various treatment programs designed for each child.

Behavioral evaluators do not ignore the occurrence or value of internal or private events, but they are aware of the problems inherent in ascribing causal attributes to those events and of the limitations in measurement afforded by such referents. Covert events may be operationalized in the same ways as overt events, but the client is the final judge as to their occurrence or nonoccurrence. For example, a young girl may report that she thinks other children are rejecting her, that they don't like her, that she's different from everyone else, and that she feels anxious or unhappy around them (all covert behaviors). These thoughts may be verbalized and quantified in questionnaires. The child may be able to monitor their occurrence and give rough estimates of the length of time the thoughts are maintained and the intensity of anxiety they arouse. But no one else will be able to verify their existence, frequency, duration, or intensity, thus resulting in an obvious biasing of the data. In the case of the anxiety feelings, verification is more feasible if the evaluator has access to telemetric equipment, but there are problems of reliability and validity in this area as well (Lang, 1971; Mason, 1972).

ESTABLISHMENT OF TREATMENT GOALS

A behavioral assessment cannot be carried out without consideration of the therapeutic ends. Behavior is not increased or decreased for its own sake, but for a specific far-reaching purpose. For example, a child may be taught to breathe slowly in response to a request to "relax." We expect this specific behavior to increase, but the therapeutic goal for this exercise is that of having the child use the relaxation response when confronted with anxiety-eliciting events. Likewise, when we consider the therapeutic goal, procedures other than regulated breathing might be used, such as closing one's eyes, leaving the situation, talking to someone, or sleeping. The point is that the goal is more important than the individual exercise. It is easy to focus exclusively on the exercise, and forget the end toward which one is working.

Referral sources, including parents, often have not conceptualized the specific outcomes they hope will be reached through treatment, but suggest such generalities as "help him be a happy child," "teach me to cope with her," "stop him from going off the wall," and "make her normal." In translating goals into realistic treatment plans, the behavioral evaluator considers the qualities of specificity, workability, and relevance. Let us consider each of these qualities in turn.

Specificity

Each goal expressed by the referring source must be redefined through a consideration of each element necessary to achieve it. The process of making these goals more specific not only helps to put expectations into realistic focus, but also helps to clarify the dimensions of the child's requirements, delineates the limitations and extensions of the therapy model, and suggests ways of evaluating the child's progress throughout treatment. Further, such a process ensures that all persons involved in treatment agree on the meaning of the goal.

Workability

It must be possible to achieve the goals specified. The child's abilities, the resources of the facility, and the realities of the environment must be taken into consideration in the goal-setting process. Often goals are set that are beyond the range of each of these elements. For example, vocational program goals that are directed at complete self-sufficiency and independent living usually are not realistic and cannot be met. On the other hand, it is tragic if goals are set too low. This situation arises for a variety of reasons. In some cases treatment teachers are unduly influenced by pessimistic labels. Sometimes meeting the goal requires a great deal of energy or the application of an unfamiliar procedure, and the teacher is unwilling to put in the necessary time. In still other instances, a treatment teacher may be concerned about meeting a goal in time for the next meeting with parents and deliberately sets the goal too low in order to show some success.

Relevance

The goals must be established in terms of performance necessary for survival in a wide variety of complex environments. They exclude the esoteric, the impractical, the superfluous, and those programs educators sometimes include in their curricula that are based on personal affinity or superstition. They require the development of an individualized curriculum that is age appropriate, functional, and cohesive.

With these elements in mind, a behavioral evaluator seeks to establish specific goals in the following mutually inclusive curriculum domains:

1. Independent living
   a. Self-care skills, including feeding, washing, dressing, hygiene, toileting, food preparation, and domestic tasks (e.g., washing dishes and clothes, dusting, vacuuming,), including the use of household equipment.
   b. Job-related skills, including sorting, matching to sample, counting, and working within fixed and variable time limits.
   c. Self-control ability, including response to instructions from others and self, which is manifested by waiting, tolerance of previously frustrating or provoking stimuli, relaxation of self on cue, and so on.
   d. Adaptation to physical limitations/disease, including wearing or using necessary aids and taking necessary medications.
2. Social interaction
   a. Social stimulus values—including physical appearance, gait, "peculiar" mannerisms, grooming skills, and dressing style—which will allow the child to be comfortable in "normal" environments and others to be at ease with the child.
   b. Methods of communication/interaction, including conversation sequencing, eye contact, giving greetings, giving and accepting compliments, and appropriate responses to humor.
   c. Recreation and play skills, including appropriate solitary and group play, sequencing skills, response to visual and aural stimuli, and appropriate functioning at community events.
3. Idiosyncratic problem behavior
   a. Repetitive behavior patterns, including body rocking, hand flapping, finger flicking, object twirling, object hoarding, mouth noises, and toe walking.
   b. Violent destructive behaviors, including head banging, self-picking, kicking, attacks on others, running away, throwing objects, stabbing, and verbal threats
   c. Tantrums, including kicking at objects, screaming, crying, fist banging, and tearing clothes.
   d. Others

Many of these curriculum domains covered by a behavioral evaluation overlap with information obtained in other evaluation systems. Particularly relevant to the development of a treatment plan are the medical assessments, speech and language measures, physical therapy reports, and educational and vocational assessments. Psychological, social history, and psychiatric reports may also provide useful information about conditions influential in the child's learning. It is important that a behavioral evaluator have access to the information provided by other professionals and incorporate those data into an integrated behavioral treatment plan.

ESTABLISHING PRIORITIES AMONG BEHAVIORAL DOMAINS

Within the array of problems presented by a child with autism, it is often necessary to establish some priorities for behavioral targets. This is so even though a treatment program is designed to cover each area comprehensively. Often one or two behaviors are of life-threatening magnitude, either to the child (e.g., self-abusive activities) or to others (violent or destructive behavior), and they occur very frequently. In these cases this behavior has top priority, and all the energies of the treatment staff must be concentrated on those particular problems, almost to the exclusion of all other areas.

If the abusive or destructive behaviors occurred intermittently or at a moderate or low frequency, their treatment would be equal in priority to a program that would increase the frequency of desirable behaviors that will maximize the child's reinforcers and/or maximize the flexibility of the child's repertoire to achieve long-term individual and social benefits (Myerson & Hayes, 1978). Improvements in a child's social stimulus value and social skills training are probably the best examples of useful and reinforcing experiences for both the child and the teacher. A high priority is assigned to this behavioral domain. Sometimes it is wise to focus efforts here and delay for a time intervention for behaviors that fall into the area of idiosyncratic problems.

Occasionally it is a good idea to place high priority on a behavior that is relatively easy for the teacher to modify. If that behavior is also one that is highly irritating to family or staff (usually because it takes place at a high rate), success with its modification may have far-reaching benefits for both the child and the treatment teacher.

Ultimately, of course, individualized goals must be established in each of the curriculum domains outlined. These goals are set according to the performance level of the child, as determined by baseline assessments.

PRESENT PERFORMANCE LEVEL: BASELINE ASSESSMENT

The child's performance level in each domain is assessed by observation in both structured and unstructured settings, and by eliciting responses to various task-relevant forms and inventories. Along with a determination of the actual behavior configuration, it is also essential, whenever possible, to determine the *frequency* of the occurrence of the targeted behaviors, their *intensity*, the *duration* of the occurrence, the *latency* between a stimulus presentation and response, and the *schedule* on which the behavior occurs. Measures of each of these variables provide us with a baseline against which we may determine the degree of change a child exhibits over time. For instance, over a six-week evaluation period, the frequency of a behavior may not have diminished, but its intensity may have decreased. Or the evaluator may find that a child who once was quickly stirred to violence by an event, can remain calm for several minutes after the stimulus presentation, and that the violent action is over more quickly than in previous experiences. Indeed it may well be that these data are more important to establishing progress than is a simple count of frequency.

Antecedent and Consequent Events

During an initial evaluation period, the evaluator tries to get an idea of the behaviors that set the occasion for the behaviors of concern (antecedents) and those that maintain it (consequences).

Antecedent events may be overt (e.g., a sharp verbal reprimand by a parent) or covert (e.g., the thought that "I'll be in trouble if I do this"). In delineating antecedent events to a response or set of responses, the evaluator considers several factors. One factor is the presence of *instructional stimuli*, those rules or demands given by the child (to himself) or by others. Another factor is the presence of *discriminative stimuli,* events that provide the child with information about the likelihood of a possible consequence conditional upon performing a behavior (e.g., "Daddy is in a bad mood and may be angry enough to punish me if I do that"). It is especially important to ascertain differences among the treatment setting, the home, and community environments since it is apparent that children discriminate differently in each setting, depending on the arrangement of consequences. Thus we often find that a child will easily perform some task (e.g., self-dressing) in one environment, but not in another. A third factor involves the existence of *potentiating variables,* procedures that might be undertaken to assure the effectiveness of a reinforcement (e.g., depriving a child of access to a favorite activity until a task is completed).

The evaluator acquires information about each of these elements by observation, by asking the child directly, by asking family members or staff, and by role playing or doll play. Once having established what looks like a pattern, the evaluator formulates a hypothesis and tests it in structured situations containing the hypothesized antecedent events in various stages. The child is engaged in each situation and notes are taken on the intensity, duration, and consistency of the responses to the various antecedent stimuli. For example, if we hypothesize that refusal of an item or event by a treatment teacher regularly provokes tantrum behavior, the treatment teacher is asked to refuse the child access to a toy, an edible, an activity, and so forth. Various "styles" of refusals may be tested, such as a softly delivered statement of "not now, but later"; a firm "no, stop that"; a statement designed to distract the child into another area, such as "not that toy, but how about this one?" With a series of such contrived situations within the naturally occurring activities of the day, the evaluator acquires confidence in the hypothesis and the ensuing program recommendations are based on data.

When looking at antecedent events, it is important to consider the existence of *facilitating stimuli,* tools that are the essential prerequisites for the occurrence of a response (e.g., children must learn the basics of social intercourse, such as making eye contact, giving greetings, and so forth, before they can master the advanced art of conversation). Thus it is necessary to determine what assets the child has, and so the evaluator asks the following questions: Is this child equipped with the skills necessary to reach the desired goals or must new behaviors be learned? How well does the child generalize from one situation to another? Is the child able to use objects for their intended purposes? Does there seem to be a desire to please others? Is the child able to recognize emotions or feelings in others (such as happiness, sadness, anger, annoyance)? Is he able to identify his own feelings appropriately? Can the child stay with an assigned task? For how long? What tasks are of greater interest? What style of learning does the child demonstrate—a molar or molecular approach? Can the child learn by modeling, by written instructions, by verbal cue, by gesture, or by some combination of these?

The evaluator also tries to specify those behaviors, called *consequent events*, which seem to be responsible for increasing or decreasing the target behaviors. There are four categories of consequent events, each with a different method of presentation. Two categories deal with ways in which a behavior is increased, and concern ways in which a behavior is decreased.

When there is an increase in behavior or behavior is being maintained at a steady rate, we say that the response has been reinforced. It may be positively reinforced or negatively reinforced, but in either case there is an increase in or maintenance of the response. When a behavior has been positively reinforced, a stimulus (usually something valued by the individual) has occurred immediately after the response. For example, a child finds that being disruptive is likely to ensure that some request will be granted, and so the disruptive behavior increases in frequency. This is an incidence of *positive reinforcement*.

When a behavior has been *negatively reinforced*, a stimulus unpleasant for the individual has been withdrawn as a result of the person's response. For example, the teacher of the disruptive child finds the behavior aggravating and gives in to the child simply to stop it. Thus the teacher's behavior—fulfilling the child's request—increased because it resulted in a termination of the aversive event (i.e., negative reinforcement), whereas the disruptive behavior increased because the child obtained what he wanted (i.e., positive reinforcement). Much of our behavior in daily life is controlled by events arranged in a negative reinforcement paradigm. We may fasten our seat belts while in a car to stop the buzzing noise. We may drive at the appropriate speed limit to avoid a heavy fine. We pay our taxes by April 15 to avoid investigation by the IRS.

For decreasing behavior the two categories of consequent events are aversive events and extinguishing events. Aversive events (also referred to as "punishing events") are stimuli presumably unpleasant to the individual that take place immediately after the response is made. For example, if, after a child was disruptive, the teacher spoke sharply, stopped smiling, and told the child to stop, and if that sequence of events occurred consistently and often, the child would probably change tactics. It is important to note that the aversive event follows the performance of the behavior and the behavior decreases as a result. This is in contrast to negative reinforcement, where the behavior increases as a result of the termination of an aversive event that is presented prior to the performance of the behavior.

Many times, of course, behavior decreases simply because there is no longer any reinforcement attached to its performance. For instance, a teacher who consistently responds to a disruptive child by giving in to the child's demands may come to ignore other, more appropriate behaviors. Thus the sporadic appearance of a child's "good" behavior may be eliminated. This process is called extinction—the use of neutral events (e.g., ignoring someone) with a behavior previously maintained by positive reinforcement.

In practice, during the initial assessment period, the behavioral evaluator looks for what consequences appear to maintain the target behaviors exhibited by a child and tries to ascertain which may be used effectively in the child's treatment plan. For instance, does contingent deprivation of a favorite food or toy result in a decrease in behavior? Is a verbal reprimand a strong aversive event? Does the child respond negatively to an unusual item, such as the odor of perfume or the taste of mayonnaise? What does the child avoid? To what does the child react in a negative way? Does the child dislike being ignored? Thus the evaluator is not only looking at a performance picture, but is trying to get an idea of tools available for use in designing an effective treatment strategy.

BEHAVIORAL OBSERVATION

The primary method of behavioral assessment is direct observation. To the extent that it is feasible, this is the most useful of all the assessment procedures. Observations are usually made by people trained in the techniques or by those most in contact with the client (teachers, parents, hospital aides). In using direct behavioral observations, it is first necessary to develop some sort of classification system, so that attention may be drawn to specific aspects of the environment, as well as to the individual's response to it. For example, in trying to determine the amount of social interaction among a group of children with autism, the evaluator must think through and list the various behaviors that are relevant to social interaction and those that are observable. Inferences about intention or meaning must be limited because they can easily lead an evaluator into fitting other independent observations into a global pattern that may be difficult to ignore later.

On the other hand, inferences that lead to hypotheses that are testable by further observation are useful. In the context of hypothesis testing, inferences are necessarily tentative and eventually will be supported or disproved by reliable evidence. The evaluator, above all, is a complex, thinking, organism observing another complex, thinking organism. As Baron (1984) points out, good observers analyze contextual variables around a response that includes, for example, the time of day a tantrum occurs—in the early morning, after a long bus ride, before going home. They will also look for accompanying behaviors around the target response that might provide a clue to effective intervention. If a scream, for example, is accompanied by an attempt to establish eye contact, extinction might be the treatment of choice for reducing the screaming, while simultaneously teaching the child an alternate method of communication.

Various measures are taken during behavioral observations, depending upon the type of response being recorded, the limitations of the physical environment, and the purupose of the recording. In most behavioral programs, the observer uses either a frequency count or a measure based on how long the target response lasts (called interval recordings).

Frequency Measures

Frequency measures concern *response rate*, the number of times a behavior takes place in a given period of time. A frequency measure is particularly useful when the target behavior is discrete, when the response takes a relatively constant amount of time each time it is performed (e.g., head banging), and when it is unnecessary or impractical to measure antecedent or consequent events. The response has a clearly delineated beginning and end that separate instances of it may be counted. The measure is not useful for ongoing behaviors, such as smiling, talking, or periods of long screaming. The advantages of the frequency measure are that (1) it is relatively simple to score for work in natural settings, (2) it readily reflects changes over time, and (3) it expresses the amount of behavior performed and so is related to goals of increasing or decreasing the number of times a behavior occurs. It can also be used to determine the number of individuals who perform a given behavior, such as using eating utensils at meals or participating in recreational programs.

Interval Recordings

With interval recordings behaviors are measured during short periods of the total time they are performed. For example, an observer might want to record the amount of time a child is paying attention in class. Using a predesignated block of time, the observer simply charts whether or not the behavior occurred at the various established intervals. Or an observer might be interested in the length of time it takes for a child to respond to a stimulus event, such as a reprimand, which previously triggered aggressive behavior.

Interval recordings are one of the most widely used strategies in applied settings today (Kazdin, 1976). They have these advantages: (1) They are flexible, and so any behavior can be recorded. (2) The resulting observations can easily be converted into a percentage.

For the reader interested in further details about recording procedures, the book by Sulzer-Azaroff and Reese (1982) is recommended.

A CONTEXTUAL EXAMPLE

Let us next examine the context within which the behavioral evaluation might occur—a daytime or residential treatment center for children with autism. Upon being referred, a child is assigned a temporary placement in a group of children of about the same age who are functioning at or above the newcomer's level in the areas of self-help, language, and social skills. Experience has indicated that a child benefits more from placement in a group that appears to be slightly more advanced. This initial placement may be changed if the evaluation data do not support it.

Relationship factors are important elements in behavioral programs. The evaluator must take time to develop a positive experience for the child because it is within that context that the child's best performance will be evident. It is never enough to observe the typical level of functioning; it is as necessary to know that which a child is capable of doing. A positive relationship establishes the evaluator as a powerful source of reinforcement that often permits a high degree of control over behavior. Praise and approval from, and time to spend with, the evaluator become important to the child.

For these reasons the first week of the four-week evaluation is devoted primarily to the establishment of some level of rapport with the child. The evaluator spends exclusive time with the child, engaging in play or pleasant activities, attending to the child at lunch or snack times, and allowing free access to activities, toys, and snack foods. The child is introduced gradually into the routines of the group program, but is not required to participate, although spontaneous participation sometimes takes place.

A second goal of the first week is to ascertain the child's initial response to the educational environment. This is realized by exposing the child to various aspects of the program, and observing the response to naturally occurring positive events (reinforcements), such as praise, greetings, smiling, and attention, and to naturally occurring environmental stresses, such as one child being reprimanded or the tantrums of another child. Attention is given to the speed with which a child may acquire behaviors not in the child's repertoire, such as finger flicking, on the negative end of the scale, or waiting in line, on the positive end.

During this week the evaluator also sets the evaluation machinery in motion by making appointments with specialists in medicine, language skills, fine and gross motor functioning, intellectual development, educational status, and recreational and vocational skills. The family is also seen for a psychiatric evaluation. These evaluations are conducted not in laboratory settings, but in the more natural surroundings of the treatment center, the community, and home. Each specialist writes a detailed report of his/her findings and recommendations, which is incorporated into the treatment program designed for each child by the behavioral evaluator. The child is videotaped in ten-minute segments in each of these situations: alone in a free play setting, with another child, and with a treatment teacher engaged in some simple task. If feasible, examples of severe behavior problems may also be taped. The child's performances in each of these situations are regarded as baseline data. More important, the tapes provide an accurate and vivid visual record to which one may refer in order to document progress. The tapes also serve as valuable visual reminders to staff, parents, and public officials of the extent of the problems presented by children with autism and of the gains they are able to make with good treatment. Since behavior changes slowly over time, we cannot trust this process to memory.

During the second week, the previous observations made by the evaluator are formalized into hypotheses and tested. The behavioral evaluator then begins to collect data on the performance picture presented by the child within the context of the overall goals that will be the focus of the child's program.

HOME VISIT

While the process of data collection is ongoing, the evaluator makes an initial home visit. The visit provides an opportunity both to ascertain the extent and type of the problems with which the family must cope and their ways of dealing with and relating to the child, and to form an initial alliance with the family. Often the information obtained from the family differs qualitatively from the information acquired during the child's stay in a treatment setting. For instance, the family often reports more intensity and more disruption than the evaluator has observed. On the other hand, it is often the case that the family has developed some effective methods of working with the child, which may be passed on to the treatment personnel. This is also the time to determine what particular problems the family may have separate from those related to the care of the child. It is important at this point to avoid comparisons between the child's behavior at home and at the treatment center. One must also be careful in discussing the child's successes at the center. It often happens that if the child's behavior in the treatment setting is better than the home behavior, the family will try to impress on the evaluator that any observed change will not last (which is usually true) and that the child is worse than the initial data indicate (which is not necessarily true). The family is usually not yet receptive to the idea that an arrangement of environmental circumstances can help to produce more appropriate behavior in their child. It seems best to enlist the family members' help in the child's programs and to demonstrate gradually how much control they actually have over the child's behavior. When it is possible to discuss differences between the child's behavior in the home and in the center, it is useful to focus on the child's obvious ability to discriminate about contingencies occurring in each environment and the flexibility of the child's behavioral repertoire.

When observing parent–child and sibling interactions in the home, it is helpful to impose some structure on the family members. Environmental structure will be useful in reducing interference from incompatible events, such as television, the telephone, meals, and outside visitors, and in ensuring that the evaluator does indeed get a sample of interaction behavior. It is too easy for a family to be on its best behavior and avoid a demonstration of the typical process of interaction. The most frequent structure imposed is to limit the family to two rooms, restrict interference from competing events, keep the child in view (and not relegated to his own room), and have specific questions in mind to which the family may respond individually. The observations of interactions will be ongoing during the interview. Sometimes it is helpful to have a team of two teachers visit the home. One member should be the behavioral evaluator; the other might be the social worker, a significant administrator (e.g., the school principal), or the speech evaluator. This team approach allows for more observations: While one person is talking to the family, the other may direct attention elsewhere. Later, observations may be compared and enriched. The contact with this other person will be more permanent than that with the evaluator, who will complete the task within several weeks and go on to another child.

During the third and fourth weeks, the evaluator begins interventions for selected targets. This is done at a relatively cursory level in order to provide preliminary information to the staff members who will actually be involved in working with the child. The evaluator tries to determine which procedures seem effective for certain behaviors, and thus will test the effects of various kinds of reinforcers, including praise, food, tactile interactions, and attention. The effects of negative events also will be tested including verbal reprimands, loss of attention, and loss of objects and food. Data are collected on each intervention and are included in the child's evaluation report.

A SAMPLE BEHAVIORAL EVALUATION

By the end of the fourth week, the behavioral evaluation is written, along with the Individual Program Plans (IPPs) and the reports from the consultant team. An example of a behavioral evaluation is presented in Figure 2-1. Excluded from this report for the sake of brevity are the IPPs and the consultant reports. Samples of IPPs are presented in Chapter 6, which deals with educational systems.

Behavioral Assessment

Figure 2-1, A Sample Behavioral Evaluation*

Name: John Child
Address: 600 Road Ave.
 Barrington, R.I.
Date of Birth: 12/19/73
Age: 12

Date: October 1985
Sex: Male
Height: 55¾ inches
Weight: 63 pounds
Admission Date: 9/8/85

Referral Source: Dr. M. D. Thorough, Baltimore, Md.

History of Treatment
1/75–11/76   The General Hospital, Boston, Mass.
9/77–6/78   Project Pre-School, Greenfield, Mass.
9/78–10/79   Memorial Hospital, Springfield, Mass.
10/79–8/81   Youth Center, Smith, N.H.
9/81–3/85   Children's Center, Baltimore, Md.

Evaluation History: Summary Data

9/79   Hospital Records, Memorial Hospital, Stanford-Binet: Standard Score (SS) = 72, Peabody Picture Vocabulary Test: three years, 11 months

6/14/80   Psychoeducational. Youth Center. John's strengths are in auditory and visual sequential memory and auditory and visual association (three year level), WPPSI, verbal age 5.1, vocabulary, age 4.5, arithmetic, age 4.11, picture completions age 5.5, and geometric designs, age 5.11.

3/14/81   Psychiatric Evaluation, Children's Center. John has autisticlike characteristics (hand flapping, mouthing objects, hitting himself) with developmental delay.

---

*Data in this report do not pertain to a single person, but are a composite of the reports of several children. All institutional names are ficticious.

During observation he made occasional eye contact, but often stared into space. When asked, he could speak in complete sentences but has little spontaneous speech. Fine and gross motor skills appeared adequate.

2/82 — *Social Service Report*, Children's Center. Principal concerns are to provide support to help the family in integrating John back into the household after having been in a highly structured residential setting.

9/18/72 — *Social Service Report*, Children's Center. Because John had had anxieties in his move to a new home and new school, a meeting was held to discuss John's expected change from a day program to an extended day program. All aspects of the evening program were explained. We felt John had made good progress in the past year and had shown a feeling of trust about the school.

3/9/82 — *Psychological Evaluation*, Children's Center. PPVT C.A. 8-3, M.A. 3-10, Bender Visual Motor Gestalt, 4-5. Although John still has a short attention span, he has shown tremendous improvement in controlling his own behavior and in responding well to increased structure and limits. Gross motor and language competence has also improved. Spontaneous speech occurs only when he wants something.

1/29/83 — *Psychological Evaluation*, Children's Center. Stanford-Binet C.A. 9-1, M.A. 5-2, S.S. 56, PPVT C.A. 9-1, M.A. 5-5 John is functioning at the low end of a mildly limited range of intelligence (55–70). Although he has shown significant progress, John continues to exhibit autistic behaviors.

5/7/83 — *Audiology Report*, Hearing and Speech Center., Baltimore.
Hearing is within normal range.

12/83 — *Speech and Language Evaluation*, Hearing and Speech Center, Baltimore. Severe receptive and expressive language delay and severe articulation disorder. Recommendation: treatment session on weekly basis.

12/5/83	*Medical Report*, Children's Center. Diagnosis—autism.
8/84	*Speech & Language Evaluation*, Hearing and Speech Center, Baltimore. Recommendation: John should be seen two times a week for half-hour sessions.
1/85	*Social Work Progress Report*, Children's Center. The school has had a good relationship with the family and assistance is recommended in the transition period when the family moves out of state.
9/29/85	*Staff Meeting Report*, Children's Center. The purpose of the meeting was to provide assistance for John's at-home behaviors. Mrs. Child felt she needed help and guidelines were provided for her to deal with John's "not listening" behavior (these guidelines are not specified in this report).
12/20/85	*Audiology Report*, Hearing and Speech Center Baltimore. Hearing is within normal limits. Recommendation: Retest in one year.

Behavioral Evaluation Format

It is our belief that observation and interaction with a person over an extended period of time and in a variety of environments have proved to be the best methods for evaluating a person's performance level. During the first four weeks of John's attendance, various behavioral assessments were conducted in the areas of community skills, social skills, and daily behavior patterns. Structured evaluations were administered in the following areas: education, medical, physical therapy, psychology, recreation, vocational, and speech and language. A home visit provided information on the nature and level of John's interaction with family members, helped to identify potential reinforcers for use at school, and determined whether any help or guidance was needed by the family. Additional assessments were performed in the community (at the local YMCA, restaurants, etc.) to evaluate levels of social skills, self-awareness, awareness of others, and general affective development.

EVENTS FOUND TO BE REINFORCING

Listed below is a variety of activities, social reinforcers, and food items that appear to be effective in increasing John's behaviors. This list was compiled from (1) items and requests made by John, (2) items he selected when given a variety of options, and (3) items listed on a Special Needs Reinforcement Survey Schedule (Dewhurst & Cautela, 1980) completed by John's mother.

Activities:	Putting self-sticking colored dots on paper, time in the lounge, magazines, familiar music, singing.
Social:	Riding in vans, going to McDonalds, gym.
Food:	Goldfish crackers, orange soda, pickles, cake, doughnuts, french fries, milkshake, drink of water. (These items have intermittent reinforcing value and are low on the list of reinforcers.)
Tokens and/or stars:	John understands the concept of tokens and/or "stars," which may be used to obtain a future reward. Because of that understanding, a token or star contract has been found effective in John's program and will be used for certain classes of behavior, such as touching people and flicking.

EVENTS FOUND TO BE AVERSIVE

The following consequences were effective in varying degrees for decelerating certain inappropriate behaviors.

1. *Response cost.* Loss of a reinforcing activity or tangible reinforcer was effective in decelerating the frequency of touching other people.
2. *Aversive odors.* An odor aversive was put on John's hand as a contingency to throwing objects and biting his hand or biting other people.
3. *Verbal reprimand.* A firm reprimand of "hands down" was given whenever John "flapped" or "flicked" his hands.

CURRICULUM DOMAINS

Behavior is assessed in the following categories

Independent Living Skills

SELF CARE

John has all the dressing skills, except that of tying his shoes. When he washes himself, occasional verbal cues are needed to remind him not to play with the water. He can independently get himself ready for his swimming class, and remember afterward where his locker and clothes are. Bathroom skills are excellent, although occasionally he's "lazy," preferring to pull his pants down instead of unbuttoning or unzipping them. At home he is allowed to play outside alone, and usually stays within the confines of the yard. It is necessary, though, that the family keep constant watch on him because he has previously run away. He is aware of the danger of the street. Except for a home program for shoe tying, no further work in this area seems necessary.

SELF-CONTROL

This category has two aspects: (1) learning to respond to the instructions of others, and (2) learning to relax as an alternative response to disruptive or anxiety-evoking situations (such as loud noises from peers), when experiencing an urge to flap or flick his hands, and as a way to facilitate waiting skills. There are two programs directed at these areas: (1) mobility training and (2) relaxation training.

Mobility Training. John was tested on his responsivity to instructions under various distracting conditions. John's performance in the program has been generally good, with few lapses. He seems to have the most difficulty when he is outdoors. On John's first trip to a restaurant, his behavior was appropriate until the end. He stood in line, ordered from the waitress, sat, and ate his food. When he was finished with his meal, he threw the salt shakers and napkin on the floor and ran around among the tables.

Training in the program will continue, coupled with the use of tangible reinforcers/praise as contingencies when he does respond to the instructions of "wait" or "come here." Gradually John's program will be extended to other stimulus conditions, such as waiting in line at a restaurant, delivering messages between teachers, and following a schedule.

Relaxation Training. John demonstrated an ability to respond to instructions to relax all his body parts when the response was modeled by a teacher. Further work will include relaxation on cue without modeling and self-initiated relaxation.

ADAPTATION TO PHYSICAL LIMITATIONS

A recent eye examination indicated the need for John to wear corrective lenses. John has, however, refused to wear glasses. Whenever they are given to him, he throws them down and steps on them. To date he has broken six pairs of glasses. The parents have requested help in getting John to wear his glasses and to care for them appropriately (i.e., cleaning them, using the case). While engaging John in a play activity he enjoyed, the evaluator tested John's reaction to a pair of glassless frames under two stimulus conditions: (1) a firm command, and (2) a gentle request to put on the glasses. Two consequent conditions were also tested when John threw the glasses down: (1) a firm request to pick them up and put them on, while the play activity stopped; and (2) response cost (loss of a token).

Of the two stimulus conditions, John threw his glasses down more often when he was given a gentle request (eight times out of ten trials), than when he was firmly instructured to put them on (four times out of ten trials). John more often complied with the request to pick the glasses up when it was clear that his enjoyable activity would not be continued until that condition was met.

The evaluator also tested John's response in a less enjoyable activity (arithmetic) and found that again John responded better when given a firm command. The consequent delay of the activity continued to be effective because John was not allowed to go on to the next preferred activity after arithmetic until he complied with the instructions and completed his academic work. We recommend that before each activity requiring glasses, John be routinely instructed to put on the glassless frames. As he complies more and more frequently, plain glass may be inserted into the frames, followed by glass of gradually increasing strength.

Social Interaction

SOCIAL STIMULUS VALUE/STRENGTHS

John has many strengths in the behavioral, academic and social areas. He is a winsome, good-looking young man who is extremely well dressed and neat and clean. He quickly established a good relationship with his treatment worker and at home referred to her as his "friend." Early in the evaluation, he indicated a good understanding of contracting and expressed a desire to know ahead of time what the daily schedule would be. By using contracting compliance was maintained at a high rate during all testing and work sessions. John is able to work alone at a desk or in a room alongside another student. He demonstrates various leisure skills, such as solving puzzles, addition problems, and peg tasks, stringing beads, and playing with Tinker Toys and Lincoln Logs.

METHODS OF COMMUNICATION/INTERACTION

John's verbal skills are fairly good on a receptive level. He is able to comment appropriately when necessary. He rarely initiates interaction with his peers or with adults, however. His expressive language is used mostly to ask for things he wants and to comment on his own behaviors or the behavior of his peers. These remarks are usually not directed at anyone in particular; they are initiated on an average of 16 times a day.

The primary intervention in this area will be designed by the speech and language therapist. An additional program will consist of giving John the responsibility of running the classroom store where interaction is necessary in order for the students to buy the rewards they earn. Staff will verbally cue John when necessary. A regular game period will be scheduled to provide John with more opportunity to interact with his peers.

Idiosyncratic Problem Behaviors

REPETITIVE BEHAVIOR PATTERNS

These problems include the following: tapping objects to teeth, mouthing structures (e.g., walls, chair legs), twirling, staring, squinting at light, shadow playing, body rocking, hand flapping and flicking, loud noises, floor touching, food and object touching to stomach, circling food and objects around body, retracing steps, repeated tapping when walking, repeated circling of poles.

Example: Hand Flapping. From this array the evaluator selected the behavior of hand flapping or flicking for detailed assessment, assuming that if environmental control could be demonstrated over one pattern, the others could be systematically eliminated later. John demonstrates this behavior under a variety of circumstances: if he is excited and happy (as when anticipating a visit to a fast-food restaurant), when there is a disruption in the classroom, upon presentation of certain games that are played with male teachers. Sometimes no antecedent event is evident and he demonstrates this behavior when he is just sitting quietly.

During the first two weeks of assessment, flicking occurred at an average rate of 50 times during six three-hour observation periods. A verbal clue of "relax your hands" was given during the third week (once John had demonstrated in other settings the skill of relaxing his hands on cue) every time John flicked his hands, and the average rate during the same time period was reduced to 40 times, still a high rate. During the fourth week, a verbal reprimand of "hands down" or "hands at your side" was used and flicking during this same three-hour period occurred an average of 22 times. The teachers continued to consequate this behavior with a verbal reprimand for the next month and the problem was reduced to approximately 12 times during a three-hour period per day.

VIOLENT/DESTRUCTIVE BEHAVIORS

Hand Biting (Self). John bites either hand in the area of the palm near his wrist, but does not bite hard enough to break the skin. Antecedent events were difficult to determine. John has bitten himself when he has been unsuccessful at some task, when happy and excited at an announcement that he was going somewhere he wanted to go, when peers exhibited disruptive behavior, or just when working quietly on a task or when walking with his teacher.

During the first two weeks of assessment, John's biting took place at an average rate of 35 times in a three-hour period. During his third week, we intervened by putting Thum (a commercially available aversive taste used to prevent thumb sucking) on both hands in the area usually bitten. (His parents had given permission for this intervention.) His hand biting was then reduced to 15 times during the same three-hour period, but he did not visibly react to the taste. He later reported that he liked having the Thum put on his hands because he thought we were making them "all better." When John began to request Thum, we switched to an odor aversive. This reduced the biting to five times in a three-hour period the third week and two times in a three-hour period for the fourth week.

Throwing Objects. This behavior occurs under a variety of conditions. John may be sitting at a desk and will throw anything within his reach; he may get out of his seat and go after something specific and throw it; or he may just throw the first object he touches. This behavior occurred most often (99 percent of the time) when John was participating in a group activity and a peer was acting in a disruptive manner. (John is extremely upset by loud voices.)

During the first two weeks of assessment, John threw various objects eight times per week. During the third week, an intervention program was implemented whereby John received a dab of an odor aversive on his hand whenever he threw something. This procedure reduced his throwing to five times the third week, four times the fourth week, and twice a week for the next month.

SEXUAL TOUCHING OF OTHERS

John demonstrated this behavior to most females who worked with him. The touching was accompanied by a correct verbal identification of the body part or area and an occasional obscene reference. In the beginning it happened at a rate of seven times per day.

Intervention consisted of a contingency contract, employing stars as rewards for refraining from touching and using sexual language. John was able to earn a predetermined number of stars during a specific period for a high reinforcer. If he touched, he lost the high reinforcer, but could continue to work for a lower reinforcer. This reduced the touching to zero during structured teaching sessions. During group sessions and field trips, touching still occurred at a rate of seven times a day. The intervention program was then expanded to include these settings. The use of these procedures resulted in a reduction of touching to an average of once per day for the next few months.

TANTRUMS

The components of John's tantrums included loud screams, kicking, throwing objects, drawing his knee up to his mouth and licking it, followed by a repertoire of repetitive speech,—"Who made John cry, what is the matter, put kitty in the tree, cross the street, down the cellar." Antecedent events for tantrums involved asking John to do something, being told a flat "no" when he wanted to have or do something that was not appropriate at the time, or a peer touching him.

During the first week of assessment, John's tantrums occurred on the average of five a day, and lasted an average of eight minutes. During the second week, an intervention program was implemented using an overcorrection procedure that reduced the tantrums to four per day. The technique, however, was difficult to promote, did not shorten the length of the tantrum, and was disruptive to the classroom routine.

The next intervention program, implemented during the third and fourth weeks, involved the use of an aversive odor. It was placed on John's hand when a scream occurred. This reduced tantrums to an average of four a day, but again, it did not decrease the length of the tantrum and seemed to provide added opportunity for John's repetitive speech repertoire, which is a component of his tantrum. This procedure also heightened the noise level of his tantrum.

During the final week, relaxation was attempted in a response cost paradigm. The relaxation program had already been incorporated into John's curriculum and the teacher had observed him initiating deep breathing on his own. Because John prefers sitting to standing, whenever he screamed, he was asked to stand, count, and take three deep breaths. If he complied, he was allowed to sit down and continue what he was doing. Praise specifically addressing his "good behavior" and a tangible reward were given after a short time had elapsed. The results of this strategy indicated that the length of the tantrums decreased from an average of eight minutes to one minute. The deep breathing provided an alternative positive behavior for the repetitive speech pattern that followed the more aggressive aspects of the tantrum. Tantrums decreased to an average of three a day during this time, and eventually diminished to about twice a month.

SUMMARY

The foregoing report details John's behavioral repertoire during his evaluation at the Groden Center. Additional reports from the physical therapy, medical, speech and language, psychological, and educational consultants have been completed and are included in his file. Individual Program Plans designed for each of the areas discussed in this report have been prepared. This evaluation is used as the basis for John's treatment plans, which are expected to change as additional information becomes available. It does not serve as the definitive word on treatment interventions, but only to point to various directions the teaching staff may take over the year in working with John.

A FINAL COMMENT

Too often behavioral assessments appear as mechanistic and detailed descriptions of behavioral excesses and deficits in task-analyzed sequences. It is certainly important to make reliable observations in an empirical context, to specify objectives and interventions, and to establish a data base as the foundation upon which judgments must be made. But this empirical attitude and these empirical accoutrements must be embedded, indeed fully ingrained, in a context of "clinical creativity." The behavioral evaluator must be flexible, be interested in the vagaries of the human condition, be an excellent observer, possess a scientific attitude, be knowledgeable about psychological principles, and have high ethical standards. It is hoped that this chapter has demonstrated a way to integrate these qualities into a workable evaluation for children with autism.

REFERENCES

Baron, M. G. (1984). Personal communication.

Dewhurst, D. L. T. & Cautela, J. R. (1980). A proposed special needs reinforcement survey schedule. *Journal of Behavior Therapy and Experimental Psychology*, 11, 109–112.

Hayes, S. (1978). *Principles of behavioral assessment*. New York: Gardner Press.

Kanfer, F. (1972). Assessment for behavior modification. *Journal of Personality Assessment*, 36, 418–423.

Kazdin, A. (1976). *Behavior modification in applied settings*. New York: Dorsey Press.

Lang, P. J. (1971). The application of psychophysiological methods to the study of psychotherapy and behavior modification. In A. E. Bergin and L. L. Garfield (Eds.), *Handbook of psychotherapy and behavior change*. New York: Wiley.

Lanyon, R. & Goldstein, L. (1971). *Personality assessment*. New York: Wiley.

Mason, J. W. (1972). Organization of Psychoendocrine mechanisms: A review and reconsideration of research. In N. S. Greenfield and R. A. Steinbach (Eds.), *Handbook of psychophysiology*. New York: Holt, Rinehart & Winston.

Myerson, W. A. & Hayes, S. C. (1978). Controlling the clinician for the client's benefit. In J. E. Krapfl and E. A. Vargas (Eds.) *Behaviorism and ethics*. Kalamazoo, Mich.: Behaviordelia.

Sulzer-Azaroff, B. & Reese, E. P. (1982). *Applying behavior analysis: A program for developing professional competence*. New York: Holt, Rinehart & Winston.

CHAPTER 3

Behavioral Programming
EXPANDING OUR CLINICAL REPERTOIRE

Grace Baron, Ph.D.
June Groden, Ph.D.
Joseph R. Cautela, Ph.D.

The Current Behavioral Repertoire
  Basics of Behavioral Programming
  Choice of Intervention
The Expanded Behavioral Repertoire:
  Self-Control Procedures
  Relaxation Training
  Covert Conditioning
Conclusions
References

It has been two decades since Lovaas' pioneering work in applying operant learning strategies to the understanding and modification of the behavior of children with autism. In that time the prevailing interpretation of autism has changed from that of an essentially psychogenic disorder to a more eclectic view that the term autism represents any number of physiological disorders with significant impact on psychological functioning. Behavioral technology is now a relatively standard component, if not the treatment of choice, in many treatment programs throughout our nation. Various texts and literature reviews (Koegel et al., 1982; Lovaas et al., 1978; Ritvo, 1976; Webster, et al., 1980; Puluzny, 1980), as well as tutorials and training programs (Schreibman & Koegel, 1981; Lovaas, 1981; Foxx, 1980; Donnellan et al., 1977; Sailor et al., 1980), provide richly detailed guides to the clinician and researcher who wish to learn the principles and procedures of effective behavior change for persons with autism.

Twenty years ago the primary question asked by clinicians and educators regarding behavioral interventions with these children was, "Will they work?" The questions of the 1980s are quite different. An increasing appreciation of the heterogeneity of characteristics and needs of these children and their families requires that one ask, "What is the behavioral intervention that will work best for this particular child?"

Emphasis on the personal and social significance of behavior change (Bailey & Lessen, 1983; Kazdin, 1975; Wolf, 1978) has led to the question "How meaningful is a chosen behavioral intervention?" Since effective, reality-based, and lifetime services for persons with autism is still an ideal (Thompson, 1981, p. 338), we must ask, "How must our existing technology change or expand to meet an individual's full life needs?"

This paper suggests procedures within the areas of behavioral analysis and intervention which help us to answer these important questions and can broaden the scope and validity of our current clinical repertoire with clients who have autism or other severe disorders.

THE CURRENT BEHAVIORAL REPERTOIRE

Our current repertoire of behavioral interventions still owes much to Ferster (1961) and Ferster and DeMyer's (1961, 1962) first theoretical and experimental analysis of autism as a function of environmental variables. The implications of the operant and respondant conditioning paradigms for intervention with autism have been most recently summarized by LaVigna and Donnellan (1986). The intervening years have provided repeated experimental demonstrations that behavioral procedures such as positive reinforcement, shaping and fading, extinction, punishment and negative reinforcement can alter the behavior of persons with autism.

The applied use of this powerful and efficacious technology is no small task and requires attention to (1) the "basics" of good behavioral programming, (2) the process of choosing the best possible intervention; and (3) an expanded awareness of what kinds of interventions may even be possible with clients who are autistic and severely behaviorally disordered.

Basics of Behavioral Programming

Effective behavioral programs for clients with autism usually reflect adequate preparation; precise execution; a commitment to personalization, or individualizing the procedures to meet the needs of the client; and a planned strategy for generalization of treatment effects.

1. *Preparation.* Good behavioral programs do not come naturally. Clinicians must prepare themselves, first, with a rationale—knowing "why" they are doing what they are doing. The rationale may be as simple as "to shape the individual to brush his own teeth independently," or more complex and dynamic, such as "to learn procedures of self-control and to learn to use them in actual life situations." Nevertheless, such a rationale guides and gives purpose to the instructional process. Second, good preparation requires familiarization with a written detailed intervention plan. As emphasized in Chapters 8 and 9 the clinician must also ensure through staff training and supervision that those carrying out the program have the skills to do so. Finally, the clinician should choose and prepare a facilitative environment for the behavioral program. Some programs demand an instructional setting that is devoid of interfering cues or distractors; others require the enrichment of natural cues and reinforcers. The clients themselves (because of their unique perceptual characteristics, i.e., attentional deficits, self-stimulation) must often be prepared to receive instruction by reinforced practice of orienting toward, imitating, and receiving reinforcement from the clinician. The possible influence of physical and programmatic features of the environment (e.g., noise level, number of

persons in environment, amount of "dead time" or unprogrammed activity) should be anticipated and monitored in behavioral programs (Olley, 1981).

2. *Precision.* Distinct learning trials are a distinguishing feature of good behavioral programming. Instructional activities as diverse as learning pincer grasp movements in a vocational task, relaxing tense muscles while doing an academic program, or learning a complex social interaction can all be facilitated by use of distinct learning trials. A number of training manuals (Donnellan et al., 1977; Lovaas, 1981; Luce & Christian, 1981; Foxx, 1980) detail the precise operant technology that is the basis of much of the good behavioral programming with persons with autism. In this book, the reader can review the techniques of operant conditioning by referring to Chapter 2 on behavioral assessment. Whether one is employing positive or negative reinforcement to increase response frequency or extinction or punishment to decrease response frequency, precision in such instruction can mean delivery of clear, precise instructions; the use of necessary, but not extraneous, prompts; an operational definition and specific criterion for the target behavior; an immediate and contingent delivery of an effective reinforcer; and pacing (intertrial interval) of learning trials to maximize client attention and motivation. On a larger scale, for each program there is also a precise balance that should be sought between the use of distinct learning trials (and the "controlled" environment implicit in such trials) and learning and practice in "natural" settings.

3. *Personalization.* As in any clinical behavioral intervention, programs for persons with severe handicaps are successful to the extent that the clinician (a) does an individualized assessment of needs and strengths in a client's behavioral repertoire and (b) carries out and objectively evaluates an individually tailored set of interventions designed to build on these strengths and to change problem behavior. As detailed in Chapters 2 and 9, such personalization demands that the clinician first take time to observe the client in a number of functioning environments using a range of observational methods and tools. Second, the individual client's responses to interventions should be systematically recorded and analyzed. Third, personalization is maximized if one coordinator oversees and reviews on a regular basis all of the clients' program areas, so that behavioral progress or difficulties in various sites and with various members of the treatment team can be compared and coordinated. Finally, personalization can mean involving the client to the fullest extent possible in the therapeutic process (as exemplified later in this chapter).

4. *Planned strategy for generalization.* A good behavioral program actively prepares for generalization of treatment effects (Stokes & Baer, 1977; Haring et al. 1983). Rather than use what Stokes and Baer (1977) call the "train and hope" method, a number of strategies are suggested for conceptualizing and actively pursuing generalization effects. Alternatives include training in a number of settings ("sequential modification"); including different types of antecedents ("training sufficient exemplars"), such as when a response is learned to a variety of verbal cues; "training loosely" or using relatively little control over the stimuli presented and the correct responses allowed; and using intermittent schedules of reinforcement that produce "indiscriminable contingencies" that maintain responding since a client is unable to discriminate whether or not a response is likely to be reinforced. Stokes and Baer even suggest that we can train "to generalize," that is, that generalization should be considered as a response itself and reinforced as such. This procedure seems at odds with most established instructional methods (Haring et al., 1983) since a learner would not be reinforced for learning a new skill, but only for generalized responding. However, one can see it as a variant of "shaping" new, creative responding. The most dependable of all generalization programming procedures detailed by Stokes and Baer is to introduce the individual to "natural maintaining contingencies," usually by teaching behaviors that will normally be maintained after training. For example, teaching a child with autism to play a table game might be naturally maintained by sibling interaction. In instances where no natural reinforcers are available, Stokes and Baer say that semicontrived or redesigned "natural" reinforcement will have to be arranged.

A final strategy "mediating generalization" includes teaching an individual to talk, think (self-talk), or act in ways to facilitate generalization. "In essence, it requires establishing a response as part of the new learning that is likely to be utilized in other problems as well, and will constitute sufficient commonality between the original learning and the new problem to result in generalization" (Stokes & Baer, 1977, p. 360). The behavioral literature on self-control and self-management is built on this strategy of mediating generalization.

Choice of Intervention

What behavior we target for change and the means by which we choose to effect that change have become an increasingly important

Figure 3-1
Decision-making Guidelines for Behavioral Program

Child's Name: _____ Unit: _____
Supervisor: _____ Date: _____

Complete the following information when choosing an intervention

1. What is the targeted behavior? _____
2. Has baseline data been collected and analyzed? _____
   Results? _____
3. What is the goal for the behavior? _____

4. What alternate or incompatible behavior has been targeted? _____

5. What interventions were considered? _____

6. What is the proposed intervention? _____
   Why was it chosen over the others? _____

7. Has it been approved by the Human Rights Committee? _____
8. Does the literature support the use of the intervention to be the best one available for the targeted behavior? _____ If not, what is the rationale for using it? _____

9. Has the proposed intervention been previously used with the client? _____
   If yes, what were the results? _____

10. Is the proposed intervention experimental? _____ If yes, what support is there for using it? _____

11. If the intervention is aversive, have positive or less aversive interventions been tried? _____ If yes, describe the intervention(s) and results: _____

concern for behaviorists. The acquisition of functional and age-appropriate skills in relevant, real-life settings has become the ideal goal in behavioral programs (Brown et al., 1979; Koegel et al, 1982; Thompson, 1981). Achieving this goal will require that we clarify, and possibly expand, the procedure by which we choose the intervention that can best effect a behavior change in an individual client.

It is most helpful to adopt a predetermined decision-making sequence to ensure that choice of intervention is based on justifiable need; current client data and past literature; input by the client, family, and all members of the treatment team; and effective communication, implementation, recording, and review procedures, and in every way conforms to guidelines protecting the individual human rights of the client. Moreover, a predetermined decision process ensures that ques-

If not, explain the rationale for first going to an aversive intervention:_____

12. Are there any possible risks to the client or others from the intervention?_____ If yes, describe them and the safeguards being taken:___

13. Is the intervention compatible with the team's professional and personal values?_____ If not, how will this be resolved?_____

14. Describe the possible impact on treatment team members administering the intervention:_____
What safeguards are being taken to counteract any negative impact?_____

15. Does the team have sufficient knowledge and ability to carry out the intervention?_____ If not, how will they be trained?_____

16. Has the client been involved as much as possible in the decision-making? _____ If yes, describe how:_____

17. Does the intervention permit placing more responsibility on the client? _____ How is this accomplished?_____

18. If the intervention succeeds, what changes will be made for generalization?___
    For maintenance?_____

19. Is the intervention likely to be supported in other settings?_____
    Describe:_____

20. Are there any alternative intervention plans if this one does not work? _____ Describe:_____

    General comments:_____

tions such as those listed in Figure 3-1 are answered before an intervention is chosen. These questions allow the clinician to address the following key issues in choosing an appropriate and effective behavioral intervention.

1. *Has priority been given to the choice of a positive intervention?* The behavioral literature appears heavily weighted toward the use of aversive procedures (Scibak et al., 1983). The need for and practical utility of such procedures is very much in question, according to LaVigna and Donnellan, (1986). They argue that behavioral psychology's very success with aversive interventions has selectively reinforced a priori deci-

sions to use aversive, rather than positive, interventions. Furthermore, they cite the relative ineffectiveness of aversive interventions if one measures variables such as generalization, maintenance, and functional skill acquisition rather than just behavior deceleration.

In general, one does a severe injustice to a client not to consider, implement, and evaluate positive alternatives before implementing an aversive procedure. However, one can still argue that an aversive event should be used if a positive reinforcement procedure is thought not to be appropriate or found to be ineffective. Generally, changing the frequency of an undesirable behavior with positive reinforcement involves a large number of learning trials. In some cases, by the time the frequency of a problem behavior is reduced, a child could seriously injure himself or others, or experience serious interference with learning. Another reason it is often difficult to rely solely on positive reinforcement is that sometimes a dearth of reinforcement is available to severely disturbed children. The decision to use an aversive intervention procedure, however, must not, if possible, be made too hastily. A clinician at least should take the reasonable caution that aversive events are not employed to decelerate undesirable behaviors until antecedent conditions to these behaviors have been thoroughly analyzed.

Such analyses provide information about what conditions may be maintaining a behavior and the possible function that behavior may serve for the individual (e.g., communication, social attention, avoidance, sensory feedback). The purpose of the analysis is for ensuring that a modification of the conditions would not be sufficient to reduce or eliminate the behaviors and for guiding the clinician in choosing interventions to fit the communicative function of the behaviors.

Furthermore, an undesirable behavior that has been targeted for deceleration must always be paired with a desired behavior for acceleration. The selection of the appropriate desired behavior is based on an analysis of the function of the problem behavior and assumes that the client is an active learner who can learn a new, more appropriate, behavior to serve the necessary function, e.g., communication. (The reader is referred to Carr (1977) and Donnellan et al., (1984) for more extensive discussion of the analysis of the possible functions of aberrant behaviors and implications of such analysis for treatment.) In any case, the desired behavior must be as well-defined as the undesired behavior, with precise descriptions of what actions will be taken to promote the desired behavior and what reinforcement will be used to teach and maintain it in the client's repertoire.

2. *Have environment changes or alternative instructional strategies been*

tried to reduce problem behaviors? Environment changes can often be incorporated into a treatment program to help achieve a desired goal. If, for example, after a careful behavioral analysis one sees that some variable such as noise, crowding, or time of day, seems related to the onset of problem behaviors, one should systematically alter that variable to see its effect on behavior. A child who persistently has tantrums at the beginning of the school day may be doing so because he is hungry or tired after a long bus ride. Providing breakfast or some physical activity when the child arrives might prevent tantrums and allow opportunities for positive instruction or communication. A behavioral program that alters environmental variables to produce a desired behavior change is in accordance with both principles of ecological psychology (Risley, 1977; Rogers-Warren & Warren, 1977) and the operant analysis of stimulus control (Sulzer-Azaroff & Mayer, 1977, p. 162).

Alternative instructional strategies can also often be used to reduce problem behaviors. The particular perceptual needs and learning styles of severely learning-disabled clients often result in extreme frustration with or disinterest in more traditional instructional strategies. Disruptive behaviors can often be eliminated or reduced by using errorless learning channels and more reinforcing instructional settings, materials, or pace or level of instruction.

3. *How much is the behavioral program guided by an appreciation of each individual client's role "in the physical and contingency milieu" (Rogers-Warren & Warren, 1977) of his everyday life?* Would the planned intervention significantly alter the reciprocal relationships the client has established between him and others in the environment? What will be the impact of a behavior change in this complex network of reciprocal relations between an individual client and his environment? Prizant (1983), Carr (1977), and Lovaas (1981) each point out that often the "problem behaviors" of clients with autism serve significant social, stimulatory, and communicative needs. Similarly, Cautela (1984) emphasizes the balance of reinforcers that is required in each individual's life. All would argue for the consideration of such variables before the onset of an intervention procedure.

4. *How much control does the client have in managing his own behavior?* A final issue that is important to the choice of an appropriate intervention is the role the client can assume in controlling himself. The special-needs individual is subject to a wide range of externally controlled contingencies. These include broad-impact variables such as court decisions regarding placement; or teacher-imposed daily activity schedules; and also narrower impact variables, such as the use of tokens

and public checks or cues to behavior. Furthermore, the reasoning and current technology used in most behavioral intervention programs for special-needs individuals assume (often implicitly) the necessity for externally based control procedures.

Though behavioral technology provides the primary and most effective intervention strategy for persons with severe behavior disorders, procedures based on self-control, or internally managed contingencies, remain conspicuously absent from this growing technology. In the same spirit in which we worked to remove environmental barriers for the physically handicapped and educational barriers for all persons with handicaps, we can rethink our decision-making and treatment strategies for special-needs individuals to remove, as much as possible, the constraints of external control. Donnellan (1981, p. 71) suggests as a strategy for deciding what to teach children with autism that teachers should ask themselves, "If this child does not learn to perform this skill, will someone have to do it for the child?" In the same spirit, the clinician should ask, "If this child does not learn to make self-controlling responses, what external controls will have to be put into effect during this child's life?" Existing literature (Drabman et al., 1973) supports the advantages of teaching self-controlling responses to normal children as an aid to generalization of treatment effects. Also, in our culture a person's social value is enhanced to the extent that the person appears autonomous or capable of managing his own life. Increasing self-control in developmentally disabled persons would provide the added advantage of increasing personal dignity and worth. The remainder of this chapter details two strategies, relaxation training and imagery-based covert conditioning, which can be implemented in programs designed to increase self-control in this population.

The Expanded Behavioral Repertoire: Self-Control Procedures

Is self-control possible? Behavioral researchers have presented a variety of definitions of the term "self-control" or "self-regulation" (Cautela, 1969; Kanfer, 1977; Thorenson & Mahoney, 1974). The behavioral literature (e.g., Cautela, 1969; Rimm & Masters, 1974; Thorensen & Mahoney, 1974) includes under the term "self-control" procedures or strategies such as *self-monitoring* (as when a person records the number of laps jogged or the amount of piece work completed); *self-instruction* (as when an individual verbally directs his own behavior during assembly of an intricate machine or as one prepares to approach an anxiety-provoking situation); and *self-reinforcement* (as when one rewards oneself with leisure time after completing a difficult assignment). One can even broaden the definition of self-control to mean involvement by the client even in the choice of behaviors to be modified or intervention to be employed. To put it another way, we say that a child with autism has made a self-controlling response whenever (1) he has learned to make a new, more apropriate response, and (2) this new response is made in the apparent absence of external cues, prompts, or contingencies. With this definition we assume not that self-control is a "higher" personal quality or ability that is only possible for individuals within a select cognitive range, but that it is a group of responses that any individual can learn to make. Another assumption we make is that all individuals, normal or with special needs, have the right to as much "freedom" as possible from externally imposed and controlled contingencies over their behavior.

Both relaxation training and covert conditioning (a set of imagery-based procedures for increasing or decreasing response probabilities) are treatment strategies that exemplify a behavioral approach to teaching self-control. Each strategy teaches the client to observe himself and to take a central role in changing his own behavior.

Relaxation Training

The behavior of persons with autism often includes disruptive, stereotypic, or self-injurious responses. If such a client could learn to make a relaxation response, this response could function as a more adaptive behavior that would be incompatible with disruptive, stereotypic, or self-injurious behavior. Furthermore, the client could learn to discriminate the presence in himself of muscle tension, which, it seems, is a component, and often a precursor, of disruptive behavior. With teacher cues a client could replace the tense behavior with a relaxation response. Eventually, with the gradual fading of external cues, the client would independently respond to muscle tension with the relaxation response.

ADAPTING RELAXATION TRAINING TO SPECIAL-NEEDS CHILDREN

As Cautela and Groden (1978) point out in their book *Relaxation: A Comprehensive Manual for Adults, Children, and Children with Special*

Needs, a number of adaptations of the traditional relaxation procedure (Jacobsen, 1938) are needed to accommodate the learning requirements of a special-needs population. The instructional sequence is changed so that the child first learns to tighten and relax gross motor areas (e.g., the arms) before more difficult parts, such as the forehead. The teaching procedure often includes more touching and manipulation as students are physically guided through steps (e.g., tightening the arm) of the procedure. Gradual shaping and fading of cues are often required. Concrete reinforcers such as food, tokens, and pleasant activities are sometimes employed in addition to social reinforcers (e.g., praise, smiling). Instructions are simplified and geared to the receptive skills of the individual. Special apparatus may be needed to facilitate and gradually augment responding. For example, a squeeze toy can facilitate the learning of tensing the hand muscles. Whistles or straws can be used to shape and amplify the deep breathing response. Physical handicaps often necessitate the elimination or modification of some step in the procedure. In such cases it is sometimes necessary to consult a physical therapist. Individual differences (e.g., attention span, distractibility) often necessitate shortening (and gradual lengthening) of the session.

TEACHING THE RELAXATION RESPONSE

Clients are taught the relaxation procedure, usually in a one-to-one teaching session lasting approximately 15 to 20 minutes, in an area with minimal distraction and noise. The practice session is a regularly scheduled event built into the client's daily schedule. The relaxation training procedure includes teaching readiness skills such as quiet sitting, eye contact, generalized imitation, and following simple locomotor instructions. Then the client learns to tighten and relax the arms, hands, and legs, and to do deep breathing in a sitting position. The client is then taught relaxing without tensing. Finally, the client is taught to tighten and relax all remaining muscle groups of the body—eyes, mouth, lips, stomach, nose, jaws, back, forehand, chest, and below the waist. All the previous skills are taught first in a sitting position, then in a standing position, then while walking, and finally while lying down.

Since it is a goal to have the client use the relaxation response in a variety of environments, it must be taught and practiced with maintenance and generalization in mind. While a rich schedule of positive reinforcers accompanies the acquisition of any step of the tense–relax sequence, after a particular skill (e.g., tighten–relax the arm) is acquired, it is maintained in a client's repertoire through intermittent reinforcement. After becoming proficient in tensing and relaxing major muscle groups, the client then practices these new skills in a variety of environments and with increasingly larger groups of children with similar proficiency levels. Often, when using a desensitization model (Wolpe, 1958), antecedent stimuli (e.g., a feared object, a change in the daily routine, or a new staff member) are presented in gradually increasing intensities, durations, or proximities while the child is cued to relax.

When cueing the use of relaxation outside the teaching session (e.g., just prior to or during a disruptive behavior or an anxiety-provoking situation), the clinician teacher should keep in mind the following guidelines:

1. Using a calm voice and gentle manner, cue relaxation response verbally (e.g., "Take a deep breath and relax") and physically (e.g., signal "relax" in sign language).

2. Instruct client how to do an appropriate alternative behavior while remaining calm and relaxed.

3. Use social and, as necessary, tangible reinforcers after client displays relaxation response.

Once having learned to relax various muscle groups, the child is verbally cued to perform the relaxation procedure in a number of situations. For example, *during* an episode of disruptive behavior (e.g., head rolling), the child could be cued to relax the head. *Before* entering a situation (e.g., a field trip or a testing situation), the child could be reminded to relax, and perhaps imagine having a good time. *After* a disturbing episode has happened (e.g., another child disturbs the environment), he could be cued to relax and return to whatever activity was being performed prior to the disturbing incident.

The relaxation training procedure can be learned by persons with autism and other severe behavior disorders in just a few sessions, or may require continued incremental daily practice for many weeks, depending on the client's level of functioning. A number of reports are available that demonstrate the use of relaxation training to treat a number of behavior disorders in clients with developmental disabilities (Graziano & Kean, 1971; Steen & Zuriff, 1977).

The use of relaxation as an integral part of a therapeutic program for a special-needs child has some very positive effects on the human service or home ecosystem in which it is employed. First of all it provides a *positive intervention strategy* for dealing with behaviors (self-injurious behaviors) that are traditionally (Forehand & Baumeister, 1976) dealt with by use of punishment procedures. Punishment procedures sometimes result in avoidance of persons doing the punishing; often produce a child with rigid, ill-at-ease or automaton-like response patterns; and since they are often quite effective in a relatively short period of time, easily proliferate in a treatment setting (Bandura, 1969). A systemwide implementation of relaxation can help avoid this self-maintaining negative modeling. Furthermore, teaching a child a calm, relaxed response style can enhance "normal" integration into home and community settings.

A second by-product of the use of relaxation procedures by all staff in a treatment setting or by family members in a child's home is its effect in producing a pleasant living or learning environment. Treatment staff or parents who have been shaped into using ineffective louder and louder reprimands can learn to use such reprimands only as planned contingencies, and can use a calmly presented cue to relax instead. Given the tensions often inherent in working or living with behaviorally disordered children, the relaxation response provides an effective self-management tool for the care giver. A calm clinician or parent is more likely to make good treatment decisions and to interact with a child efficaciously.

Finally, when a child has learned to self-initiate a relaxation response, and that response is observed by others, he can be perceived as someone capable of controlling (albeit sometimes in a very limited way) his own behavior. This contrasts with the often obtrusive and sometimes impractical interventions employed with this population in public settings. The self-control that results from the use of relaxation training enhances not only the personal dignity, but also the social attractiveness of persons with autism and behavior disorders.

Covert Conditioning

Much of the research with individuals with autism or other behavioral disorders shows effective intervention with overt operant procedures, that is, procedures in which the response to be decelerated or accelerated and the consequence naturally occur in or are presented to the person's physical environment. We have explored the use of an imagery-based operant conditioning paradigm called *covert conditioning* (Cautela, 1973; Cautela & Baron, 1977). In covert conditioning procedures, a client is asked to imagine performing a behavior that is to be modified, such as making bizarre body movements (a deceleration target) or initiating a social interchange (an acceleration target). The client is then asked to imagine a consequence designed to decrease or increase the probability of that behavior. These procedures are labeled covert sensitization, covert reinforcement, covert negative reinforcement, covert response cost, and covert modeling, and are analogous to the operant conditioning procedures. Preliminary clinical interventions and experimental data have provided evidence that (1) clients labeled autistic or psychotic or severely behaviorally disordered can cooperate in learning and using procedures that involve imagery, and (2) these procedures are effective in reducing problem behaviors (Cautela & Baron, 1973; Groden & Cautela, 1984; Workman & Dickinson, 1979) and increasing deficit behaviors (Groden, 1982).

These positive findings have encouraged us in our efforts to broaden our clinical repertoires with many children with autism so that imagery-based procedures now serve as a standard intervention strategy. Moreover, our successes have supported our growing awareness of the role of these children's "inner lives" or private behaviors in the shaping and controlling of their lives.

ASSUMPTIONS/RATIONALE

The authors have outlined elsewhere (Baron & Cautela, 1983; Groden & Cautela, 1984) the working assumptions supporting the use of imagery-based procedures with special-needs children. These include the radical behaviorist perspective that *private events such as imaging (and thinking and feeling) obey the same laws of learning* and have equal status in the explanation and control of behavior. These private events are differentiated from public, observable events primarily by their location and relative inaccessibility to public confirmation. This means that imaging is a behavior that can be assumed to increase or decrease in frequency depending on the contingencies applied. Another important assumption is that the *behavior of imaging can be taught* if it is not already in a child's repertoire. In other words, the fact that a child is labeled as "special needs," or at first cannot cooperate with a therapist's instructions to imagine something, or at first does not appear to have self-generated imaging responses in his repertoire, should not prevent the therapist from attempting to use clinical procedures involving imagery.

Finally, the nature of imagery (i.e., it is a private event and unobservable per se) and the nature of our clients' verbal repertoires (i.e., they may be mute or possess deficient communication skills) required that we make another assumption about how we determine that a child is imaging.

Assessment of imaging may focus on certain classes of external events that cue an observer that imaging has occurred or is occurring in an individual's repertoire. These observable events support the inference that a child is imaging. These events are actions, or behaviors, that a child either does, or does not do. For example, a child who is asked to imagine eating an ice cream cone may make throat and lip movements, thus indicating the following of instructions. Sometimes imaging can be observed via the impact of imaging on a child's behavioral repertoire—as when remembering that cookies are in the cupboard results in opening the cupboard. Therefore, one can observe objective concomitants of imaging and/or objective consequences of performing an imaging behavior. Cautela (1982) and Groden and Cautela (1984) have made some suggestions for activities that help assess a client's imaging capabilities. Also, at the Groden Center a battery of imaging assessment procedures has been developed (Baron & Cautela, 1983) for use with normal and special-needs children. As part of this imagery assessment, parents, teachers, and other clinicians are asked to provide observations of a child's use of imagery in day-to-day activities such as play and classroom learning. The Functional Imagery Checklist (Baron & Cautela, 1983) also allows the clinician to examine the reliability of imaging across settings and provides an overview of the spontaneous imagery already in a client's behavioral repertoire.

INVESTIGATIVE STUDIES ON COVERT CONDITIONING

A few clinicians and investigators (Cautela, 1982; Groden & Cautela, 1984; Groden, 1982; Guralnick, 1973) have successfully treated children who are retarded or have autistic-like characteristics with clinical procedures that involve imagery. A series of studies done by Groden (1982) and Groden and Cautela (1984) systematically investigate the impact of covert conditioning procedures (Cautela, 1973; 1982) with children who are labeled retarded or autistic.

Groden and Cautela (1984), in a multiple baseline design across behaviors, demonstrated the effectiveness of covert procedures to reduce socially aberrant behaviors in students labeled "trainable retarded." Specifically, covert reinforcement and covert modeling procedures were used in a therapeutic, nonclassroom setting to change behaviors in a classroom setting. The design of the study included the following elements: a two-week baseline period, treatment of behavior 1, demand phase on behavior 2 in which the experimenter strongly requested that the student desist from the targeted behaviors, treatment of behavior 2, demand phase for behavior 3, treatment of behavior 3.

Subject one was a 15-year-old blind boy with multiple handicaps. Behaviors targeted for him included loud nose honking, wrist bending, and rocking. Covert reinforcement procedures were used in the treatment conditions for this subject. A typical covert reinforcement scene follows:

Imagine you are working on braille with your teacher. You feel your arm about to move toward your nose so that you can blow through your nose. You say to yourself, 'No, I'm not going to make that sound with my nose, it's not good for my ears. I'd better just put my hand back on the braille.' You feel your hand moving back to the braille and you feel the dots on your fingers. (The therapist then asks the student to raise his right index finger when the scene is clear. The therapist then describes the reinforcement.) Now, imagine you are eating your mother's sugar cookies right from the oven with a glass of delicious, cold milk; imagine biting into that cookie and thinking how good it tastes. Smell the cookie, try to taste the cookie and that cold milk. Think how good and cool it feels in your mouth.

Subject two was a 13-year-old girl with Down syndrome. The three behaviors pinpointed for her were keeping her head low on her chest, excessive nose picking, and tongue chewing. Covert modeling procedures were used to reduce these behaviors.

For treatment each child was seen by a therapist-experimenter for three 15-minute sessions each school day for six months, as part of the ongoing school curriculum. Covert modeling or covert reinforcement scenes were presented during these sessions. During the course of the study, daily recordings were taken in the classroom in three different situations: subject working alone, subject in a group situation, and subject working one to one. Interrater reliability was obtained.

There were no changes as a result of the demand condition. However, results indicated dramatic changes for both subjects in each of the targeted behaviors as the imagery procedures were employed. Both covert modeling and covert reinforcement techniques were equally effective. In addition to the fact that the socially inappropriate behaviors were significantly reduced by these techniques, the results also suggest that imagery procedures can be utilized effectively with retarded individuals in a school environment. It is suggested that the implications for changing in-class behavior with verbally mediated imagery treatment outside of the classroom are far-reaching in terms of mainstreaming and integrating special-needs children.

Another study (Groden, 1982) investigated the impact of covert conditioning in increasing peer social interaction in children and adolescents with autism. The dependent variable was positive verbal behaviors (initiations, responses, and continuations) in a play context. Covert reinforcement (Cautela, 1970) scenes such as the following were employed with each client in the two groups of three clients (Group I—ages = 14–21 years, IQ = 47–85; and Group II—ages = 8–13 years, IQ = 34–49).

Peter, imagine you are in the playroom (describe the room, tell me what toys you see). Picture yourself in the room (what are you wearing?). Imagine taking the matching cards, you feel the cards in your hand (what card do you have?). You say to John and Mark, come and play this game with me. You sit at the table and wave your hand to John and Mark (can you feel your hand waving to John and Mark?). Now imagine you are eating a chocolate ice cream cone (tell me how it feels in your mouth; can you smell the ice cream?).

The observations of peer interaction were made daily through a one-way mirror in a playroom setting for 20 minutes. The intervention was carried out twice daily in 15-minute sessions with a therapist not associated with the playroom setting activities. The study included baseline, demand-control, and intervention phases. The results indicate that for three (of the six) students, a combination of therapist request, modeling, and covert reinforcement significantly increased verbal interaction. For the three other students, covert reinforcement alone seemed to be the critical factor in increasing interactions.

Drucker (1980) extended Groden's research and again used a single case design to examine whether covert reinforcement could effect a similar positive change in social interaction in a more natural setting as it had in a laboratory setting. Her study was conducted in the children's classroom as part of their daily program. Four autistic or autistic-like students, whose verbal capabilities ranged from short phrases to complete and meaningful sentences, participated in daily play sessions (baseline). Frequency of appropriate initiations, inappropriate behaviors, and episodes of eye contacts were recorded. Two students took part in daily 15-minute sessions (just prior to the play sessions), during which they practiced a number of covert reinforcement scenes that exemplified peer interaction.

The students' number of appropriate initiations increased significantly from the baseline to treatment phase. During the last eight treatment sessions, student one made an average of 16.25 initiations compared with 4.25 average initiations during an eight-day baseline. Student two increased from a daily average of one initiation during a seven-day baseline to a daily average of 3.86 initiations during the last seven days of treatment. Furthermore, inappropriate behaviors (e.g., irrelevant talk, stereotypic movements) began to decelerate and the amount of eye contact increased, even though neither of these behaviors was targeted for treatment. Two students served as controls; that is, they did not receive covert reinforcement treatment and showed no increase in initiations from baseline to treatment.

A number of other topics invite further research in the use of covert conditioning with clients with severe behavior disorders. First, though there is some evidence of positive impact of such procedures with this population, what client characteristics (communication ability or imagery skills of the client, type of problem behavior) are indicative of probable success of such an intervention? Second, covert conditioning procedures are themselves an active social process. What features of this process are critical to the success of the procedures? Groden and Cautela's (1984) use of the "demand" control phase presents some evidence that the instructional, or even self-instructional, aspect of covert conditioning has some role in the procedure's effectiveness. And finally, and perhaps most important, do self-control procedures that involve covert conditioning facilitate maintenance and generalization of learning, as do their overt counterparts?

WHEN ARE IMAGERY PROCEDURES APPROPRIATE?

The behavioral evaluator and clinician must first determine that (1) a child has both the necessary cooperation and communication skills and (2) there is some evidence that the child's behavioral repertoire includes imaging before choosing to use an imagery-based clinical procedure. We define cooperation as the child having the ability to, and actually does, follow the clinician's instructions for a minimum of two to three minutes. The instructions may include requests to (1) sit or lie down in a relaxed manner, (2) close the eyes (or allow the eyes to be covered with a cloth), (3) listen to instructions, and (4) carry out instructions. The child must have a communication system. We have worked, so far, primarily with children with oral communication; however, imagery procedures can be adapted to a sign or pictorial communication system. The Functional Imagery Checklist, cited earlier, provides the clinician with evidence of a child's day-to-day use of imagery abilities. The clinician may elect to do a more intensive assessment (Baron & Cautela, 1983), specifically noting the child's abilities in labeling, remembering, imitating–pretending, sequencing, describing an image, and stopping and starting an image (all components, or subskills, of imaging).

Imagery-based procedures may be appropriate in any of the following situations or problem behaviors.

1. *Limited opportunity to practice a correct response.* Some behaviors occur at a low frequency and present a limited opportunity to practice correct responding. For example, a child has an extreme fear of injections, but only visits a doctor annually. In such a case, a procedure such as covert reinforcement (Cautela, 1970) or covert modeling (Cautela, 1976) would allow repeated practice in approaching the feared situation and responding in a nonfearful way. Similarly, a child who is preparing for transition to another program may be prepared not only by actual visits to the other program, but also by the repeated successful visits presented via covert reinforcement. Here a child could imagine, for example, working alone at a desk (a behavior to be increased), or feeling the urge to flap his hands in front of his eyes (a behavior to be decreased), but relaxing his hands instead (i.e., making a self-controlling response).

2. *Self-injurious behavior.* Often self-injurious clients are not presented with much opportunity to practice correct responding or self-controlling behavior because of the severity, and sometimes the low frequency, of the problem behavior. In these situations punishment procedures are generally the treatment of choice. Imagery-based procedures can be used advantageously in these situations to increase non-self-injurious appropriate behavior. For example, as with one adolescent client labeled schizophrenic (Cautela & Baron, 1973), a combination of covert sensitization (Cautela, 1967) and covert reinforcement was used to teach self-control of severe self-injury (eye poking and lip biting and tearing). Similarly, covert reinforcement was effective with a four-year-old verbal child with autism whose response to changes in routine usually was a severe tantrum, which, in turn, led to intense asthmatic episodes. This child was taught to respond, via picture books, to variations in certain routines (e.g., bedtime preparation) with a relaxed response (i.e., taking a deep breath and saying "relax"). Tantrums and asthmatic episodes diminished in frequency and intensity as a result.

3. *Imagery as a component of the problem.* Clients who are autistic or severely disturbed sometimes show phobic reactions to certain stimuli or an intense preoccupation with an object. One can certainly hypothesize that the child's imaging may have a role in the maintenance of these problems. One eight-year-old mildly retarded, autistic-like boy was obsessed with flowers. His interest in flowers was so intense that he talked about, drew pictures of, and tried to pick any flowers he saw. Thwarting such actions led to severe tantrums. Along with the use of overt extinc-

tion and reinforcement procedures, this boy practiced, three times daily, tape-recorded imagery scenes in which he ignored flowers and continued his work or play, and his interest in flowers has been decreased to a manageable level.

SUGGESTIONS FOR FUTURE USES OF IMAGERY PROCEDURES

To date our experiences with imagery procedures have focused on the use of covert conditioning procedures in a child's treatment program. These initial successful efforts have encouraged us to explore further the advantages of using imagery-based procedures for individuals with autism and mental retardation.

For example, since imagery processes are assumed to play a central mediating role (Paivio, 1971) in learning, one can use imagery to expand educational strategies with our clients. A child's imagery skills can be incorporated into the child's academic, play, and social skills curricula. One can also consider the advantage of teaching imagery skills as a standard component of the life curriculum of our clients—that is, *prescriptive programming* in imagery skills development. Rather than preclude the use of mediational methods such as covert conditioning with individuals with autism, clinicians and teachers should consider imagery-based techniques as viable procedures with this population.

CONCLUSIONS

This chapter has presented a picture of current behavioral technology as it applies in the clinical treatment of persons with autism and other severe behavior disorders. It details two procedures, relaxation training and imagery-based covert conditioning, that hold much promise for expanding clinical endeavors with this population.

Both of these procedures are helpful in meeting the needs of clients to learn to function effectively under real-life circumstances. These procedures can provide clients training in controlling and managing their own behavior, thus minimizing dependency on external control by others. Such self-control procedures are particularly helpful in programs that require functional skills in real-life settings where an external controlling agent (i.e., a teacher who gives verbal praise, a token system dispensed on a pre-fixed schedule) is either intrusive or impractical. It is, in fact, our expectation that these self-control procedures will aid the individual with autism to bridge the gap between the ideal of community integration and the reality of adjustment in community-based settings.

It is the authors' hope that this review succeeds in giving the reader an appreciation of both the actual and potential contributions of a behavioral perspective in the treatment of children with autism and other behavioral disorders.

REFERENCES

Bandura, A. (1969). *Principles of behavior modification.* New York: Holt, Rinehart and Winston.

Baron, G. & Cautela, J. R. (1983). Imagery assessment and special needs children. *Imagination, Cognition and Personality,* 3(1), 17-30.

Brown, L., Branston, M., Hamre-Nieutupski, S., Pumpian, I., Certo, N. & Gruenwald, L. (1979). A strategy for developing chronological age-appropriate and functional curricular content for severely handicapped adolescents and young adults. *Journal of Special Education,* 13, 81-90.

Carr, E. (1977). The motivation of self-injurious behavior: A review of some of hypotheses. *Psychological Bulletin,* 84, 800-816.

Carr, E. G. (1977). The motivation of self-injurious behavior: A review of some hypotheses. *Psychological Bulletin,* 84, 800-816.

Cautela, J. R. (1967). Covert sensitization. *Psychological Reports,* 20, 459-468.

Cautela, J. R. (1969). Behavior therapy and self-control: techniques and implications. In C. Franks (Ed.), *Behavior therapy: Appraisal and status.* New York: McGraw-Hill, pp. 323-340.

Cautela, J. R. (1970). Covert reinforcement. *Behavior Therapy,* 1, 33-50.

Cautela, J. R. (1973). Covert processes and behavior modification. *The Journal of Nervous and Mental Disease,* 157, 27-36.

Cautela, J. R. (1976). The present status of covert modeling. *Journal of Behavior Therapy and Experimental Psychiatry,* 7, 323-326.

Cautela, J. R. (1982). Covert conditioning with children. *Journal of Behavior Therapy and Experimental Psychiatry,* 13(3), 209-214.

Cautela, J. R. (1984). General level of reinforcement. *Journal of Behavior Therapy and Experimental Psychiatry,* 15(2) 109-114.

Cautela, J. R. & Baron, M. G. (1973). Multi-faceted behavior therapy of self-injurious behavior. *Journal of Behavior Therapy and Experimental Psychiatry,* 4, 125-131.

Cautela, J. R. & Baron, M. G. (1977). Covert conditioning: A theoretical analysis. *Behavior Modification,* 1, 356-368.

Cautela, J. R. & Groden, J. (1978). *Relaxation: A comprehensive manual for adults, children, and children with special needs.* Champaign, Ill.: Research Press.

Donnellan, A. M. (1981). An educational perspective of autism: Implications for curriculum development and personnel development. In B. Wilcox and A. Thompson (Eds.), *Critical issues in educating autistic children and youth.* (Washington, D.C.: NSAC, pp. 53-88).

Donnellan, A., Gossage, L. D., LaVigna, G. W., Schuler, A. & Traphagen, J. D. (1977). *Teaching makes a difference: A guide for developing successful classes for autistic and other severely handicapped children.* Sacramento, Calif.: California State Department of Education.

Donnellan, A. M., Mirenda, P. L., Mesaros, R. A. & Fassbender, L. L. (1984). A strategy for analyzing the communicative functions of behavior. *Journal of the Association for Persons with Severe Handicaps,* 9(3), 201–212.

Drabman, R. S., Spitalnik, R. & O'Leary, K. D. (1973). Teaching self-control to disruptive children. *Journal of Abnormal Psychology,* 82, 10–16.

Drucker, W. C. (1980). *The use of covert reinforcement procedures to increase the verbal interaction of autistic children in the classroom setting.* Unpublished undergraduate thesis, Wheaton College, Norton, Mass.

Ferster, C. B. (1961). Positive reinforcement and behavioral deficits of autistic children. *Child Development,* 32, 437–456.

Ferster, C. B. & DeMyer, M. K. (1962) A method for the experimental analysis of the behavior of autistic children. *American Journal of Orthopsychiatry,* 32(1), 81 - 98. Reprinted (1967) in S. W. Bijou & D. M. Baer, (Eds.) *Child development: Readings in experimental analysis.* New York: Appleton-Century-Crofts.

Ferster, C. B. & DeMyer, M. K. (1961). The development of performances in autistic children in automatically controlled environment. *Journal of Chronic Disorders,* 13, 312–345.

Forehand, R. & Baumeister, A. A. (1976). Deceleration of aberrant behavior among retarded individuals. In M. Hersen, R. M. Eisler, and P. M. Miller. (Eds.), *Behavior modification.* New York: Academic Press.

Foxx, R. M. (1980). *Effective behavioral programming: Procedures for educating and training retarded persons.* Champaign, Ill.: Research Press.

Graziano, A. M. & Kean, J. E. (1971). Programmed relaxation and reciprocal inhibition with psychotic children. In A. M. Graziano (Ed.), *Behavior therapy with children.* Chicago: Aldine.

Groden, J. (1982). *Procedures to increase social interaction among autistic adolescents: A multple baseline analysis.* University Microfilms International no. 8215479.

Groden, G. & Baron, G. (1987). *Autism: Strategies for Change.* New York: Gardner Press.

Groden, J., Baron, G., Pentecost, A. & Stevenson, S. (1987). A systems approach to implementing educational curricula and treatment for persons with autism. In G. Groden & G. Baron (Eds), *Autism: Strategies for change.* New York: Gardner Press.

Groden, J. & Cautela J. R. (1987). Use of imagery procedures with students labeled 'trainable retarded.' *Psychological Reports,* 54, 595–605.

Guralnick, M. J. (1973). Behavior therapy with an acrophobic mentally retarded young adult. *Journal of Behavior Therapy and Experimental Psychiatry,* 4, 263–265.

Haring, N., Liberty, K., Billingsley, F., Butterfield, E. & White, O. (1983). *Investigating the problem of skill generalization.* Seattle: University of Washington/Washington Research Organization.

Jacobson, E. (1938). *Progressive relaxation.* Chicago: University of Chicago Press.

Kanfer, F. H. (1977). The many faces of self-control or behavior modification changes its focus. In R. B. Stuart (Ed.), *Behavioral self-management.* New York: Brunner/Mazel.

Kanfer, F. H. & Saslow, G. (1969). Behavior diagnosis. In C. M. Franks (Ed), *Behavior therapy: Appraisal and status*. New York: McGraw-Hill.

Kazdin, A. E. (1975). Characteristics and trends in applied behavior analysis. *Journal of Applied Behavior Analysis, 8,* 332.

Koegel, R. L., Rincover, A. & Egel, A. L. (1982). *Educating and understanding autistic children.* San Diego, Calif.: College-Hill.

LaVigna, G. & Donnellan, A. M. (1986). *Alternatives to punishment: Non-aversive strategies for solving behavior problems.* New York: Irvington.

Lovaas, O. I. (1981). *Teaching developmentally disabled children: The me book.* Baltimore: University Park Press.

Lovaas, O. I.,. Young, D. B. & Newsom, C. D. (1978). Childhood psychosis. Behavioral treatment. In B. B. Wolman, J. Egan, and A. O. Ross (Eds.), *Handbook of treatment of mental disorders in childhood and adolescence.* Englewood Cliffs, N.J.: Prentice-Hall, pp. 385–420.

Luce, S. C. & Christian, W. P. (1981). *How to reduce autistic and severely maladaptive behaviors.* Kansas: H & H Enterprises.

Mahoney, M. J. & Thorensen, E. E. (Ed.) (1974). *Self-control: Power to the person.* Calif.: Brooks/Cole.

Nelson, R. O. (1983). Current status and new developments in behavioral assessment. In A. E. Kazdin (Chair), *Behavioral assessment: Historical development, advances and current status.* Symposium conducted at the meeting of the Association for Advancement of Behavior Therapy, Washington, D. C.

Olley, J. G. (1981). A behavioral approach to childhood autism: Have we overlooked some things?. Paper presented at the meeting of the Association for Behavior Analysis, Milwaukee, Wis.

Paivio, A. *Imagery and verbal processes* (1971). New York: Holt, Reinhart & Winston.

Prizant, B. (1983). Echolalia in autism: Assessment and intervention. *Seminars in Speech and Language, 4,*(1), 63–77.

Puluzny, M. J. (1980). *Autism: A practical guide for parents and professionals.* Syracuse, N.Y.: Syracuse University Press.

Rimm, D. C. & Masters, J. C. (1974). *Behavior therapy: Techniques and empirical findings.* New York: Academic Press.

Risley, T. R. (1977). The social context of self-control. In R. B. Stuart (Ed.), *Behavior self-management: Strategies, techniques and outcomes.* New York: Brunner/Mazel.

Ritvo, E. R. (Ed.) (1976). *Autism: Diagnosis, current research and management.* New York: Spectrum Rogers-Warren, A., & Warren, S. (1977). The developing ecobehavioral psychology. In A. Rogers-Warren and S. Warren (Eds.), *Ecological perspectives in behavioral analysis.* Baltimore: University Park Press.

Sailor, W., Wilcox, B. & Brown, L. (1980). *Methods of instruction for severely handicapped.* Baltimore: Paul H. Brookes.

Schreibman, L. & Koegel, R. L. (1981). A guideline for planning behavior modifcation programs for autistic children. In S. M. Turner, K. S. Calhoun, and H. E. Adams (Eds.), *Handbook of clinical behavior therapy.* New York: Wiley, pp. 500–526.

Scibak, J., Bertsch, G. & Zane, T. (1983). Decelerative techniques and factors influencing their aversiveness: Clinical judgements. In T. Zane (Chair). *Aversive procedures: Reconciling human rights, research, and effectiveness.* Symposium conducted at the meeting of the Association for Behavior Analysis, Milwaukee, Wis.

Steen, P. L. & Zuriff, G. E. (1977). The use of relaxation in the treatment of self-injurious behavior. *Journal of Behavior Therapy and Experimental Psychiatry*, 8, 447–448.

Stokes, T. F. & Baer, D. M. (1977). An implicit technology of generalization. *Journal of Applied Behavior Analysis*, 10, 349–367.

Sulzer-Azaroff, B. & Mayer, G. R. (1977). *Applying behavior analysis procedures with children and youth*. New York: Holt, Rinehart and Winston.

Sulzer-Azaroff, B. & Reese, E. P. (1982). *Applying behavioral analysis: A program for developing professional competence*. New York: Holt, Rinehart and Winston.

Thompson, R. P. (1981). Afterword. In B. Wilcox and A. Thompson (Eds.), *Critical issues in educating autistic children and youth*. Washington, D. C.: NSAC.

Thorensen, C. E. & Mahoney, M. J. (1974). *Behavioral self-control*. New York: Holt, Reinhart & Winston.

Webster, C. D., Konstantareas, M. M., Oxman, J. & Mack, J. E. (Eds.) (1980). *Autism: New directions in research and education*. New York: Pergamon Press.

Wilcox, B. & Thompson, A. (Eds.) (1981). *Critical issues in educating autistic children and youth*. Washington, D. C.: NSAC.

Wisocki, P. (1987). Behavioral assessment procedures for the evaluation of children with autism. In G. Groden and G. Baron (Eds.), *Autism: Strategies for change*. New York: Gardner Press.

Wolf, M. M. (1978). Social validity: The case for subjective measurement or how applied behavior analysis is finding its heart. *Journal of Applied Behavior Analysis*, 11, 203–214.

Wolpe, J. (1958). *Psychotherapy by reciprocal inhibition*. Stanford, Calif.: Stanford University Press.

Workman, E. A., and Dickinson, D. J. (1979). The use of covert conditioning with children: Three empirical case studies. *Education and Treatment of Children*, 2, 245–259.

CHAPTER 4

Intellectual Functioning and Assessment

Gerald Groden, Ph.D.
Leesa Mann, M.A.

Intellectual Functioning
   Level of Functioning
   Pattern of Functioning
   Specific Cognitive Deficits
Intellectual Assessment
   Choices of Instruments
   Dealing with Behavioral and
      Attentional Deficits

Utilization of Assessment Results
   A Behavior Sample
   Basis for Discussion with Parents
   Individualized Program Planning and
      Evaluation

INTELLECTUAL FUNCTIONING

Level of Functioning

AFTER AUTISM WAS FIRST IDENTIFIED as a syndrome, it was assumed that children with autism had potentially normal intelligence (DeMyer, 1976). The reasons for that assumption were many. One of the most compelling was that the children often demonstrated isolated skills that were far above the level of other skills, especially language skills. For example, they sometimes had excellent memory for auditory stimuli, such as numbers, phrases, or sentences. Some persons with autism could perform tasks that appeared quite complex and beyond the ability of most normal adults, such as giving the day of the week upon which a specific date in the past had fallen or would fall in the future. Others, though nonverbal, could perform at age level or above on nonlinguistic, visual-motor items such as puzzles or complex block patterns.

Other reasons for attributing to children with autism the potential for normal intelligence included their normal physical appearance and good motor dexterity; they tended not to show the physical characteristics that identify many retarded children, and their gross and fine motor skills were usually relatively intact. In addition, the tendency of children with autism to avoid physical contact and to attend selectively to some stimuli, while showing no response to other stimuli, often created an impression that their failures in evaluative and learning situations reflected inadequate motivation, rather than impaired ability.

Now it is generally accepted among serious students of the syndrome that children with autism have significant, measurable developmental and intellectual deficits that are obvious early in life, and, to a great extent, remain throughout life (DeMyer et al., 1981). The deficits, which will be discussed in greater detail in the following, can be reduced if appropriate instructional methods are applied, but they can rarely be eliminated (DeMyer et al., 1981). Most children with autism function below the average range on psychological tests, and on other types of measures as well, and will continue to lag behind their chronological age peers. They are not children who have withdrawn from contact with others simply as a result of certain environmental events, nor are they hiding normal cognition behind a facade of ritualistic behavior. They have real intellectual deficits that have been, and must continue to be, carefully and scientifically explored.

On standardized intelligence measures, such as the Wechsler Intelligence Scale for Children—Revised (WISC-R) (Wechsler, 1974) and the Stanford-Binet Intelligence Scale (Terman & Merrill, 1972), children with autism show significant delays. DeMyer and colleagues (1974) reported that 94 percent performed in the retarded range. Of these, 75 percent had standard scores below 51, and most fell within the moderately to severely retarded range. Less than 6 percent of children with autism were average to above average on global measures of cognitive ability. There appears to be a higher proportion of female to male children at very low intellectual levels than at higher levels (Lord, 1985).

Test scores for children with autism have been shown to have predictive utility. Lockyer and Rutter (1969) found that IQ measures of young "psychotic" children were useful predictors of later functioning, and also were useful in predicting behavioral outcome and social adjustment in adolescence and young adulthood. The long-term stability of IQ measures for their population of psychotic youngsters was, in fact, comparable to stability measures for normal children. DeMyer et al. (1974) showed that there was a significant correlation between IQ estimates and severity of symptoms, and that IQ scores were good predictors of school performance and of response to treatment.

There is some question arising from recent reports of the effects of early intervention on intelligence scores of children with autism. Groden and colleagues (1983), and Lovaas and co-workers (1987), for example, have provided data suggesting that such intervention may produce large increases in intelligence scores in some children. Also, Freeman and colleagues (1981) as well as other investigators (Bartak & Rutter, 1976) have also reported that children with autism can differ with regard to types of behaviors, depending on IQ level.

Pattern of Functioning

Children with autism have shown considerable variability among subtest scores. Rutter (1966) reported on testing of normal children, and of children with retardation and autism. He found that children with autism showed the most variability, with some of them having a spread of five standard deviations among individual subtests.

Further analysis of subtest scores for children with autism shows a pattern that is unique to this population. These children as a group tend to perform relatively well on tasks that require fitting and assembly (DeMyer, 1976), visuo-spatial understanding, (Bartak et al., 1975), or space performance ability and perceptual organization (Lockyer & Rutter, 1969), such as the block design and object assembly subtests of the WISC-R. They have greater difficulty with nonverbal subtests that require language mediation, sequencing, and abstraction, and generalization, or that in general require "mental manipulation" beyond immediately available cues. Thus children with autism do poorly on such tasks as WISC-R picture completion, and especially WISC-R picture arrangement (which requires putting pictures in an order that will tell a story). The more severe the language deficit, the more obvious is this pattern of test performance (Rutter, 1966).

In the verbal tasks of the Wechsler scales, these limitations can also be seen. Children with autism perform relatively well on rote immediate auditory memory tasks, such as digit span. They have marked difficulty with more abstract tasks, such as vocabulary, similarities, and especially comprehension. Other standardized assessment instruments yield similar results.

The Leiter International Performance Scale (Leiter, 1969), an entirely nonverbal measure designed for use with deaf or non-English-speaking children, includes a number of visuo-spatial-motor items such as block designs. In the experience of the authors, many children with autism can complete these items—even the more complex ones—with impressive speed and accuracy. But other Leiter tasks require the extraction of a rule, or generalization, from one set of objects to another set. For example, at Year VI the child must recognize a pattern of increasing size in a set of circles, and must reproduce this pattern with a similar set of squares. Even if a child with autism is able to complete visuo-spatial tasks within the higher age ranges of the test, he is likely to fail abstract items such as this one at lower age levels, this demonstrating the discrepancy that exists between the two types of skills (Maltz, 1981).

It is also well established that autism can meaningfully be distinguished from the broader area of mental retardation. Children with autism differ from the nonautistic retarded population in the pattern and range of their scores on intelligence tests (DeMyer et al., 1974), in their use of meaning in retention tasks (Hermelin & O'Connor, 1970), and in their language patterns (DeMyer et al., 1972). The two groups share some of the same behavioral characteristics, but children with autism show social indifference that is not typical of children with retardation. Although autistic deficits and behaviors may certainly be found to have multiple causes, experimentation has upheld the validity of autism as distinct from other diagnostic categories.

Specific Cognitive Deficits

Experimental studies of learning and cognition in children with autism have shed additional light upon the information gained from standardized assessment. Although it is beyond the scope of this chapter to provide an extensive review of the literature on cognitive functioning in autism, those studies most pertinent to psychological test data will be discussed.

RULE MAKING

Hermelin and O'Connor (1970) have studied cognitive deficits of children with autism intensively. They warn against attempting to isolate a single deficit that is specific to autism and that underlies the multiplicity of problems that persons with autism demonstrate. But they have identified one very broad and basic deficit—an inability to extract rules. Children with autism have difficulty placing objects into a meaningful sequence, as in the Leiter task that requires ordering of squares by size, because they cannot extract the rule that characterizes a set of stimuli. This type of difficulty was previously referred to in the discussion of subtest performance.

Other researchers have identified deficits that are similar in nature. Although different terms may be used by various investigators, it appears that the child with autism has a strikingly limited ability to relate one stimulus (or one set of stimuli, or one experience) to another. Breger (1965) cited the inability of persons with autism to generalize. Wing and Wing (1971) referred to a problem in manipulating abstract symbols. Rimland (1964) describes a failure to integrate and derive meaning from separate experiences and an inability to relate new stimuli to remembered experiences. O'Connor and Hermelin (1971) report a lack of integration of input and stored material. According to these authors, children with autism can memorize rotely, but the memorized or stored material is not modified, categorized, or otherwise processed in storage. Similar stimuli are not connected or associated with one another; the similarities are not noted, or at least not utilized, by the child. Fein and colleagues (1985), on the other hand, have suggested the presence of a short-term memory deficiency in these children.

LANGUAGE

Impaired ability to extract similarities or rules, and thus a failure to generalize from one stimulus to another, may also be a major factor in the language problems—both deviance and delay—that are among the more striking deficits in autism. Kanner (1943) and subsequent investigators (Hermelin & O'Connor, 1970; Pierce & Bartolucci, 1977) have noted the literalism and concreteness of language in autism, and a failure to learn to use synonyms or to understand connotations of words. Ricks and Wing (1975) describe difficulty in comprehending and using parts of speech that change with the context or the speaker, such as prepositions, pronouns, and verb tenses. Such words convey relationships rather than concrete objects or events; they relate a speaker to an object or to another person, or an action to an event in time. They vary with circumstances.

This last point deserves elaboration. Language acquisition requires a great many prerequisite skills, primary among which are generalization and discrimination. In order to recognize a thing as belonging to a category, its similarity to other objects in that category must be recognized. Having learned, for example that the family pet is called a "dog," the toddler happily begins to label all four-legged creatures "dogs". Gradually, as parents correct his errors, the child learns precisely which features define that category of four-legged creatures known as "dogs," and which features (size, shape, and so on) eliminate others from that category. A constant process of generalizing and discriminating is operating. One stimulus after another is examined and its features duly noted. Comparison is made with other stimuli encountered, either in the past or simultaneously. An object acquires a label on the basis of qualities or features or properties that it shares with others. If the commonality (the sharing) of the feature or features is not noted, if no association is made between the two stimuli, if the child does not generalize from one to the other, then the assignment of that object to a category, and indeed the understanding of the category of objects (or concept, or class) as a whole, will surely be impaired.

This may be part of the reason that persons with autism have difficulty with the subtleties of verbal language, and with other forms of symbolic communication. They may understand and use certain aspects of language, but in a relatively concrete and limited fashion. They fail to extract the rules that govern language. Having associated the words "Do you want some candy?" with the experience of receiving candy, the child with autism echoes "Do you want some candy?" to make the request. He does not know that the pronoun and the form of the question change with the speaker, and refers to himself by his first name, as he frequently hears references to himself, and may also refer to others by their names, rather than use the pronouns "I," "me," and "you." If asked "How old are you?," the child may recognize the words as one of a set of familiar sentences that requires one of a set of highly practiced responses. On occasion, however, the child may confuse these responses and give his name or address instead of age, showing almost no true comprehension of the actual content of the question. From the myriad of language experiences to which the child with autism has been exposed, perhaps a number of simple associations may have been gleaned, but the complexities elude him. The child's language is "wooden," lacking in flexibility.

It has been suggested (Churchill, 1972) that autism can be explained as a language disorder, similar to, but more severe than, the disorder found in children labeled "aphasic," or simply language impaired. However, Bartak and colleagues (1975) dispute this contention and make a strong case for maintaining separate diagnostic categories for children with autism and those with language disorders. They were able to demonstrate that, although there are children who do not clearly fit into one category or the other, children with autism show a more severe and extensive language deficit, more deviant (as opposed to merely delayed) language, less use of language for communication, less relevant language, and less skill in the use of gesture. Children with autism also showed a different pattern in test scores, even when matched with children with language impairments on nonverbal IQ measures. Clearly these are characteristics peculiar to autism that largely are not shared by aphasic groups, in spite of their similarities.

STIMULUS OVERSELECTIVITY

Lovaas, and co-workers (1971) have investigated another feature of autism that may be related to, and indeed may underlie, the problems in rule extraction and generalization. Children with autism show "stimulus overselectivity"—that is, in a learning situation, they often attend and respond to only a single aspect of a complex stimulus. If the aspect to which they attend is removed, the stimulus no longer produces the learned response.

In the Lovaas et al. (1971) study, normal children, and children with autism and retarded children, were taught to press a bar upon the appearance of a complex stimulus, such as a light and a sound presented simultaneously. Subsequently, when these stimuli were presented in isolation, the normal children responded to them singly as they had responded to them in combination, indicating that they had attended to both stimuli; their behavior was then under the control of both. The children with autism characteristically responded to only one of the cues, indicating that they attended only to one or the other of the stimuli, but not to both. The children with retardation responded between these two extremes. Stimulus overselectivity has also been demonstrated to occur within, as well as between, sensory modalities, and was investigated in follow-up studies by Schreibman and colleagues (1977), Koegel and Wilhelm (1973), Reynolds and co-workers (1974), and Koegel and Schreibman (1977). Within the visual modality, Koegel et al. (1982) felt that overselectivity may reflect a type of tunnel vision.

One can easily see how overselectivity will affect rule extraction; perceiving relationships requires attention to multiple aspects of the stimuli. Its implication with regard to generalization is also readily apparent. In generalizing from one stimulus to another, a child responds to a new, slightly different stimulus in the same manner as the child learned to respond to the original stimulus. If the original response was based upon a single, perhaps irrelevant, aspect of that stimulus, and if that aspect is not part of the new stimulus, generalization will not occur.

Suppose that a child with autism has learned to respond to a line drawing of a man with the word "man," and suppose that the mouth of the man is represented by a straight line. The child is now shown a drawing that is identical, except that the mouth in the new drawing is represented by an upwardly curved line. If the mouth line in the first drawing is the aspect of the drawing to which the child attended, the child will not identify the second drawing as a man. Furthermore, if the child is taught to label the second drawing as a "man," the new learning is not facilitated by the past learning. Overselectivity has profound implications not only for general intellectual development, but also for development in other areas, including language. At a very basic level, new words are taught by pairing the word with the object it represents. If the child attends to only a limited portion of each stimulus, learning will be greatly impaired.

In spite of these findings, there is probably no one disability that can explain all of the characteristics of autism, such as limited social interaction or stereotyped behaviors. In fact some investigators argue that many of the reported deficits previously mentioned can be explained on the basis of IQ, and disappear when this factor is carefully controlled (Baker, 1979). The reader is referred to Sindelar, and colleagues (1981) for a recent review of this topic.

INTELLECTUAL ASSESSMENT

Chapter 2 describes an initial evaluation procedure that includes intellectual assessment. Although assessments may be performed in a setting apart from ongoing therapeutic-educational activities, there should be considerable exchange of information between the examiner and other personnel working with the child. Prior to the first testing session, the examiner should review relevant records concerning the child, and if not already familiar with the child, should speak at length with personnel already familiar with the child and observe the child engaged in various activities. Following assessment, the examiner makes use of the findings to assist staff and the family in furthering the child's development. This aspect will be discussed in more detail in the following section.

Choices of Instruments

The problems encountered in intellectual assessment of children with autism are as varied as the difficulties that define the syndrome. They are similar to the obstacles encountered by any examiner who works with the developmentally disabled, but often are more acute. More children with autism have been labeled "untestable," or have been evaluated with inappropriate test instruments, than any other single segment of the developmentally disabled population, including the severely and profoundly mentally retarded.

One primary difficulty is choosing an appropriate test. Since many children with autism are relatively low functioning, tests suited to their chronological ages are often not appropriate to their developmental levels.

For example, if a child is given the Wechsler Intelligence Scale for Children—Revised (WICS-R) and his scores fall below the norms on most or all of the subtests, little has been learned about that child's abilities, or relative strengths and weaknesses. If the test is above the ability level, the examiner has identified an upper limit, but has not explored the lower limits or the full range of the child's skills.

It is most informative to use tests that tap skills appropriate to the child's developmental or "mental age." In some cases, because of a limited range of chronological ages in the standardization population of a particular test, this will mean sacrificing standard scores in favor of age equivalents.

When a test is beyond the ability level of a developmentally disabled child, test results are of little value. For example, Brian, a 6½-year-old child, had previously been evaluated on two separate occasions, once using the Wechsler Preschool and Primary Scale of Intelligence (WPPSI) (Wechsler, 1967), standardized on children 4½ to 6½ years old, and once with the WISC-R, standardized on children aged 6½ years and older. On the first occasion, the psychologist called Brian "basically untestable;" the test was terminated when he was unable to respond to WPPSI terms, which include such questions as, "How many ears do you have?"

A second psychologist who attempted to administer the WISC-R, terminated because the child "refused to respond." The psychologist also attempted a projective test that requires interpreting ink blots. This effort was equally unsuccessful. Finally, on the basis of a Vineland Social Maturity Scale, which taps self-help and other adaptive skills, the psychologist labeled Brian as functioning at a "mild to borderline intellectual level." He was placed in a class for children who are educable mentally retgarded, where the teacher noticed that he performed far below the level of his classmates.

A third evaluation, using the Bayley Scales of Infant Development (Bayley, 1969) and portions of the Stanford-Binet Intelligence Scale, yielded more accurate and useful information about Brian. Visuo-spatial-motor skills (block constructions, drawing, puzzles, formboards, and the like) were generally at a 24- to 30-month level, too low to be tapped by the Wechsler scales. Language skills were even less well developed, and ranged from about 12 to 20 months. His verbal repertoire consisted of perhaps three meaningful words and a few imitations. He was found to be severely to profoundly retarded, and was subsequently placed in a class for children performing at a similar developmental level, where daily activities could be geared to his interests and abilities.

The discrepancy between language and other skills could then be addressed.

Age equivalents (or "mental ages" or "test ages") are a less satisfactory statistic than standard scores in many ways, but they can be used judiciously for description and comparison. Age estimates are often the most easily understood statistic to give to a parent or a treatment teacher, especially since they apply to a continuum (age) with which we are familiar. It is more meaningful, and often more helpful, for the primary care givers of a handicapped child to know, for example, that his language comprehension is similar to that of a child 12 to 18 months of age, than to be told that he received a General Cognitive Index of less than 50 on the McCarthy Scales of Children's Abilities (McCarthy, 1972).

The relatively low verbal functioning of many children with autism adds to the difficulty of choosing an appropriate test and completing a psychological assessment. Tests that combine a variety of skills—verbal, visual-motor, memory, and so on—into a single global scale can yield scores that are virtually meaningless for the language-impaired child. Such tests include the Bayley Scales of Infant Development and the Stanford-Binet Intelligence Scale. Poor language functioning can depress the child's overall performance, while good rote memory or visuo-spatial-motor skills can enhance it, and the result can be an "average" that masks both the deficit and the strength.

Michael, for example, was a 3½-year-old boy with a severe language delay. His Stanford-Binet score of 66 placed him in the "mildly retarded" range. However, this global estimate provided very little information about Michael. Only an examination of his successes and failures revealed that he succeeded on every nonlanguage item on the Binet up to Year III-6, but failed every language item above Year II. The statistic 66 conveys nothing of the variability in his functioning.

Therefore, when the instrument of choice is the Bayley or the Binet, it is helpful to extract items that reflect certain specific skills and to examine the child's performance on those clusters of items. A language comprehensive cluster on the Bayley, for example, includes such items as pointing to shoes on request and identifying body parts by pointing; imitating simple block constructions and putting two halves of a picture together are visuo-spatial-motor items from the Binet.

Such analyses must, of course, be done cautiously. The instruments were not originally designed for this purpose. Many skills in which the psychologist might be interested are not evenly represented throughout the scales, and the tests tap different skills at different age levels. For example, the Binet becomes increasingly verbal at higher age levels. In spite of the drawbacks, however, an examination of clusters of skills can help the psychologist to extract more than just a global statistic from these assessment tools. Sattler (1982) and Valett (1964) have done a good deal of work in interpreting the Binet and other standard instruments in this manner, and the interested reader should examine their analyses.

Those scales designed to differentiate between verbal and nonverbal skills—such as the Wechsler scales and the McCarthy Scales of Children's Abilities—can sometimes be particularly useful in the assessment of children with autism. Some children can achieve a meaningful standard score on a nonverbal scale (the performance scale of the Wechsler or the McCarthy) even though they are functioning far below the norms of the verbal scales. More information on specific tests is presented in the following.

The most critical point to consider is that many so-called "untestable" children can respond cooperatively and appropriately to test items that are within their development range (Alpern, 1967). The label "untestable" might legitimately reflect the presence of strong competing behaviors or severe attentional problems, but it often indicates an attempt to use an inappropriate assessment device and the presentation of items that are too difficult for the child to manage. Another reason children are "untestable" may be the inherent structure of the testing situation itself; that is, it is usually a sustained (30–45 minutes) interaction with one individual. Persons with autism often do not engage in even short interpersonal contacts, and have limited practice in turn taking. Moreover, their learning histories are usually characterized by short sessions, and not long interactions, even with materials.

There is no "typical" assessment battery for children labeled autistic. Each evaluation is individually tailored to the child, the estimated developmental level, behavioral characteristics, previous diagnoses and tests, and any specific questions that may have arisen about his programming needs. Following are brief descriptions and a discussion of several of the instruments that have proved most useful in assessing these children, and some of the advantages and disadvantages of each for use with youngsters who are behaviorally disturbed. The list is by no means exhaustive.

Bayley Scales of Infant Development, Mental Scale

The Bayley is useful for many children who are behaviorally disturbed because of the high-interest manipulative activities that it offers and, more important, because it taps skills as low as a one-month level and as high as 30 months. It can yield developmental estimates for children who are chronologically about 30 months, and should be considered for use with children who are young, nonverbal, and/or lower functioning. One disadvantage is that children may fail items appropriate to younger children simply because they have passed the developmental age at which a particular item is likely to elicit a specific response—for example, manipulating a table edge in an exploratory manner, investigating a pegboard by fingering the holes, or turning a bell over to examine the clapper or other details. Other disadvantages include the age range, in that some children fail to achieve a ceiling on the Bayley, and the fact that it is not continuous with any of the other childhood scales.

Stanford-Binet Intelligence Scale

The Stanford-Binet is the "grandfather" of intelligence tests, and, after two revisions, a 1972 restandardization, and a 1985 revision, it continues to be widely used. For this reason it is often useful in comparing a child's current functioning with past evaluations. It taps a broad age range, from the two-year level to the adult level. However, all versions of the Binet prior to 1985 consist of a wide variety of items that tap a multiplicity of skills, and yield only a single, global statistic, the "IQ" score. The Binet can be used to give a "mental age" as well, but since the restandardization, when many items were found to have changed in difficulty level, the mental age is no longer considered a valid statistic. The "IQ" score itself has limited meaning for children with great variability in their performance or with significant differences between language and nonlanguage skills. For the Binet to be most useful, the evaluator must dissect a child's performance in an effort to specify strong and weak skills. The 1985 revision of the Binet introduced a change in format such that items are grouped into subscales (Thorndike et al., 1985). At this time, however, few reports, if any, are available on the use of this version with the autistic population.

Leiter International Performance Scale

The great advantage of the Leiter, mentioned earlier, is that it is totally nonverbal, as it was developed for use with children who, for a variety of reasons, lack vocal speech or speak only a foreign language. As it encompasses a wide age range, it is useful for children who have severe language impairments but fairly well-developed visual-spatial skills. It is a cleverly conceived and constructed test in that it requires no verbally administered instructions and only minimal gestural cues; the materials themselves provide most of the guidance that the child requires to understand the nature of the test, assuming that the evaluator begins it at a comfortable, easy level for the child. Early items permit a good deal of demonstration and correction, enabling the evaluator to teach some of the very basic skills needed to take the test. The lowest level items are matching tasks, but gradually the tasks become more and more conceptual and complex.

Disadvantages of the Leiter include the age of the scale and of its norms. Questions have been raised (Werner, 1965) as to the adequacy of the standardization sample, especially for lower level items. Shah et al. (1985) compared Leiter and WISC-R scores of a group of 18 children with autism and found high positive correlations between the Leiter and WISC-R full-scale and performance "I.Q.'s". There was no significant difference between Leiter and WISC-R performance "I.Q.'s", but significant differences were found between Leiter and WISC-R full-scale and verbal "I.Q.'s". Those who use the Leiter should be familiar with both its strengths and its statistical limitations.

McCarthy Scales of Children's Abilities.

The McCarthy yields separate standard scores for verbal, perceptual-performance, memory, and quantitative, and motor skills. It then combines these scores into a General Cognitive Index (GCI) with a mean of 100 and a standard deviation of 16. The materials are modern and are intrinsically interesting to most children.

Comparison with other common tests is somewhat limited by the fact that the lowest standard score on each of the scales, including the GCI, is only three standard deviations below the mean. There are no scores for children who function below the level of "mild mental retardation." Another problem in using the McCarthy, particularly with children with autism, but for other groups as well, is that memory items appear on all the scales. Children with exceptionally good rote auditory memory can achieve inflated scores on the verbal or quantitative scales simply by repeating words or digits accurately.

Wechsler Intelligence Scale for Children—Revised (WISC-R)

The WISC-R is another widely used scale that yields separate standard scores for verbal and nonverbal skills, as well as a global or full-scale score that combines the two. The WISC-R is appropriate for children six years of age and up. If the child's verbal functioning is too low to permit testing with the verbal scale, it still might be of interest to attempt some of the nonverbal items from the perceptual performance scale. As we have seen, the WISC-R has been found useful as a predictive and diagnostic tool, since analysis has produced evidence of a pattern of scores on the WISC-R that is peculiar to children with autism. The WISC-R is especially useful for higher functioning, older children, but can be too difficult for lower functioning and younger children.

These scales can be easily supplemented with a variety of other tests and subtests. Among these are the Peabody Picture Vocabulary Test-Revised (PPVT-R) (Dunn and Dunn, 1981), which assesses receptive vocabulary and requires choosing a requested picture from a set of four, and the Hiskey-Nebraska Test of Learning Aptitude (Hiskey, 1966), which can be given with gestural rather than verbal instructions and has separate norms for children with normal hearing and for children who are deaf. For low-functioning individuals, the previous version of the Peabody Picture Vocabulary Test (Dunn, 1965), tends to underestimate Stanford-Binet scores (Groden & Mann, 1976). Until further research is conducted on the PPVT-R, caution should be exercised in equating scores from the Peabody with those from other instruments such as the Binet.

The Developmental Test of Visual-Motor Integration (Beery, 1967); the Goodenough-Harris (human figure) Drawing Test (Harris, 1963); the French Pictorial Test of Intelligence (French, 1964); and portions of the Illinois Test of Psycholinguistic Abilities (Kirk et al., 1968) are also useful.

The concept of global "intelligence" has increasingly been called into question. In the field of autism and other severe behavioral disorders, the idea that there is an innate measurable capacity that can be considered "intelligence" is particularly meaningless. Persons with autism show such extreme variability in their skills, and such an atypical pattern of abilities, and in addition often demonstrate behaviors that are so detrimental to an assessment, that any global measure of ability must be treated with caution.

Dealing with Behavioral and Attentional Deficits

Even if a test instrument is chosen that is appropriate to the child's developmental level, the psychologist is likely to encounter some degree of atypical, competing behavior that will interfere with a reliable assessment. The unfamiliarity of the testing room and of the examiner, or lengthy sessions, can elicit anxiety, distress, and avoidance. Difficulty and failure are, to some extent, a necessary part of a psychological evaluation, but even minor frustration can lead to tantrums or an increase in self-stimulatory or self-injurious behavior. Social reinforcers, such as smiling, touching, and praise, are often ineffective, and sometimes even aversive. Children with autism can have severe deficits in attention and may avoid focusing visually on test materials. The child who demonstrates highly selective attention in learning and in assessment situations may respond to a request only if it is worded in a particular, familiar way. The child may respond to the instruction "Look at me" but not to "Pay attention" or "Watch me," or may comprehend "Put your finger on the dog" but not "Point to it," "Show me," "Touch the dog," or "Where is the dog?"

Before beginning an evaluation, the psychologist should be familiar with techniques that have been used effectively with the child by treatment teachers, parents, and others. Such preparation will help to circumvent potential problems and can show the evaluator how to take advantage of the child's strengths.

Both prior to and within the assessment, there are a variety of other ways to help children display their ability and to reduce the negative effects of anxiety, overactivity, avoidance, sterotypic behavior, disinterest, and variable attention. Many children who are behaviorally disturbed are distressed by unfamiliar persons and places, and changes in their routine. Even if the child is not unduly disturbed by novelty or change, many aspects of the assessment situation can remind the child of unpleasant experiences in the past, particularly if the evaluation takes place in a hospital or clinic setting. Parents may feel apprehensive, too, about the implications of an assessment. Parental uneasiness can increase the child's own misgivings. To alleviate parents' concerns, it is helpful to discuss the assessment with them in advance. Removing the mystique of intellectual assessment by means of a straightforward discussion, using lay terminology, and clarifying what psychological tests are and what they can and cannot reveal, usually reduces parental tension.

For the child who might react with anxiety or resistance, desensitization can be used, either informally or in a more methodical and systematic manner. Informally the child might simply be introduced to the assessment setting, and to the person who will conduct the evaluation, one or more times prior to the appointed date. In more extreme cases, the child can be exposed to carefully graded successive approximations of the test setting, over a period of several days or weeks. Concomitantly, the child can be provided with reinforcers that are not compatible with anxiety, such as favorite foods or comforting and cuddling (if these are desirable to the child). If desensitization is ineffective and the child's anxiety severe, the wisest alternative might be to perform the assessment in a setting that is familiar and comfortable. Children can be tested in a hospital lobby, in waiting rooms, in classrooms, and at home.

Relaxation procedures can also be employed to reduce tension, anxiety, and overactivity and to promote good attending and reflective problem solving. If a child's record indicates that these behaviors might be expected to occur in an assessment situation, and might interfere with achieving a reliable estimate of ability, the child can be taught relaxation on cue prior to the testing date.

In many cases it is beneficial to have a treatment teacher or aide present in the testing room. These familiar care givers may have established good stimulus control over the child's behavior, and the control may not yet have generalized to other adults. The opposite, of course, can also be true—treatment teachers or parents can elicit negative behavior. The decision to include or exclude others from the assessment room has to be made on an individual basis.

UTILIZATION OF ASSESSMENT RESULTS

The ideal assessment device would be one that measures the skills most critical for success in important life tasks such as school and the workplace, and that yields data that can be translated directly into remedial methods. The ideal test, in other words, would provide us with specific information on how to teach a particular child. Many researchers (Valett, 1964; Sattler, 1982) have developed methods of using standardized intelligence test results to design remedial programs, but in general the tests have not been of great value to the classroom teacher, as most of them were not developed for that purpose.

A Behavior Sample

Intelligence tests, however, do serve several useful purposes for the severely behaviorally disturbed population in that they provide a sample of a child's developmental functioning under standard conditions. Given the problems of assessment of these children, one must take care in interpreting the results and make such interpretations only in the context of additional information from other sources. A psychological evaluation is a good observation ground, a "window" from which to begin to investigate the child and his needs. Each scale requires a "basal" level at which the child is comfortably competent, and a "ceiling" level at which the child fails several consecutive items. Tests provide an interesting sample of the child's behavior and responses to gradual increases in difficulty and frustration levels, and how these behaviors relate to the types of tasks and the modalities involved.

Thus, as part of an initial evaluation-observation period, tests help to place the child on the developmental continuum, which assists in determining class placement and level of instruction in initial teaching phases. The information that tests provide allows the treatment teacher to eliminate some of the trial and error that would otherwise be necessary if no information about the child's level of functioning were available in conjunction with other information. Test results can also help personnel in the determination of appropriate therapeutic approaches. Imagery approaches, for example, should be considered very cautiously with a child whose general level of development and individual assessment items indicate possible insufficient symbolic functioning for such procedures.

Basis for Discussion with Parents

Intellectual assessment results also provide an excellent basis for discussion with parents. Among children who are severely disturbed and autistic, parents have often been given a great deal of confusing, conflicting, and incorrect information. They have usually heard an overwhelming amount of technical jargon—psychosis, neurosis, schizophrenia, emotional overlay, visual processing problems, primary emotional disturbance, failure of maternal–infant bonding, and so on. They may have been exposed to one or more of the painful, and potentially damaging, myths that abound in the field—for example, that they are the cause of their child's problems, or that the low-functioning child is potentially average but cannot or will not demonstrate his true ability. They may very well be confused by the variability in their child's abilities, and they may tend to attribute certain failures or difficulties to obstinancy or poor motivation.

A thorough assessment by a qualified psychologist, followed by a carefully planned conference with the child's parents or other primary care givers, serves several purposes. It can give parents an accurate perspective on the child's level of functioning in several different skill areas, thereby helping them to understand relative strengths and weaknesses and shaping appropriate expectations about the child's day-to-day behavior. This in turn can help to relieve guilt and anxiety about the parental role, particularly in autism, but in other behavioral disturbances as well. For example, when a three-year old makes elaborate block constructions and learns almost independently to recite or to read letters and numbers, the failure to make eye contact or to communicate verbally with others in a meaningful way is likely to be interpreted by parents as a rejection, caused by something they have done wrong. They may blame themselves for allowing the child to view marital disagreements, or for disciplining the child, or for spending insufficient time with the child in the earliest years of life.

Individualized Program Planning and Evaluation

To be useful to the parent, child, and treatment teacher, an assessment must address the child's strengths, as well as weaknesses or deficits. Specifying competency areas (for example, well-developed artistic, musical, or spatial and mechanical skills) helps the treatment teacher to plan activities that will continue to build on those skills, thereby making the most of the child's strengths and, one hopes, increasingly the expectancy of success.

In addition, when strong skill areas are identified, they can be used to help compensate for deficit areas. For example, a child who has no vocal speech, but who has spontaneously developed a simple gestural system, can be taught to communicate by means of a program that combines sign and vocal speech. The introduction of sign is often exciting and reinforcing for a formerly nonverbal child, and gains in sign have often been accompanied by gains in expressive vocal communication as well. The child's strength—the use of rudimentary gestures for communication—can be utilized to build another, weaker skill.

Activities in which the child is most skilled are usually reinforcing.

They can be used on a contingent basis to improve behavior or to teach other skills, or on a noncontingent basis simply to add to the quality of the child's daily life.

For the older child, psychological test results can aid in vocational planning. By delineating the major strengths and weaknesses in the young person's test profile, the psychologist can rule out some occupations from consideration and suggest others. A youngster who has limited language ability or is echolalic will have difficulty with work that requires meaningful, independently generated speech. The adolescent with poor spatial reasoning may not be an appropriate candidate for a program in automobile mechanics or complicated piecework in a factory.

As has been earlier stated, DeMyer and colleagues (1974) have shown that, even for youngsters who are behaviorally disturbed, test results have a fair degree of test–retest reliability and predictive validity. Thus they can be useful prognostic indicators, particularly for older, lower functioning children. It is important for parents, other care givers, and treatment teachers, as well as other service providers, to have a realistic understanding of the likelihood that a particular child will "catch up" developmentally and perform at a level commensurate with the child's chronological age. Parents of a cognitively limited child, who have not had the advantage of a candid discussion of psychological testing of their child, can endure years of anxiety and frustration as they await the anticipated gains in mental and academic ability.

Psychological test performance of children can also be one means of assessing program effectiveness. Although we cannot realistically expect at this time that remedial programs will produce large IQ gains, we do know that inferior care and institutionalization have been related to decrements in IQ scores. Thus psychological test data constitute one factor worthy of consideration in program evaluation.

To summarize, traditional psychometric instruments can be helpful in providing services to children with autism and their families. They can help to confirm or discredit theories about intellectual development in autism; identify the level of general developmental functioning, as well as strengths and weaknesses; and help in parent counseling and program planning. They were not designed, however, for careful, scientific exploration of specific areas of cognitive operations. The most precise and enlightening data on autism are coming from the experimental laboratory. The ongoing study of autism—and of cognitive functioning in other disabled groups as well as in normal children—will require a combination of efforts, a wedding of traditional assessment techniques and laboratory studies. Reliable and valid assessment needs to be firmly grounded in carefully executed experimental work, such as the elegant studies done by Hermelin and O'Connor (1970) in their investigations of autism. Experimentation, it is hoped, will eventually lead to the development of even more useful standardized assessment instruments.

REFERENCES

Alpern, G. D. (1967). Measurement of "untestable" autistic children. *Journal of Abnormal Psychology, 72*, 478–486.
Baker, A. M. (1979). Cognitive functioning of psychotic children: A reappraisal. *Exceptional Children, 45*(5), 344–348.
Bartak, L. & Rutter, M. (1976). Differences between mentally retarded and normally intelligent autistic children. *Journal of Autism and Child Schizophrenia, 6*, 109–120.
Bartak, L., Rutter, M. & Cox, A,. (1975). A comparative study of infantile autism and specific developmental receptive language disorder: I. The children. *British Journal of Psychiatry, 126*, 127–145.
Bayley, N. (1969). *Manual for the Bayley Scales of Infant Development.* New York: Psychological Corporation.
Beery, K. E. (1967). *Administration and scoring manual: developmental test of visual-motor integration.* Chicago: Follett Educational Corp.
Breger, L. (1965). Comments on "Building social behavior in autistic children by use of electric shock." *Journal of Experimental Research in Personality, 1*, 110–113.
Churchill, D. W. (1972). The relation of infantile autism and early childhood schizophrenia to developmental language disorders of childhood. *Journal of Autism and Childhood Schizophrenia, 2*, 182–197.
DeMyer, M. K. (1976). Motor, perceptual-motor, and intellectual disabilities of autistic children. In L. Wing (Ed.), *Early childhood autism.* New York: Pergamon Press.
DeMyer, M. K., Barton, S., Alpern, G. D., Kimberlin, C., Allen, J., Yang, E. & Steele, R. (1974). The measured intelligence of autistic children. *Journal of Autism and Childhood Schizophrenia, 4*, 42–60.
DeMyer, M. K., Barton, S. & Norton, J. A. (1972). A comparison of adaptive, verbal, and motor profiles of psychotic and non-psychotic sub-normal children. *Journal of Autism and Childhood Schizophrenia, 2*, 359–377.
DeMyer, M. K., Hingtgen, J. N. & Jackson, R. K. (1981). Infantile autism reviewed: A decade of research. *Schizophrenia Bulletin, 7*(3), 388–451.
Dunn, L. M. (1965). *Peabody Picture Vocabulary Test Manual.* Circle Pines, Minn.: American Guidance Service.
Dunn, L. M. & Dunn, L. M. (1981). *Examiner's Manual: Peabody Picture Vocabulary Test—Revised.* Circle Pines, Minn.: American Guidance Service.
Fein, D., Waterhouse, L., Lucci, D. & Snyder, D. (1985). Cognitive subtypes in

developmentally disabled children: A pilot study. *Journal of Autism and Developmental Disorders, 15*(1), 77–95.
Freeman, B. J., Ritvo, E. R., Schroth, P. C., Tonick, I., Guthrie, D. & Wake, L. (1981). Behavioral characteristics of high- and low-IQ autistic children. *American Journal of Psychiatry, 138*(1), 25–29.
French, J. L. (1964). *Manual: Pictorial Test of Intelligence.* Boston: Houghton-Mifflin.
Groden, G., Domingue, D., Chesnick, M., Groden, J. & Baron, G. (1983). Early intervention with autistic children: A case presentation with pre-program, program and follow-up data. *Psychological Reports, 53*, 715–722.
Groden, G. & Mann, L. (1976). Relationships between Peabody Picture Vocabulary Test and Revised Stanford-Binet performance in young handicapped children. *Perceptual and Motor Skills, 42*, 1227–1232.
Harris, D. B. (1963). *Children's drawings as measures of intellectual maturity: A revision and extension of the Goodenough Draw-A-Man Test.* New York: Harcourt, Brace & World.
Hermelin, B. & O'Connor, N. (1970). *Psychological experiments with autistic children.* Oxford: Pergamon Press.
Hiskey, M. S. (1966). *Hiskey–Nebraska Test of Learning Aptitude.* Lincoln, Neb.: Union College Press.
Kanner, L. (1943). Autistic disturbances of affective contact. *Nervous Child, 2*, 217–250.
Kirk, S. A., McCarthy, J. J. & Kirk, W. (1968). *Examiner's manual: Illinois Test of Psycholinguistic Abilities.* Urbana, Ill.: University of Illinois Press.
Koegel, R. L., Rincover, A. & Egel, A. L. (1982). Stimulus overselectivity and stimulus control: Problems and strategies. In *Educating and understanding autistic children.* San Diego, Calif.: College-Hill Press.
Koegel, R. L. & Schreibman, L. (1977). Teaching autistic children to respond to simultaneous multiple cues. *Journal of Experimental Child Psychology, 24*, 299–311.
Koegel, R. L. & Wilhelm, H. (1973). Selective responding to the components of multiple visual cues by autistic children. *Journal of Experimental Child Psychology, 15*, 442–453.
Leiter, R. G. (1969). *General instructions for the Leiter International Performance Scale.* Chicago: Stoelting.
Lockyer, L. & Rutter, M. (1969). A five-to-fifteen-year follow-up study of infantile psychosis: III. Psychological aspects. *British Journal of Psychiatry, 115*, 865–882.
Lord, C. & Schopler, E. (1985). Brief report: Differences in sex ratios in autism as a function of measured intelligence. *Journal of Autism and Developmental Disorders, 15*(2), 185–193.
Lovaas, O. I. (1987). Behavioral treatment and normal educational and intellectual functioning in young autistic children. *Journal of Consulting and Clinical Psychology, 55*, 3–9.
Lovaas, O.I., Schreibman, L., Koegel, R. L. & Rehm, R. (1971). Selective responding by autistic children to multiple sensory input. *Journal of Abnormal Psychology, 77*, 211–222.
Maltz, A. (1981). Comparison of cognitive deficits among autistic and retarded children on the Arthur adaptation of the Leiter International Performance Scales. *Journal of Autism and Developmental Disorders, 11*(4), 413–426.

McCarthy, D. (1972). *Manual for the McCarthy Scales of Children's Abilities*. New York: Psychological Corp.

O'Connor, N. & Hermelin, B. (1971). Cognitive deficits in children. *British Medical Bulletin, 27*, 227–232.

Pierce, S. & Bartolucci, G. (1977). A syntactic investigation of verbal autistic, mentally retarded, and normal children. *Journal of Autism and Childhood Schizophrenia, 7*, 121–134.

Reynolds, B. S., Newsom, C. D. & Lovaas, O. I. (1974). Auditory overselectivity in autistic children. *Journal of Abnormal Child Psychology, 2*, 253–263.

Ricks, D. M. & Wing, L. (1975). Language, communication, and the use of symbols in normal and autistic children. *Journal of Autism and Childhood Schizophrenia, 5*, 191–221.

Rimland, B. (1964). *Infantile autism: The syndrome and its implications for a neural theory of behavior*. New York: Appleton-Century-Crofts.

Rutter, M. (1966). Behavioral and cognitive characteristics of a series of psychotic children. In J. Wing (Ed.), *Early childhood autism*. Oxford: Pergamon Press.

Sattler, J. M. (1982). *The assessment of children's intelligence and special abilities*. Boston: Allyn & Bacon.

Schreibman, L., Koegel, R. L. & Craig, M. S. (1977). Reducing stimulus overselectivity in autistic children. *Journal of Abnormal Child Psychology, 5*, 425–436.

Shah, A. & Holmes, N. (1985). Brief report: The use of the Leiter International Performance Scale with autistic children. *Journal of Autism and Developmental Disorders, 15*(2), 195–203.

Sindelar, P. T., Meisel, C. J., Buy, M. J. & Klein, E. S. (1981). Differences in cognitive functioning of retarded children and retarded autistic children: A response to Ahmad Baker *Exceptional Children, 47*(6), 406–411.

Terman, L. M. & Merrill, M. A. (1972). *Examiner's Manual: Stanford-Binet Intelligence Scale—1972 Norms Edition*. Boston: Houghton Mifflin.

Thorndike, R.L., Hagen, E. & Sattler, J. (1985). *Examiner's Manual: Stanford-Binet Intelligence Scale: Fourth Edition*. Chicago: Riverside Publishing Co.

Valett, R. E. (1964). A clinical profile for the Stanford-Binet. *Journal of School Psychology, 2*, 49–54.

Werner, E. E. (1965). Review of the Arthur adaptation of the Leiter International Performance Scale. In O. K. Buros (Ed.), *The sixth mental measurements yearbook*. Highland Park, N.J.: Gryphon Press.

Wechsler, D. (1974). *Manual for the Wechsler Intelligence Scale for Children—Revised*. New York: Psychological Corp.

Weschler, D. (1967). *Manual for the Wechsler Preschool and Primary Scale of Intelligence*. New York: Psychological Corp.

Wing, L. & Wing, J. K. (1971). Multiple impairments in early childhood autism. *Journal of Autism and Childhood Schizophrenia, 1*, 256–266.

CHAPTER

5

Teaching Communication to Children with Language Impairment

Suzanne Swope, Ed.D.
Marie Chesnick, M.Ed.

PURPOSE OF CHAPTER
A Developmental-Ecological-Behavioral
   Model
   Principle I
   Principle II
   Principle III
   Principle IV
   Principle V
   Principle VI
Evaluating Language Disorders in
   Children with Autism
   Referral
   History
   Behavioral Observations
      (Communication Emphasis)
   Content
   Comprehension
   Production
   Alternate Forms of Communication
   Other Considerations
Interpretation of Test Results

Treating Language Disorders in Children
   with Autism
   Setting Goals
   Reevaluation to Note Progress
   Effectiveness of Treatment
Specific Treatment Contexts
   Language in Play
   Communication in Daily Routines
Summary
References
Further Reading

NEARLY ALL CHILDREN WITH AUTISM evidence a communication problem, whether it be labeled a communication disorder or a speech–language problem. A communication disorder may in fact be inherent to the definition of autism. Parents and teachers experience a major concern over the lack of language development in children with autism—a concern second only to behavioral problems.

PURPOSE OF CHAPTER

This chapter presents a developmental-ecological-behavioral approach to the treatment of language disorders. It defines the clinician's role in diagnosis and treatment, describes treatment strategies, and presents examples of programs that can be implemented by parents and teachers. Further, the authors (1) examine autism as a multiply handicapping disorder and outline the principles of language development that relate to the treatment of language disorders in children with autism; (2) discuss the unique features of diagnosis and language therapy for children with autism; (3) briefly review measurement tools used to assess the effectiveness of language therapy; and (4) describe therapy strategies that provide language learning opportunities in play and daily routines.

A DEVELOPMENTAL-ECOLOGICAL-BEHAVIORAL MODEL (ASSUMPTIONS ABOUT LANGUAGE THERAPY)

Autim is a multiply handicapping disorder that affects cognitive, social, and linguistic development. Although a number of articles and books examine the nature and treatment of autism (Lovaas et al., 1973; Koegel et al., 1982; Wing, 1976), little is known about development of emerging speech and language in children with autism or the long-term success of speech or language treatment programs. The following principles are intended to serve as guides for speech–language assessment of and intervention with children with autism and other severe disorders. These principles form the foundation of programs for this population which covers a broad range in age and social, linguistic, and intellectual development.

Principle I

The labels "autism" or "behavioral disorders" do not describe the type or severity of a language disorder.

Bloom and Lahey (1978) suggest that the classification of "autism" may not suggest a unique set of language behaviors. Similarly, Condon (1975) hypothesizes an overlap or functional similarity, differing only in intensity, between autism and learning disorders; that is, both show similar errors in auditory receptivity and processing. These findings suggest that the neurological, physiological, or psychological basis for autism may be very similar to that for other disorders; and that the clinician may not be able to classify the disorder on the basis of limited observation of behavior.

Furthermore, as in normal children, language in children with autism changes as the child develops and interacts with the environment. An individual child in this population may have been given several different diagnostic labels—slow learner, atypical, retarded, developmentally delayed, and autistic. Changes in diagnostic labels do not suggest a set of defined speech and language behaviors that can be easily identified by the clinician.

Because no specific type of language disorder is inherent in any of these classifications, the language clinician cannot use the diagnostic label to define the language problem. The extent and nature of the language problem must, therefore, be determined by the clinician. Goals and intervention strategies must be based upon extensive observation and interaction with the child and principles of development and learning.

Principle II

The most important emphasis in speech and language diagnosis and intervention with this population is to assess the extent and nature of language use and the environment in which it occurs.

Speech and language therapy in the 1960s was focused on *form*; that is, the syntactic structures or sentences children should learn and the sound sequences necessary to produce those forms. In the early 1970s, clinicians shifted their emphasis to include content; that is, the cognitive basis for language learning, or what the child needs to know about objects, events, and their relationships to learn language. In the late 1970s, and currently in the 1980s, clinicians are considering the importance of language *use* when diagnosing language problems (Baltaxe, 1977; Wetherby & Prutting, 1984). Use of language or "pragmatics" is the social basis for language learning. How language is used to communicate underlying intention is the primary consideration.

The diagnosis of language disorders includes consideration of form, content, and use. However, the most important consideration for the clinician, teacher, or parent is, "How can the environment be arranged so the child will want to communicate?" To answer this question, one must examine the situation itself, identify the "communicators," and determine the purposes for which the language is being used within the situation. Diagnosis and therapy have become targeted toward "useful" communication—communication that facilitates personal, social, and educational growth.

Principle III

The model for language diagnosis and therapy should be a positive rather than a deficit model.

A distinction between a positive and a deficit model is essential for an understanding of the recommended approach for language diagnosis and therapy. A positive model is structured by the clinician on information known about cognitive, linguistic, and social development of a child within an environmental milieu. The clinician observes and strives to alter this milieu, using behavioral principles to maximize the child's overall development.

Conversely, clinicians who use the deficit model, what Bloom and Lahey (1978) call the "adult model of language," analyze behaviors of children as inadequate or incomplete forms of adult behavior. Using this model, the clinician may emphasize the child's lack of intellectual, social, or linguistic skills. Below are two paragraphs excerpted from different clinical reports that exemplify the two models.

REPORT A
 Positive, Proactive Model

Elizabeth has made significant progress during the summer session in her use of language and in her ability to attend to verbal and nonverbal tasks. She is talking more frequently and the length of her utterances has increased. She is using fewer single words and many two-, three-, and four-word phrases. She uses language to comment on events ("people fall down"; "Matthew cry"), to ask for things ("I want yellow"), to reassure herself ("Mommy out the door", "She come back"), and to ask questions ("when baby go?"). She is coding semantic relations of existence ("crackers"; "baby"), nonexistence ("all gone"), recurrence ("more juice"), and rejection ("don't"), possession ("Daddy's hat"), and locative action ("put Mommy away"). Elizabeth's attention span has increased significantly for many activities. It was at first difficult to get her to attend to simple puzzles, pegboards, and other visual motor tasks; however, with teacher encouragement, structuring, and insistence that she finish what she started, she began to increase her ability to perform these tasks and has become willing and at times eager to engage herself in them.

REPORT B
Deficit Model

George, age six, can be described as demonstrating every variety of visual and auditory problems. He is extremely hyperactive and distractible. He often runs back and forth across the classroom, slapping his hands several times on each wall. Even when he is seated, he either attends to every sound by turning toward the source of the noise or sits in his seat and rocks back and forth and appears totally deaf. Also, George does not socialize well with his classmates, demonstrating daily aggressive behavior. His language is characterized by two- to three-word utterances when he talks, but he often refuses to talk at all. Most of his speech is echolalic, continually repeating the last portion of phrases he has heard from others. His low score on the Peabody Picture Vocabulary Test yielding an IQ of 65 indicates his poor receptive vocabulary skills. The low score on the verbal expression portion of the Illinois Test of Psycholinguistic Abilities (language age = 3.0) may explain his lack of spontaneous speech. Due to George's multiple processing problems, he appears unable to function successfully in a first grade. A special needs class with an emphasis on language training and firm discipline is recommended.

In Report A, a positive, proactive model, the clinician observes the child's behavior within the framework of her overall development in a communication situation. The clinician assumes the responsibility for providing an environment conducive to learning.

Report B is written from a deficit model. In this case the clinician uses standardized test scores to account for language deficits that result in social and educational problems. The child's behavior is also seen as the reason for lack of progress.

Principle IV

The speech and language clinician assumes direct responsibility for diagnosis while serving as a "third party" in language therapy.

A speech and language diagnostic report should include a description of the language problem, together with a set of recommended long- and short-term language goals, and strategies for accomplishing these goals, including specific examples. The clinician should take the *direct* responsibility for overseeing and/or conducting the evaluation and writing the report. However, the clinician assumes *indirect* responsibility for therapy. The child's opportunity for acquiring knowledge about communication will take place with every exchange between one or more individuals as significant others assume responsibility as langauge facilitators.

The clinician can best serve the child throughout a long-term treatment program by striving to accomplish four goals:

- To assist parents and teachers or primary caretakers to appreciate communication from a developmental point of view.
- To teach others to be language facilitators by modeling and/or recommending directly or indirectly environmental conditions that are conducive to communication.
- To be an advocate for children with handicaps.
- To assist parents and teachers in becoming advocates for their respective child or student within the community.

The following diagram represents the relationships of those involved in treatment of individuals with autism or behavioral disorders. As illustrated, teachers, parents, and others directly influence the child, whereas the clinician directly influences the behavior of the teachers or other language facilitators.

	Treatment	
	Parents	
	Teachers	
Clinician	Siblings	Child
	Others	

The diagram indicates that the clinician should not expect to serve as the primary long-term provider of communication teaching. For treatment to be successful, parents, teachers, and others in the community must serve to provide language models through social interactions with language-impaired individuals in the context of daily routines (meal-time, travel, work and school activities and social activities).

Principle V

The clinician should stress the importance of data collection for determining the extent of the problem, recommending goals and strategies for therapy, and providing feedback to the language facilitator.

Data collection includes observations made in standardized testing, criterion-referenced measures, and functional and naturalistic settings. Through standardized testing the clinician attempts to compare the child's prelinguistic skills, language comprehension, and language production with those of other children. Since most children described in this book have noticeable language disorders, and many are nonverbal, standardized measures are used primarily as a means for determining present status and as a measure of growth after a period of language therapy. Examples of recommended standardized measures are mentioned later in this chapter.

Another assessment technique used frequently is criterion-referenced measures. The clinician determines a present level of performance on certain tasks. These same tasks will be presented before and after treatment to determine a child's progress. The clinician sets the criteria for successful completion of the task on the basis of the literature and a clinical judgment of what is considered a necessary level of performance that might indicate whether the goals of therapy have been achieved. These measures are most useful for determining specific therapy goals, developing strategies, or assessing improvement on specific tasks.

In an effort to ensure that the data are both reliable and valid, the following should be considered:

1. *Assess context as well as performance.* Because most forms of communication, both verbal and nonverbal, take place in a social setting, the child's performance must be evaluated taking into consideration the contextual support, familiarity with the individual conducting the testing, and the opportunity presented for interaction on a nonverbal basis.

2. *Assess performance in natural settings.* To judge whether a child has learned what the clinician intended to teach, the clinician analyzes communication performance based on language samples collected from the child in a natural setting.

Parents and teachers should be asked to collect language samples. However, in most cases they require training to master this task. For example, they must be encouraged to:

- Let the child initiate communications, if possible.
- Phrase questions that may elicit more than one-word responses.
- Provide a situation or encourage activities that are likely to elicit communicative interaction.

Emerick and Hatten (1974) have developed a series of guidelines for collecting language samples that can be helpful for parents, teachers, and beginning clinicians.

Principle VI

The role of the speech and language clinician in consultation with parents and teachers is to evaluate, assess, and recommend the type of communication (gesture, sign, verbal, communication-board) that can be most effective from a social, psychological, educational, and vocational perspective.

Combining a variety of communication methods (for example, sign language with oral language) has also been attempted. A series of cases has been reported in which children who were taught sign language later began to exhibit oral language (Barrera et al., 1980; Barrera Sulzer-Azaroff, 1983). Results suggest that the clinician must determine which communication system is the best facilitator for communication development and effectiveness for each child with autism.

Shane and Bashir (1980) developed a decision matrix that lists questions about cognitive, linguistic, and social development that help to determine a child's potential for various levels of communication. The questions ask about the child/adult's chronological age, presence or absence of oral reflexes, level of cognitive development, amount of language and motor speech production, speech intelligibility, presence of emotional factors, previous therapy indicators, speech imitative ability, and implementation factors. These questions are arranged in a hierarchical matrix for selecting the most feasible communication system for the child/adult. The Bashir and Shane matrix determines whether to "elect, delay, or reject an augmentative communication system."

The principles suggested provide the basis for a developmental-ecological-behavioral model (DEB) to language evaluation and treatment. In essence the clinician using the DEB model takes a positive, proactive approach and:

1. Views the child's total integrated development with the realization that the language behavior is an outgrowth of cognitive, social, and linguistic development and not an isolated phenomenon.

2. Observes the child's behavior from the perspective that any single behavior is part of development that proceeds in an organized manner.

3. Assumes that the clinician can facilitate development based on the child's current skills rather than be frustrated by the clinician's own unfulfilled expectations based on adult intuition.

4. Plans therapy goals and strategies based on observations of the child, which are then related to knowledge about development of normal children.

5. Views individual language behaviors as part of language development, which, as with any other aspect of development, may vary in rate but occur in stages.

6. Plans language therapy on the basis of what the child can do given the level of development.

7. Plans therapeutic strategies based on observations of the child's behavior with sensitivity to the environmental conditions under which the child is learning.

8. Is sensitive to ways in which the child's daily environment can be structured so as to maximize learning opportunities.

EVALUATING LANGUAGE DISORDERS IN CHILDREN WITH AUTISM

The therapist plans and implements the speech and language evaluation and writes the report. The components of the evaluation are traditional. However, several special considerations are important to the successful completion of the evaluation with this population. Comments on and examples of the evaluation components and processes focus on these considerations.

The evaluation has three major purposes: (1) to determine the extent of the speech and language problems; (2) to develop goals for therapy; and (3) to determine strategies that might be successful in achieving the goals. The emphasis of the evaluation for this population was the development of goals and strategies for therapy since the students evaluated are severely language impaired. When possible, however, standardized tests are given to determine the extent of the problem. Also, these tests are repeated after a period of therapeutic intervention to determine the extent of progress.

Table 5-1 outlines the components of the evaluation and lists standardized tests or criterion measures most frequently used. Each of these components is discussed in terms of the special considerations needed to evaluate this population.

Referral

This section contains a short rationale for conducting the speech and language evaluation and summarizes previous therapy, including the

Table 5-1.
Components of the Speech and Language Evaluation

Components	Suggested Measures/Procedures
I. Referral	. Determine reason for referral
II. History	. Gather case history
III. Behavioral observations (communication emphasis)	. Observe child in a variety of communicative settings
IV. Content	1. Conduct Cognitive Assessment Battery (Liebergott & Swope, 1977)
	2. Observe and analyze play routines (see text)
	3. Observe and analyze daily routines (see text)
V. Comprehension	. Assess vocabulary: Peabody Picture Vocabulary Tests (Dunn, 1965, 1983)
	. Evaluate language structures: Test for Auditory Comprehension of Language (Carrow, 1973)
VI. Production	. Collect spontaneous language sample (Bloom & Lahey, 1978)
	. Calculate mean length of utterance (Brown, 1973)
	. Analyze semantic-syntactic relationships (Bloom & Lahey, 1978)
	. Analyze developmental sentence Analysis (Lee, 1974)
	. Analyze language uses (Liebergott & Swope, 1977b)
	. Conduct phonological analysis: Goldman/Fristoe Articulation Test (1969, 1972)
	. Determine appropriate communication system: Election criteria for the adoption of an augmentative communication system (Shane & Bashir, 1980)
	. Conduct oral peripheral examination; voice/fluency assessment; audiological assessment (Darley & Spriestersbach, 1978)
VII. Alternate forms of communication	
VIII. Other considerations	

quantitative and qualitative results of previous speech and language assessments, as well as recommendations for language goals.

History

Since the overall case history is generally already available, the clinician's case history is limited to the history of the child's communication development. The information is collected from previous reports and by interviewing parents or treatment workers.

Behavioral Observations (Communication Emphasis)

The therapist must observe the child in a variety of settings since the child's communicative abilities vary according to communicative contexts. For example, children who appear nonverbal with a new teacher may evidence several communicative acts with parents. This means that the children must be seen in structured and unstructured settings, with a variety of people—for example, peers, parents, teachers.

Through extensive notes or videotape, the therapist records the child's behavior with others. These observations can become critical for determining effective strategies for therapy. The following behavioral observation contains several examples of communicative acts that became critical elements in planning appropriate materials and settings most conducive to the development of communication.

Jerry is a solidly built two-year-old who walks with a slightly awkward gait. He makes infrequent eye contact; during the evaluation he made eye contact with the examiner only when he removed her glasses. He smiles rarely; in the course of the evaluation he smiled twice at the picture on the wall and twice when removing the clinician's glasses.

The examiner did not directly request verbal responses from Jerry, but gradually involved him in action with some interesting toys. With this approach, he did not resist interaction. He examined objects handed to him, threw down those objects he did not appear interested in, and took the examiner's hands off objects he wanted to retrieve. When the examiner took an object in which he seemed interested away, he screamed in protest; this appeared to be the most frequent device used to get his needs met. While he did not initiate interaction with the examiner, he accepted objects from her for about an hour.

He responded inconsistently to environmental noise and linguistic stimuli; either he continued an activity without interruption or turned his head toward the sound. He appeared to focus visually on an object with greater regularity when auditory or verbal stimuli accompanied presentation of visual stimuli such as, "Jerry, look at this."

Stereotyped rocking behavior was intermittent. When playing with new objects, Jerry occasionally placed the object on the floor, took a kneeling posture above it, and rocked backwards and forwards on hands and knees. However, if the examiner than handed him a further interesting object, he immediately abandoned his rocking to examine the new toy. Therefore, it appeared that it is possible to distract him from this stereotypical behavior.

Content

As a member of an interdisciplinary team, the clinician has access to the results of cognitive testing conducted by the psychologist. When appropriate, the psychologist assesses the child's cognitive level through standardized measures such as the Arthur adaptation of the Leiter International Performance Scale (Arthur, 1969), The Wechsler Preschool and Primary Scale of Intelligence (Wechsler, 1967), or the Wechsler Intelligence Scale for Children, Revised (Wechsler, 1974).

The cognitive assessment battery developed by Liebergott and Swope (1977b) adopted from Uzgris & Hunt scales (1976) for the sensorimotor period (see Table 5-2) and from Piaget (1962) during the preoperational stage (see Table 5-3) is conducted for children who appear to be between zero and four years old in their cognitive development. The battery is conducted on a formal basis. That is, the clinician presents certain tasks to the child and records the responses. In addition, the clinician observes the child's play activities and daily routines to assist in determining the child's developmental level and to determine goals and procedures for intervention.

Following is a short description of each sensorimotor and preoperational process. The learning or prerepresentational knowledge that characterizes the sensorimotor period involves the activities of the child and is necessary for the development of representation. Prerepresentational knowledge begins with direct experience of actions on objects. Subsequent learning proceeds toward the separation of specific actions on specific objects, and therefore, allows actions and objects to exist as independent entities that can be repeated and combined. The knowledge that the child acquires at this stage is information that may eventually be represented through language.

1. *Sensorimotor processes.* The development of sensorimotor skills is evaluated through observation of the child's ability to attend, imitate, establish object permanence, and develop means–ends relationships.
   a. *Attending.* Attending is a skill that requires a child to be able to focus selectively on stimuli presented. This process begins with attention to environmental stimuli, and later to linguistic stimuli.
   b. *Imitation processes.* Imitation is a skill that can be used to extend behaviors. It requires both correct identification of elements of an act to be imitated and accurate translation of that identification into one's own actions. Imitation skills begin with imitation of self, and then others; a simple behavior, and then a series of behaviors. Both motor and vocal imitative skills are assessed.
   c. *Object permanence.* To develop the object concept, the child must acquire the knowledge that objects continue to exist independently of their immediate experience.
   d. *Means–ends relationships.* The development of means–ends relationships is measured by the child's ability to use actions, objects, or other people as a means to obtain a goal. The goal, for example, could be a request for an object, an action from another person, or another person's attention.

2. *Preoperational processes.* If a child's responses to the foregoing tasks indicate the necessary prelinguistic processes that serve as language prerequisites, the clinician assesses the cognitive skills that develop in normal children between two and four years. Cognitive learning on the nonlinguistic level during this period appears to structure and/or interact with the more formal language components. The clinician assesses the child's development in the areas of attending, representation, classification, seriation, and numeration.
   a. *Attending process.* Attending is an extension of the attending skills assessed previously. The development of attending can be observed by noting the child's ability to attend to linguistic stimuli in order to direct any actions.
   b. *Representational skills.* Drawing, symbolic play, and dreaming, as well as language, are all forms of representation. In these instances the child begins to develop the concept of double knowledge; that is, that during play a bowl can become a hat, a cotton ball can become clouds, or a word or phrase can represent an object, event, or relationship between objects and events. As a result the child increases his knowledge of the world and learns to represent this knowledge through language, drawing, and so forth, in the absence of actual events.
   c. *Classification.* Classification involves the concept that objects share at least one common element. The child demonstrates this knowledge when grouping objects together to represent the similarities that exist. In doing so the child may use several classification schemes: size, color, shape, function. The development of this skill is noted in the child's

Table 5-2.
Sensorimotor Processes: Cognitive Prerequisites for the Acquisition of Language

Area to Be Assessed	Behavior to Be Assessed
1. Attending	Turns head or makes an appropriate response to environmental noises.
	Turns head or makes an appropriate response to sound of a familiar person's voice.
	Looks at an object that is placed in front of him.
	Turns head or makes an appropriate response to the names of familiar people.
	Responds to a request to look at the teacher.
2. Imitation of gross body movements	Imitates gross body movements that are already familiar and he can see himself make.
	Imitates gross body movements already familiar and he cannot see himself make.
	Imitates a series of gross body movements that are already familiar to him.
	Imitates unfamiliar gross body movements that he can see himself make.
	Imitates unfamiliar gross body movements that he cannot see himself make.
	Imitates unfamiliar and novel series of behavior.
	Imitates a previously learned activity at some future time.

ability to use these multiple attributes within an increasing number of categories when sorting objects.

d. *Seriation.* Seriation involves the ability to arrange a group of objects into a continuous series on the basis of dimensional relationships. The process increases in difficulty when multiple dimensions of objects to seriate increases. Until able to note finer distinctions in seriation, the child is unlikely to use the morphological endings -er, -est, which code comparisons.

3. Imitation of vocal behavior	Imitates own sounds.
	Imitates unfamiliar sounds.
	Imitates familiar words.
	Imitates unfamiliar words.
4. Object permanence	Follows the movements of an object with the eyes.
	Looks at the place where a moving object has disappeared.
	Looks at the place where an object should appear after it has disappeared behind an obstacle.
	Finds a partially hidden object.
	Finds an object that is completely hidden.
	Finds an object when it is hidden consistently under one of two cloths.
	Finds an object when it has first been put under one cloth and then conspicuously put under a second cloth.
	Finds an object when it has first been put under one cloth and then moved to another. The child does not see the actual movements of the object, but sees the movement of the hand containing the object.
5. Use of objects	Performs the same actions on different objects.
	Performs different actions on the same objects.
	Makes one object act on another.
	Changes the location of an object from one place to another.

e. *Numeration.* Numeration involves the ability of the child to establish relationships between sets of objects. The child demonstrates this knowledge when grouping objects in a one-to-one correspondence. Until a child understands the relationships between sets of objects, he is unlikely to use words that code those relationships; for example, more, some, all.

Table 5-3.
Cognitive Development of the Early PreOperational Stage

Area to Be Assessed	Behavior to Be Assessed
1. Attending	Fixed attention to a concrete task of his choice.
	Fixed attention to a task but with adult help can transfer attention to receive directions. Attention is under adult control.
	Attends to a task but can transfer attention to receive directions. Attention is under child's control.
	Attends to a task while incorporating verbal directions.
2. Play	Performs his own action schema on an object in a new context (12–18 months).
	Performs his own action schema on a new object in a new context (18–24 months).
	Uses another object to perform his own action schema.
	Performs someone else's action schema on an object, without identifying him as the other person.
	Uses an object to represent another object.
	Pretends to be another person or object.
	Pretends a series of symbolic activities, where the symbolic objects are components of the whole episode.
	Pretends a series of symbolic activities with other children.

Comprehension

Although a variety of language comprehension testing techniques have been tried, comprehension is not easily measured in early stages of language development either in normal children or in those with language disorders. First, in the early stages of development, comprehension of gestures or language is tied closely to the context. Language has not developed as a representational system. Second, some of the children examined who appeared to have the cognitive abilities to develop language have limited ability to demonstrate understanding. Although comprehension is measured through some standardized measures, criterion-referenced measures are more useful for developing therapy goals.

A frequently used standardized test to measure single-word hearing vocabulary is the *Peabody Picture Vocabulary Test*—Revised (Dunn and

3. Classification	Sorts objects that are physically similar.
	Sorts objects that function together.
	Sorts objects on the basis of a single attribute.
	Sorts objects on the basis of more than one attribute.
	Completes a series of objects by finding a new object with a similar attribute.
	Completes a series of objects by finding a new object with two or more similar attributes.
4. Seriation	Arranges three items in a series that varies in one dimension.
	Arranges ten items in a series that varies in one dimension.
	Arranges three items in a series that varies in more than one dimension.
	Arranges ten items in a series that varies in more than one dimension.
	Inserts an item into a series that has already been ordered.
5. Numeration	Establishes one-to-one physical correspondence between two sets of objects.
	Establishes one-to-one physical correspondence between series of objects.
	Establishes one-to-one physical correspondence between two sets of objects by adding or subtracting objects.
	Establishes one-to-one correspondence between two sets of objects when the physical space is not familiar.

Dunn, 1981). The *Test of Auditory Comprehension of Language* (Carrow, 1973) is often used to measure the child's ability to understand different structures of language. Both of these measures require the child to respond by pointing to a picture that matches the word or utterance spoken by the examiner. Although successful for some, other children may not succeed in learning the task.

To develop goals for therapy, however, the therapist develops informal criterion-referenced measures, including attending to and following one-, two-, or multiple-step instructions in daily activities or play routines to assess comprehension.

Production

SPONTANEOUS LANGUAGE SAMPLE

If the child uses language to communicate, the clinician or teacher records an extensive language sample. The clinician often collects the samples for diagnostic purposes; however, the parent and teacher also might be taught to collect a sample. Teaching parents or teachers to collect the language data helps them focus on the child's language, and often teaches them to become better language facilitators during the therapy process. Also, since some children have minimal language or must first adapt to the clinician, the parent may have a better opportunity to collect a more representative sample. The clinician analyzes the length of utterances, the semantic/syntactic features, and the use of utterances.

SEMANTIC/SYNTACTIC ANALYSIS

A mean length of utterance (MLU) is calculated according to Brown's rules (1973). If the child produces at least 50 subject–verb constructions, linguistic forms are analyzed using Lee's *Developmental Sentence Analysis* (1974). This measure evaluates eight different linguistic forms in a developmental hierarchy. These forms include personal pronouns, indefinite pronouns, main verbs, secondary verbs, negations, conjunctions, interrogative reversals, and wh-questions.

If the child is functioning at a two- or three-word level, a semantic-syntactic analysis, as outlined by Bloom and Lahey (1978), is completed from the child's language sample.

The child's spontaneous one-, two-, and three-word combinations, and the context in which the word or words are said, are categorized into one or more of 12 semantic relationships that emerge in a child's language at the two- to three-word level. A child must demonstrate three different examples of the category before it is considered to be mastered.

USE

In all instances the therapist evaluates language use. Appropriate language use depends on one's ability to know who can say what to whom, and when, where, and how language should be used (Hymes, 1971). The therapist analyzes use by observing the nonlinguistic context of the spontaneous speech sample and evaluating the communicative intentions of the child. The variety and appropriateness of the following categories of language use are noted: (Liebergott & Favors, 1978)

1. To talk about their actions.
2. To talk about the actions of others.
3. To talk about something that has happened in the past.
4. To talk about something that will happen in the future.
5. To request objects.
6. To request actions to be performed by others.
7. To request information.
8. To gain permission (subcategory about which parents and teachers are concerned.)
9. To give information.
10. To answer other's questions.
11. To express feelings about themselves.
12. To express their feelings about others.
13. To make childlike jokes.

The Goldman-Fristoe Articulation Test (Goldman & Fristoe, 1972) is administered to assess the production of phonemes (the basic unit of sounds in spoken language) in the initial, medial, and final position of single words, as well as words in the context of sentences. The examiner records any errors that occur during this formal testing. Stimulability testing is conducted to determine if the child is capable of correctly producing the error phonemes when provided with the correct model. Also, if warranted, the examiner observes the child's spontaneous speech to determine the phonological patterns in context, using Ingram's (1981) methods for analyzing phonological processes. Intelligibility of the child's speech is also assessed to determine whether articulation therapy is warranted.

ORAL PERIPHERAL EXAMINATION AND VOICE/FLUENCY AND AUDIOLOGICAL ASSESSMENTS

These measures are standard procedures in all speech and language evaluations regardless of the type of disorder. Although important, these areas of assessment are not usually the basis for the primary communication problems in this population.

Assessment procedures in these areas are outlined extensively by Darley and Spriestersback (1978), and must be considered when goals of therapy are established. Some basic guidelines are as follows:

- Evidence of motor apraxia or dysarthria through an oral peripheral examination could impede the child's ability to use oral language as a means of communication.
- Evidence of voice problems requires that a child receive an examination by an otolarynologist prior to recommendations for voice therapy.
- Fluency problems may be evident but may not be a primary reason for communication problems in this population.
- If a hearing problem is suspected, hearing testing is critical prior to initiating therapy. If the clinician is unable to condition a child to respond to a hearing screening test, the child should be seen by an audiologist. If a hearing problem is detected, therapy goals and strategies must be provided to treat the problem.

Alternate Forms of Communication

Many children with autism are often diagnosed as nonverbal. Some children who are nonverbal do not have the necessary cognitive precursors to develop representational behavior. In these cases the clinician can recommend developing a gestural system paired with the use of a communication board. Shane and Bashir (1980) present a helpful format for developing such systems that are applicable to children who are autistic.

Other children who are nonverbal appear to have developed the cognitive precursors for language. For these children one can explore the potential for learning sign language by attempting to teach a number of signs in a meaningful context. For some, sign language provides an alternative form of communication that is most successful.

Another alternative is the use of communication boards using words and symbols. This approach is most successful for those who have the cognitive ability but not the motor ability to develop sign language.

Other Considerations

TIME

In many diagnostic centers, a speech and language evaluation is scheduled for one to two hours. However, we recommend that the clinician spend approximately four days—that is, approximately two half-days a week for a month—in observing and testing the child and interviewing parents and teachers. Although observations and interviews with parents and past teachers can begin almost immediately, formal cognitive or linguistic testing is usually not started until stimulus control is apparent and the child has begun to adapt to the environment.

TEAM APPROACH

Special-education teachers, psychologists, speech-language-hearing clinicians, and physicians are core team members. To enhance reliability, the language clinician encourages another team member to observe a portion of the language diagnostic. Feedback from team members can also enrich the recommendations for therapy strategies.

Interpretation of Test Results

Test environment, materials and the use of reinforcers often affect responses of children who are at the early stages of development. Therefore, the therapist must not draw conclusions that deviate too far from the actual test item results. For example, several children performed poorly on tests of object permanence when the item hidden was a doll; however, they did remarkably better when the examiner hid an M & M or another favorite item. Conversely, another child passed every object permanence task that the examiner presented, but when faced with a real problem in the environment, he was unable to demonstrate that knowledge. In this instance the teacher observed this child trying to put on a pair of rubber gloves. Upon his first try he placed two of his fingers in one finger on the glove. When he removed the glove, he inadvertently inverted one of the fingers on the glove. The student immediately told his teacher that one of the fingers on the glove had disappeared.

These sample results suggest that, first, the examiner must not assume that a level of cognition or language has been reached unless the behavior is evident under several conditions. Second, the child may not develop the underlying concept that the clinician intended to test even though the child passed the test item. Third, the examiner should be cautious about making rich interpretations about a child's knowledge based on the test scores of a child with autism. Most importantly, the clinician who is aware of the seemingly minor environmental stimuli that effect the response, will be able to systematically change the instructional stimuli so that the child continues to respond correctly to a range of discriminative stimuli.

TREATING LANGUAGE DISORDERS IN CHILDREN WITH AUTISM

Setting Goals

After the completion of the speech and language evaluation, the clinician analyzes the data in order to develop appropriate speech and language goals for the child. After the goals are determined, the clinician decides on short- and long-term objectives that will be incorporated into the child's overall Individualized Program Plan (IPP) for the upcoming academic year.

During the IPP meeting with the parents and teachers, the clinician explains the speech and language goals and objectives, and also the role of the clinician, emphasizing the mutual responsibility of parents, teachers, and the clinician to alter the child's communication skills. Together the clinician, parents, and teachers discuss the potentials and limitations of the child's communicative ability. They agree upon and rank order the goals for therapy and the strategies that will be used to make these changes. After discussing the child's optimal potential communication objectives, the clinician demonstrates the format of the speech and language programs that need to be conducted by the parents and school personnel, either through further explanation of the program, demonstration of the program, or observation of a video recording of the prospective program. During the IPP the clinician also tries to establish a balance between the parents' and school department personnel's optimistic or pessimistic versus realistic goals for the child's communicative growth.

Reevaluation to Note Progress

Even though the clinician reevaluates a child yearly to develop appropriate IPP goals, a complete speech and language diagnostic should be conducted at the end of every three years. The same diagnostic battery that was presented during the initial speech and language evaluation is repeated in the three-year evaluation in order to note the student's overall communication progress. A complete reevaluation is conducted, usually over a one-month period.

Within a consultant (or "third"-party) model, the speech and language evaluations are conducted by the clinician, while therapy is delivered by parents and teachers trained by the clinician, who serves as a consultant. Using the "consultant model," the speech and language therapist teaches the teacher or parent to administer the child's speech and language programs. This treatment strategy maximizes the number of treatment sessions per week for the students; for example, the teachers carry out an intensive program three or four times per week or throughout the day through incidental teaching instead of the one or possibly two sessions per week if conducted by a speech and language therapist.

Before using the consultant model approach, the clinician's role must be understood and accepted by staff and parents. One can introduce this concept through a series of workshops on language learning, stressing the importance of learning communication within the context of one's environment. In the consultant model, the clinician writes the speech and language program(s), and teaches the teachers and parents to conduct the program(s) using one or more of the following techniques.

1. Role playing the treatment program with the staff member.
2. Modeling the treatment program with the child.
3. Direct observation of a similar treatment program with another staff member and child.
4. Suggested readings.
5. In-service workshops.

In role playing the teacher acts as the student and the speech and language clinician demonstrates the format of the communication program. The clinician also explains the goal of the program; the stimuli used to elicit a response; the type of response that is considered correct, partially correct, or incorrect; the type and schedule of reinforcement; the record-keeping system; and the criteria for attaining each goal of the problem.

After role playing the communication program(s), the speech and language clinician then models the program(s) with the student in order for the teacher to gain a better understanding of the procedures.

During the modeling the clinician answers any of the teacher's questions about goals and procedures.

Also, if another child is following a similar speech and language program, the clinician recommends that the teacher observe the format of the program in the classroom to gain further understanding and insights into the goal that was to be accomplished with the child. If the teacher has any further questions after observing the similar program, the speech and language clinician should be accessible to answer them.

Another important teaching strategy is the use of directed readings. The speech and language therapist recommends reading material to the staff that would suggest various teaching procedures or strategies to facilitate the goal(s) of the program, and arranges for these materials to be available to the language facilitators.

Another means of effectively teaching the staff the intent of the student's speech and language programs is to conduct in-service workshops. The intent of the workshops is to provide basic knowledge of speech and language development and principles for facilitating this development in the student's curriculum. These workshops focus on salient aspects of overall speech and language development in order to broaden the staff members' understanding of speech and language development in normal children, as well as in children with autism.

Effectiveness of Treatment

To determine the effectiveness of the treatment programs, the teachers record data to note the child's progress in the programs. Depending on the goal or type of treatment program, various strategies are used to record the data. The teacher might record data on the frequency or number of correct and incorrect responses or the percentages of correct and incorrect responses, or use a time-sampling procedure.

Another way to note progress as a result of the treatment program is the completion of the "conference chart" (see Figure 5-1). After observing the program, the clinician determines a progress rating for the student, as well as a rationale for the rating. Also, the clinician asks the teacher for a rating of the child's progress and the possible rationales for progress. As a result of the clinician's and teacher's progress ratings and rationales, the clinician offers additional program suggestions to facilitate the student's progress. These suggestions are presented through:

Communication Therapy

Date _____

Name of Student _____   Conference Time _____

Name of Teacher assigned
to Language Program _____   Conference cancelled due to

No. & Curriculum Area
of Language Program _____   _____

PROGRESS RATING SCALE: Excellent-5; Above Average-4; Average-3; Fair-2; Poor-1

. Teacher Rating = (circle) '0'
. Language Therapist's Rating = (slash) '/'

Teacher's rationale for progress rating: _____

Language Therapist's rationale for progress rating: _____

Number of IPP short-term language goals passed: _____

Program Suggestions presented through: Explanation
_____ Demonstration w/students
_____ Role playing w/teacher
_____ Suggested readings
_____ Observations

Program Suggestions: _____

**Figure 5-1
Conference Chart**

1. Further explanation.
2. Demonstration with the child.
3. Additional role playing with the teacher.
4. Observation of a similar program.
5. Suggested readings for supplemental knowledge of the goals of the speech and language program.

To maintain maximum continuity, three copies of the conference chart are completed. One copy is for the person who supervises the child's programs, a second is for the teacher, and the final copy is for the speech and language clinician. This procedure is effective in providing direct communication and feedback among the professionals who are involved with the student's educational or vocational programs. Also, the conference chart effectively communicates any changes that are to be implemented in the treatment programs. In essence the conference chart is a helpful tool for providing feedback to parents or teachers who serve as the language facilitators.

SPECIFIC TREATMENT CONTEXTS

Language in Play

The literature (Largo & Howard, 1978; Liebergott & Swope, 1976) strongly suggests that play contexts provide an interactive and enriching environment that facilitates language learning in normal children. This same finding applies in the language learning of children with autism.

Before discussing teaching language in play, it is important to describe the levels of play that are focused on in the treatment process. Many researchers have developed a number of different descriptions of play that emerge in a child's behavior (Largo & Howard, 1978, Piaget, 1962; Liebergott & Swope, 1977a). We have chosen four categories of play that are easy for parents and teachers to differentiate.

The first level of play skills that emerge are referred to as random or practice play. In *practice play* children focus on touching, throwing, mouthing, and smelling objects or people. The second level of play is referred to as *exploratory play*, in which children begin to explore and manipulate their environment to help them learn about the properties of objects. For example, a child may pick up a new truck, turn it over, spin the wheels, explore the inside, and then place the truck on the floor. *Functional play* is the third level of play. At this level children begin using objects for what they are intended—building with blocks, rolling and throwing balls, pushing cars on the floor, placing toy furniture and people in a toy house.

The fourth and final stage of play is *symbolic or pretend play.* Symbolic play, like language, is a form of representation. In symbolic play a child demonstrates the ability to represent an action pattern the child has observed in himself or others out of the usual context of the action and eventually learns to represent these action patterns with make-believe objects or people. For example, at a rather sophisticated level of symbolic play, the child pretends to have birthday parties. A flattened piece of clay may be used as a cake and paper clips as candles, and imaginary friends invited. Symbolic play is an activity in which children engage quite frequently, and is an important vehicle for the child's learning about properties and functions of objects and how they relate to one another. In addition, the actions of play are the events that children are likely to code in language.

THE PLAY ENVIRONMENT

The playroom is organized to facilitate and teach the children play skills. The play area is divided into a number of different "active-learning" situations. This allows the children to involve themselves openly in a variety of play activities. The area of the playroom can be divided into a kitchen area; block-building space; dolls and dollhouses; numerous shelves to house toy people, furniture, transportation items, and miscellaneous toys; and floor space for the active-play items.

The play materials chosen are age appropriate, as well as functional in the children's repertoire. That is, functional play materials can be used in a number of ways and also to provide differential learning opportunities about properties of objects that would be beneficial to the student in "everyday real-life situations."

DESCRIBING DEVELOPMENT IN PLAY

In order to determine whether the treatment strategies for facilitating the children's play skills were effective, clinicians should record data for the levels of play in which the children engaged during playtime, using a "Play: Ten-Minute–Ten-Second Sample Form" (see Figure 5-2).

During one play session per week, the teacher or observer completes the form. The initial identifying information records the child's name, the date of the recording, the name of recorder (for purposes of reliability), and the time the session began and ended (to determine if the child engaged in play for the entire ten minutes and if the time of the session appeared to have an effect on the child's performance). Also, the teacher identifies the location of the play session (e.g., playroom, outdoors), who was involved during the play session, and the materials

Communication Therapy

Name: _____ Location: _____
Date: _____
Recorder: _____ Circle whichever apply: alone, with adult,
Time: Began - _____ Ended- _____   With one child - Name: _____
 With > than one child - Names: _____

In each interval, observe for 10 seconds and write play description during 50 seconds. Record by ✓ under interval if play sequence occurs during that minute. Write action/object sequence and/or verbalization in corresponding section titled play description.

Play Sequence	Interval	Play Description
Ramdom Play Practice play-throwing, banging, touching, smelling, mouthing objects or people	1 2 3 4 5 6 7 8 9 10	
Exploratory Play Explore objects by manipulation - fitting one object into another one	1 2 3 4 5 6 7 8 9 10	
Functional Play Using objects for what they are intended for - building with blocks, lids on jars, etc.	1 2 3 4 5 6 7 8 9 10	
Symbolic or Pretend Using objects to represent other things - birthday party, box as a bed or hat, imaginary people	1 2 3 4 5 6 7 8 9 10	

Figure 5-2
Play: 10 Minute—10 Second Sample Form

the child played with during the session. The teacher/observer records the child's play behavior for ten minutes. During the ten minutes, the teacher/observer observes the child's play for ten seconds during each minute, and within the remaining 50 seconds of each minute records

Figure 5-3
Summary Data of Play Skills

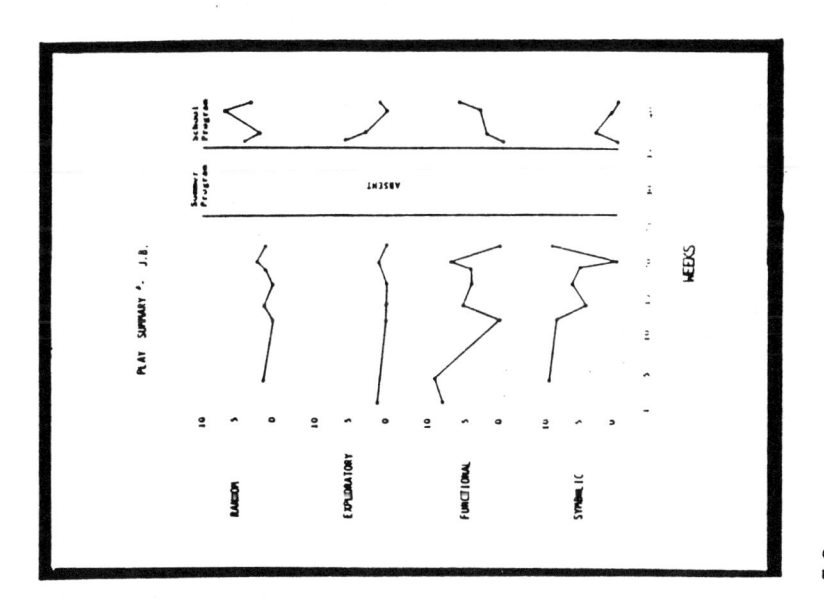

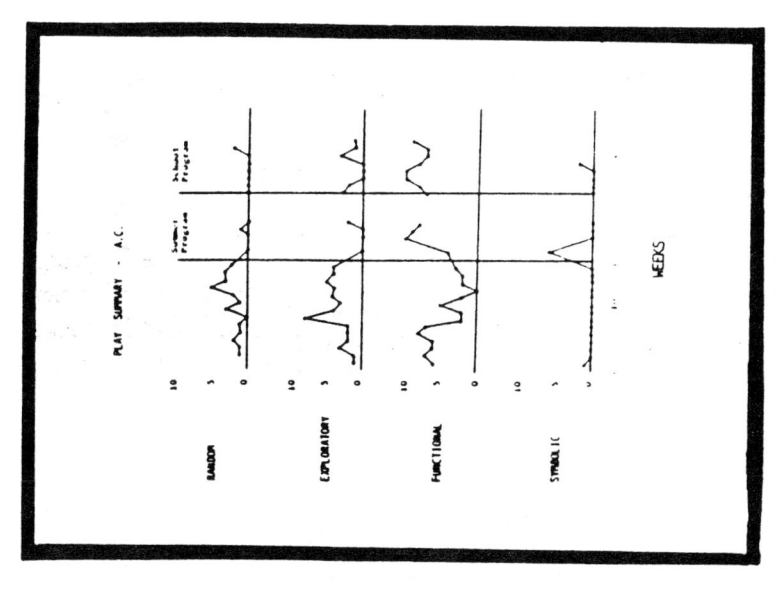

the level of play, as well as a description of the play activities and any child vocalizations/verbalizations.

The data are then transferred to a cumulative play progress chart. This descriptive summary allows the clinician to note any increases or decreases within the same level of play, as well as any new play behaviors (see Figure 5-3).

For example, the summary data in Figure 5-3 indicate that while A.C.'s random and exploratory play behavior have decreased, his functional play has increased, and a few instances of symbolic play even are beginning to emerge in the later sessions. Similarly, J.B.'s random and exploratory play occurred infrequently before his summer vacation, whereas functional and symbolic play were his primary play skills. These newly acquired play skills, however, were not maintained over the summer months. But subsequent programming regained functional play skills. Such descriptive data can help the clinician monitor a client's progress in a play program over time.

Communication in Daily Routines

Due to the complexity of the communication disorders in children and adults with autism, communication programs must be developed in their daily routines to maximize their linguistic abilities. Many of these children do not generalize language skills that were taught in isolated contexts on a three- to four-day-a-week basis. Therefore, the language programs should be designed to coordinate with the student's other programs or activities. For example, many of the speech and language programs can be carried out during the student's self-help activities, snack time, lunch, recreation, or personal hygiene, as well as "free time."

Of course, the type of program varies with the cognitive and linguistic level of the children. For children at the early developing stages of cognitive and linguistic skills, one can implement a program similar to the Lunch Time Communication Program using communication boards (see Table 5-4). Such a program will vary based on the goals being taught. However, a portion of a sample program is included to illustrate activities used to increase requests to teachers and the other children.

SUMMARY

In summary, this chapter has outlined the principles, diagnostic goals, and therapeutic considerations in treating language problems of children with autism and similar disorders. The goals and treatment strategies of this approach are guided by developmental, ecological, and behavioral principles that emphasize the arrangement of environmental conditions that are conducive to communication.

The therapist, as one member of a team, is responsible for conducting an evaluation to determine the extent of the communication problem and, most important, goals and strategies for therapy. For this population the therapist uses standardized measures when possible to determine the extent of the problems, although the emphasis of the evaluation is on goals and strategies. To this end the therapist develops and uses a series of criterion-referenced measures to assess content, semantic-syntactic, phonological, and pragmatic aspects of language. If the child is nonverbal, alternate forms of communication are considered. Whether the communication approach is verbal or nonverbal, the *use* of communication is the primary consideration when developing goals and strategies for therapy.

Language therapy must take place in a social milieu in which communication is reinforced, or there is no use in talking. Therapy is most advantageous when a child's positive communicative behaviors are consistently reinforced by others.

To develop a successful communication program, the therapist serves as a third party in the treatment. After determining goals the therapist must assist parents, teachers, caretakers, siblings—all of the language facilitators—to teach communication skills. The therapist also plays an important role in tracking and assessing progress, suggesting new goals and treatment strategies when appropriate.

Whether the child is three or 21, language therapy must take place in a meaningful context. Play and daily routines are just two settings where teaching communication can be effective. These settings are highlighted to indicate the content and language learning/teaching possibilities inherent in these activities and to demonstrate program variation, depending on the developmental level of the child.

If our interpretation of the child's behavior reflects an accurate level of cognitive and linguistic development and learning strategies, then the goals and strategies for therapy provided in a social context will be most likely to teach what the child is able to learn.

Table 5-4.
Lunchtime Communication Program Using Communication Boards

Long-term goals
A. Produce gestural requests to adults and peers to acquire present objects and subsequently objects that are not present.
B. Increase comprehension of action–object relationship.

Short-term goal
A. Increase production of requests to teacher during lunch by pointing to the appropriate photograph of the desired item.
B. Increase production of requests to other students during lunch by pointing to the appropriate photograph of the desired item.

Materials
    A. Lunchbox or bag.
    B. Lunch items cut up in small portions:
        1. Sandwich.
        2. Container of milk, juice, etc. (pour only small portions).
        3. Fruit.
        4. Cookies.
    C. Bell child can ring.
    D. Individual photographs of each child and each item.
    E. At least one other child and two teachers seated at one table.

Program suggestion:
Although this program attempts to teach the child to use communication cards, the teacher should always *model* language behavior appropriate for the task. The teacher's language should consist of simple interrogative or declarative sentences that are appropriate to the immediate context.

Program I
Goal: The child will spontaneously request desired food items by looking at the teacher and pointing to the communication card that pictures desired item.

Program suggestions
1. Teacher will place small buzzer or bell on table in front of child and child will be taught to ring the bell *spontaneously* by pressing down on it with one finger. (This behavior may need to be shaped into tapping response.) When child rings the bell and looks at teacher, the teacher will reinforce response with small bites of the sandwich, kept in front of *the teacher* but in view and out of reach of the child. If the child does not know how to ring the bell using one finger, the teacher will physically shape the response. If the child does not look at the teacher, the teacher must shape looking behavior using physical prompts.

    Criterion: Child will simultaneously ring the bell (using one finger) to receive each bite of lunch for two consecutive lunch periods.
2. The teacher will punch a hole in the *picture* of the child's sandwich and place it on top of the bell. Contingent upon the child tapping the picture (therefore ringing the bell) and looking at the teacher, the teacher will give the child part of the sandwich. Once the sandwich is eaten, the teacher will place a second bell on the table with a picture of another desirable lunch item (cookie). Contingent upon the child tapping the picture of the cookie and looking at the teacher, the teacher will give the child a bite of the cookie. If the child taps the picture of the sandwich, the teacher will say, "It's all gone." As each type of

lunch food is eaten, the teacher should introduce another picture placed on a bell but always leave the previous items on the table.

Criterion: Three consecutive lunch periods in which child taps desired food item.
3. Repeat step 2 with the following addition: Teacher will shift the pictured lunch items the child hasn't eaten to various places on the table after each response.

Criterion: Three successive lunch periods in which child taps the desired food items.
4. The teacher will repeat step 2 of Program II using the pictures of food items *without* the actual food item in view of the child.

Criterion: Three lunch periods in which child taps the desired food items.
5. The teacher will remove the pictures from the bells and placed them on the table. The child must point to a picture of the food item and look at the teacher in order to receive the actual item that is hidden from the child's view.

Criterion: Three successive lunch periods in which child taps the desired food items.
6. The teacher will place the pictures of the food items on a key chain and place them in front of the child *or* on the child's belt. The child will point to the picture of the desired item and look at the teacher in order to obtain it from the teacher.

Criterion: Three successive lunch periods in which child taps the desired food items.

Program II
Goal: Child 1 will request a desired food item from child 2 by looking at child 2 and pointing to communication card representing the food item of choice.
Staff: Two teachers
Materials: Tray for cut-up sandwiches, cookies, and fruit
Program Suggestions:
1. Two children should be seated opposite one another and one set of communication cards should be placed in front of them depicting all lunch items of both children. The actual lunch items should be placed on a tray to one side of the table, close enough for both children to reach them but close enough to one teacher so that the teacher can control the distribution of the items.

    One teacher begins by pointing to a card, looking at child 1, and saying, "I want _____." Another teacher assists child 1 in passing the desired item. If the child completes the task, it is that child's turn to request a food item. (The teacher moves the food tray closer to child 2.) Child 1 points to communication card picturing the desired food item and looks at child 2. Child 2 gives child 1 desired item. If task is successfully completed, child 2 gets a turn. The food tray is moved closer to child 1 and teacher assists child in making the communication exchange. The child should always look at the person closest to the food tray. The movement and position of the food tray become important discriminative stimuli as to whom to request food items from and when the next turn is appropriate.

    Criterion: Two children taking turns requesting all lunch items for five lunch periods.
2. Step 1 can be extended to include more children as well as being conducted in a variety of settings (such as McDonalds).

REFERENCES

Baltaxe, C. A. M. (1977). Pragmatic deficits in the language of autistic adolescents. *Journal of Pediatric Psychology*, 42, 376-393.

Barrera, R. D., Lobato-Barrera, D. & Sulzer-Azaroff, B. (1980). A simultaneous treatment comparison of three expressive language training programs with a mute autistic child. *Journal of Autism and Developmental Disorders*, 10, 21-37.

Barrera, R. D. & Sulzer-Azaroff, B. (1983). An alternating treatment comparison of oral and total communication training programs with echolalic autistic children. *Journal of Applied Behavior Analysis*, 16, (4), 379-394.

Bass, K., Brown, J. & Redmond, A. (1975). Symbolic play in normal and language-impaired children. Unpublished master's thesis, Emerson College.

Bates, E. (1976). *Language and context: Studies in the acquisition of pragmatics.* New York: Academic Press.

Bates, E., Benigni, L., Bretherton, I., Camaioni, L. & Volterra, V. (1977). From gesture to the first word: On cognitive and social prerequisites. In M. Lewis and L. Rosenblum (Eds.), *Interaction, conversation, and the development of language.* New York: Wiley, pp. 247-308.

Bloom, L. (1970). *Language development: Form and function in emerging grammars.* Cambridge, Mass.: The MIT Press.

Bloom, L. (1978). *Readings in language development.* New York: Wiley.

Bloom, L. & Lahey, M. (1978). *Language development and language disorders.* New York: Wiley.

Bloom, L., Lighbown, P. & Hood, L. (1975). Structure and variation in child language. *Monographs of the Society for Research in Child Development*, 40 (serial no. 160).

Brown, R. (1973). *A first language: The early stages.* Cambridge, Mass.: Harvard University Press.

Carrow, E. (1973). *Test for auditory comprehension of language.* Boston, Ma: Teaching Resources, 1973.

Condon, W. S. (1975). Multiple response to sound in dysfunctional children. *Autism and Schizophrenia*, 5, 37-56.

Corrigan, R. (1978). Language development as related to stage 6 object permanence development. *Journal of Child Language*, 5, 173.

Dale, P. S. (1972). *Language development: Structure and function.* Ill. Dryden Press.

Darley, F. L. & Spriestersback, D. C. (1978). *Diagnostic methods for speech pathology.* New York: Harper & Row.

Dore, J. (1975). Holophrases, speech acts and language universals. *Journal of Child Language*, 2 (1), 21.

Dunn, L. M. & Dunn, L. M. (1981). *Peabody Picture Vocabulary Test (PPVT).* Circle Pines, Minn.: American Guidance Service.

Emerick, L. & Hatten, J. (1974) *Diagnosis and evaluation in speech pathology.* Englewood Cliffs, N.J.: Prentice-Hall.

Goldman, R. & Fristoe, M. (1972). *Test of articulation.* Circle Pines, Minn.: American Guidance Service.

Greenfield, P. & Smith, J. H. (1976). *The structure of communication in early language development.* New York: Academic Press.

Hymes, D. (1971). Competence and performance in linguistic theory. In Hyxley and Ingram, (Eds.), *Language acquisition: Models and methods.* New York: Academic Press, pp. 3–27.

Ingram, D. (1981). *Procedures for phonological analysis of children's language.* Baltimore: University Park Press.

Koegel, R. L., Rincover, A. & Egel, A. L. (1982). *Educating and understanding autistic children.* San Diego, Calif.: College Hall.

Lahey, M. (1978). *Readings in childhood language disorders.* New York: Wiley.

Largo, R. H. & Howard, J. A. (1978). Developmental progression of play behaviors in children between 9 and 30 months I: Spontaneous play and imitation. *Developmental Medicine and Child Neurology.* June, 1979 Vol. 21 No. 3 p 299–310.

Lee, L. L. (1974). *Developmental sentence analysis.* Evanston, Ill.: Northwestern University Press.

Leiter, R. G. (1969) Leiter International Performance Scale. Los Angeles, California: Western Psychological Services.

Liebergott, J. W. & Favors, A. (1978). *Head start manual for children with communication disorders.* Washington: Office of Child Development.

Liebergott, J. W. & Swope, S. (1977a). An application of Piaget to language therapy: A child's play is serious work. *Communication disorders: An aduio journal for continuing education.* New York: Grune & Stratton.

Liebergott, J. W. & Swope, S. (1977b). Developmental language and assessment and teaching presentation. American Speech and Hearing Association Convention. Chicago, Ill.

Liebergott, J. & Swope, S. (1976). Symbolic play as a basis for language acquisition. *The handicapped learner: Language development = materials design = curriculum management.* New York: Charles E. Merrill.

Lovaas, I., Young, D. B., & Newsom, C. D. (1978). Childhood psychosis: Behavioral treatment. In B. B. Wolman, J. Egan, and A. O. Ross (Eds.), *Handbook of treatment of mental disorders in childhood and adolescence,* Englewood Cliffs, N.J.: Prentice-Hall, pp. 385–420.

Morehead, D. M., & Morehead, A. (1974). From signal to sign: A Piagetian view of thought and language during the first two years. In R. L. Schiefelbusch and L. L. Lloyd (Eds.), *Language perspectives—Acquisition, retardation and intervention.* Baltimore: University Park Press.

Nation, J. E., & Aram, D. M. (1977). *Diagnosis of speech and language disorders.* St. Louis: C. V. Mosby.

Piaget, J. (1962). *Play, dreams, and imitation in childhood.* New York: W. W. Norton.

Rees, N. S. (1978). Pragmatics of language: Applications to normal and disordered language development. In R. L. Schiefelbusch (Ed.), *Bases of language intervention.* Baltimore: University Park Press.

Shane, H. C., & Bashir, A. S. (1980). Election criteria for the adoption of an augmentative communication system: Preliminary considerations. *Journal of Speech and Hearing Disorders,* 45 (3), 408–414.

Sinclair, H. (1973). Language acquisition and cognitive development. In T. E. Moore (Ed.), *Cognitive development and the acquisition of language.* New York: Academic Press.

Uzgiris, I., & Hunt, J. (1976). *Assessment in infancy: Ordinal scales of psychological development.* Urbana, Ill.: University of Illinois Press.

Wechsler, D. (1974). *Wechsler Intelligence Scale for Children (Revised)*. New York: Psychological Corporation.

Wechsler, D. (1967). *Wechsler Preschool and Primary Scale of Intelligence*. New York: Psychological Corporation.

Wethersky, A. M. & Prutting, C. A. (1984). Profiles of communicative and cognitive-social abilities in autistic children. *Journal of Speech and Hearing Research*, 27, 364–377.

Wing, L. (1976). *Early childhood autism*. Oxford: Pergamen Press.

FURTHER READING

For further information about the diagnosis of speech and language problems, see:

Emerick, L. L. and Hatten, J. T. *Diagnosis and evaluation in speech pathology*. Englewood Cliffs, N.J.: Prentice-Hall, 1974.

Darley, F. L. and Spriestersbach, D.C. *Diagnostic methods in speech pathology*. New York: Harper & Row, 1978.

Fey, Marc. *Language intervention with young children*. San Diego, California: College—Hall Press, 1986.

Nation, J. E. and Aram, D. M. *Diagnosis of speech and language disorders*. St. Louis: C. V. Mosby, 1977.

CHAPTER

6

Medical Evaluation and Management of the Child with Autism

Siegfried Pueschel, M.D., Ph.D., M.P.H.

Medical History
   Family History
   Preconception and Gestation
   Perinatal Period
   Neonatal Period
   Early Development Data
Pediatric Evaluation
   Initial Observations
   Anthropometric Data
   General Physical Examination
   Neurologic Examination
   Behavioral Data

Laboratory Investigations
   Electroencephalogram
   Biochemical Evaluation
Treatment
   Drug Treatments
   Vitamin/Metabolic Therapies
   General Health Care
Conclusions
References

MEDICAL HISTORY

Family History

TO ARRIVE AT A BETTER UNDERSTANDing of the child with autism, information concerning the medical history is of utmost importance. The historical investigations usually start with obtaining a detailed family history. Although autism generally is not considered to be an inherited disease applying Mendalian concepts, twin studies have revealed that there is some evidence that genetic factors are involved in the etiology of autism. Folstein and Rutter (1978) interpreted the monozygotic and dizygotic difference in concordance for autism, and the much larger difference in concordance for cognitive disorders, as highly suggestive that genetic elements are causatively related to the development of autism. Although Hanson and Gottesman (1976) did not find any strong evidence implicating genetics in the development of infantile autism, there have been more recent efforts by Ritvo and colleagues (1982) to examine the role of genetic factors in causing certain cases of autism (a genetic subgroup).

Since incomplete penetrance and genetic heterogeneity may be prevalent factors in this disorder (Folstein & Rutter, 1978), it is paramount to explore both the father's and the mother's families in terms of known genetic diseases, neurological disabilities, cognitive dysfunction, mental deficiency, and psychiatric disorders. The ethnic origin and family composition need to be recorded and a pedigree should be obtained. The health status of the immediate members of the family, including both parents and siblings, will be assessed. Particularly, social and interfamily circumstances need to be investigated. Furthermore, the parents' education, professional involvements, and socioeconomic factors, as well as previous pregnancies and their medical and psychological elements, need to be explored.

Preconception and Gestation

Preconception medical history, as well as medical data from the gestational period of the child in question, should be reviewed. While no specific condition or circumstances before or during pregnancy have been positively identified in mothers who gave birth to children with autism, it is known that some children whose mothers had rubella during pregnancy have autistic features (Ornitz, 1978). A report from the National Institute of Neurological Diseases and Stroke Collaborative Perinatal Study (Torrey et al., 1975) found that a significantly increased number of mothers who had children diagnosed as autistic had experienced vaginal bleeding during the first and particularly during the second trimester of pregnancy. This prospective study did not uncover any correlations between other antenatal conditions and autism. However, there are a number of retrospective studies that emphasize the association between maternal antenatal and perinatal complications and autism (Campbell, 1978; Campbell et al. 1971; Cohen & Young, 1977; Fish, 1976; Fish, 1971; Folstein & Rutter, 1978; Gittleman & Birch, 1967; Greenbaum, 1970). Thus it is possible that certain gestational circumstances might be noted that could have been responsible for the child's developmental disability. Novel approaches in history taking, detailed accounts of apparently insignificant occurrences during pregnancy, and detective-like epidemiological investigations might provide clues to important etiological factors not previously considered. Hence infectious processes, environmental insults, possible exposures to chemicals, and a variety of other apparently benign aspects will need to be explored. Beyond the immediate home environment, exposures elsewhere, such as at places of work, recreation, and education, might give new leads that deserve further study.

Perinatal Period

In addition to the preconceptional and antenatal histories, perinatal circumstances also should be investigated. Since a few retrospective studies indicate that birth trauma, birth anoxia, or other insults at the time of delivery are associated with later development of autism (Campbell Fish et al. 1971; Fish, 1976; Fish, 1971; Gittleman & Birch, 1967; Greenbaum, 1970), it is important that such pertinent medical information be obtained. In the analysis of his data, Torrey and coinvestigators (1975) did not find any association between autism and the degree of difficulties during delivery, use of forceps, premedication or anesthesia, cord complications, or Apgar scores.

Neonatal Period

The neonatal period also should be described in detail. Complications that might have arisen during the first few days of the child's life should be noted. Although no positive correlations between abnormal findings on newborn physical and neurological examinations and autism have been identified, Berlin and Szurek (1973) indicate that failure in bonding during the neonatal period might be causatively related to later development of autism, which, however, is seriously questioned by Rutter (1978).

During further investigations of medical history, past medical problems of the child, including infectious diseases, endocrinologic or metabolic problems, operations, accidents, or other illnesses, will be recorded. The status of immunization should be obtained, and if incomplete, further inoculations should be forthcoming. An accurate record of medications, allergies, and nutritional intake is part of routine history taking.

Early Development Data

Most important, detailed data regarding the child's development should be provided by the parents. While it is common to obtain the available information on gross and fine motor developmental aspects, it is important also to explore the child's social and language development as these are most affected in the child with autism. Insight into the developmental circumstances of the child and their interpretation by the parents not only may result in a better understanding of the child's maturational processes and the parent–child relationship, but also will provide the physician with information for differential diagnostic considerations and the teacher with educational strategies.

Further historical events of interest relate to the behavioral aspects of the child in the home, neighborhood, school, and other places at various developmental stages. The child's response to and interrelation with people and objects need to be recorded. His progress or possible regressions need to be explored and various preoccupations, obsessions, perseverations, and other stereotypic behaviors investigated.

The first symptoms of autism might not have been recognized as such or be readily recalled by the parents. Often parents report the infant as having had a fairly normal development during the first 12 months, and only during the second year of life were symptoms and differences in development and behavior noted. But careful history taking often elicits subtle signs that had been evident much earlier. Some parents indicate that the infant cried infrequently, "was a good baby," and did not need much companionship. Other parents have described the child as overly irritable and hyperactive during infancy.

Disturbances of the child's developmental rate have been reported by many parents. They have observed sequences of developmental spurts and plateaus. With regard to language acquisition parents have reported normal language development during the first 18–24 months of life when the child had clearly said distinctive words and short phrases, but then regressed to echolalia and few word utterances.

During the second and third years of life, according to most parents, the child seems hard to reach or does not respond to affection. Some parents mention that their child became attached to an unusual object and seemed not to be interested in people. Many observed that the child avoided looking people directly in the eye or stared into space. During the first few years, parents also note that their children were preoccupied with things that spin and excessively watched the motions of their hands. Rocking, flapping the arms in a repetitive way, and toe walking are other frequent symptoms.

Beyond the history obtained from parents, it is necessary to acquire other historical records, such as birth history, previous investigations and evaluations, and past laboratory studies. These data need to be integrated into the overall assessment of the child. Children with autism often have long medical histories that document milestones and previously attempted medical interventions. Nonmedical personnel (e.g., intake specialist) can help in the organization and presentation of history details and patterns.

It is well known that accurate history taking can shed light on many facets of the child's present status, and also can provide important information concerning etiology and the natural history of the developmental disability.

PEDIATRIC EVALUATION

Initial Observations

Initial observations are essential in any comprehensive physical examination. This is particularly true in the child with autism since he most often has significant difficulties in communicating. Thus information concerning the child's well-being, behavior, and physical condition will be obtained primarily through observation. The relationship to the child's immediate environment, activity level, and other behavioral aspects should be recorded. Attention should be paid to the use of spontaneous and elicited language, if present. Other observations relate to the child's physical condition, such as skin color, possibly existing phenotypical abnormalities, or movement disorders. Although the child usually does not present with specific physical features as in chromosomal disorders or specific syndromes, he may have certain characteristics that require detailed description.

Anthropometric Data

As during the routine examinations, the child with autism will be weighed and height and head circumference measured. Ordinarily children with autism do not vary significantly in their physical dimensions from other children and there is no need for further anthropometric investigations. However, if a child should present with unusual features, other measurements—such as head breadth, head length, interpupillary distance, or arm span—might need to be obtained.

The analysis of physical measurements will often provide clues to further investigations of possibly coexisting endocrinologic diseases, metabolic abnormalities, nutritional deficiencies, or other physical disorders.

General Physical Examination

The approach to the general physical examination of the child with autism will be essentially the same as that for other children, although it might be somewhat difficult because of limited cooperation on the part of some children with autism. Yet in most instances a gentle approach and the presence of a person whom the child can trust facilitate the physical and neurological examinations. The otolaryngologic, respiratory, cardiac, gastrointestinal, genitourinary, and musculoskeletal systems are usually unaffected, and most of the patients appear to be in good general health. Particular attention, however, is paid to the ophthalmologic and auditory assessments, and occasionally consultations by specialists in these areas will be required.

The most common pathologic findings observed by the author relate to the oral cavity, where poor dental hygiene, dental caries, malocclusions, and gum problems are often identified. Also, dermatologic conditions such as infected skin lesions resulting from poor hygiene and wounds caused by self-abusive behavior are frequently observed.

Neurologic Examination

The neurologic evaluation focuses on the examination of cranial nerves, the sensory as well as the motor systems. Also, the child's coordination is tested and the deep tendon reflexes are elicited. The mental status is described, and an estimate of overall functioning is usually made.

Behavioral Data

Behavioral characteristics—in particular, stereotypic, self-stimulating, aggressive, and other pathologic behaviors—will be noted. These observations are of paramount importance in suggesting further laboratory studies or recommending specific treatment programs. A physician who examines and treats a child with autism in the context of an integrated treatment program has access to day-to-day behavioral data taken in many functional environments to guide evaluation and treatment decisions. Often the physician and behavior specialist must work together to evaluate the relative contributions of environmental and biologic factors in a behavior such as self-injury that may be preceded by eruption of teeth or some painful experience such as otitis media. Another child may have a severe attentional deficit disorder whose daily behavior suggests a need for further neurologic evaluation. Similarly, the physician can make use of detailed seizure reports completed by parents and professionals to determine the need for further neurological assessment.

LABORATORY INVESTIGATIONS

While routine laboratory investigations have not been helpful either in confirming the diagnosis of autism or assisting in the development of

Electroencephalogram

treatment, some specific tests occasionally are needed in order to study a particular symptom.

If a child, for example, has a convulsive disorder or has been observed to exhibit behaviors resembling seizurelike activities, an electroencephalogram (EEG) is indicated. Preferably it should be done in both the waking and sleep states. If such recordings should reveal significant paroxysmal discharges corroborating the clinical observations, appropriate anticonvulsive therapy should be administered. Close follow-up of such patients during which blood is taken periodically to determine drug levels and the necessity to readjust medications, is essential.

In the past several investigators have engaged in neurophysiologic studies. Kolvin and colleagues (1971), as well as Hutt and co-workers (1965), reported unusually low-voltage EEGs suggestive of hyperarousal. A carefully controlled study by Small (1975), which utilized quantitative EEG measures in seven autistic and seven normal children, found significantly less session-to-session and transhemispheric variability in the group with autism. Sleep EEGs found rapid eye movement (REM) activity to be reduced in children with autism, which, according to Ornitz and colleagues (1969), is due to a maturational defect in these children. Ornitz (1978) also suggested that the reduced organization of the REMs may reflect vestibular dysfunction since the presence of REM bursts depends on the integrity of the vestibular nuclei.

Other areas of neurophysiologic investigations have focused on sensory evoked responses, and autonomic and vestibular response studies. Noncontingent sensory evoked response studies in children with autism (Lelord et al., 1973) revealed inconclusive results; however, neurophysiologic responses to sensory stimuli involving contingencies showed large, slow positive or negative potentials resembling those evoked by movement or its anticipation, which suggests a strong motor component in the perceptual and associated processes of children with autism. Ornitz (1978) interprets the sensory-motor behavior of children with autism, as well as their tendency to learn through motor feedback, as a neurophysiologic dysfunction of a system that modulates interaction of sensory and motor processes.

While the latter studies do not find routine application in the clinical situation and are primarily of interest to the research-oriented investigator, they may provide answers to questions concerning pathogenetic mechanisms and treatment approaches in the future.

Biochemical Evaluation

Increased research activity in the field of neurochemistry attempts to elucidate biochemical aberrations in the central nervous system of the child with autism. Basic advances in the study of neurotransmitters, including serotonin, acetylcholine, and the newer compounds of enkephalins and endorphins, have provided biological strategies for investigating autism and clarifying mechanisms of actions of commonly used drugs. While much research currently is focusing on transmitter substances, there are major methodological difficulties due to a number of complex issues (Cohen & Young, 1977). For example, the metabolism of the biogenic amines is only one fragment of a biological mosaic that includes outer structural organizations, endocrine regulations, genetic control mechanisms, and complex interactions among these systems.

During recent years, several reports in the literature have linked specific biochemical and genetic disorders with infantile autism. Lowe and colleagues (1980) reported children with both autism and phenylketonuria and Coleman and Blass (1985) described four patients with autism and lactic acidosis. In addition to these biochemical disorders, several investigators observed children with infantile autism associated with fragile-X syndrome (Meryash et al., 1982; Gillberg, 1983). However, Pueschel and colleagues (1985) did not find any such chromosomal problem in the autistic population they studied.

TREATMENT

It is assumed that the results of the neurophysiologic and neurochemical investigations will provide a better understanding of the underlying pathology in autism and might give a rationale for therapeutic approaches. At present, however, there is no effective medical treatment available for children with autism. Current care and management practices are primarily concerned with the improvement of the child's symptoms.

Drug Treatments

Although the majority of children with autism do not need medications to control their behaviors, in certain circumstances a medication can inhibit or decrease negative behaviors or improve the organization and control of behavior. These children then will be more receptive to educational instructions and social interactions. Medical therapy should be used as an adjunct and should not replace other therapeutic or educational strategies. If a child is in need of medication, it is understood that this form of treatment must be individualized since no one pharmacologic agent will take care of everything that is wrong with a child.

Phenothiazines have been said to be effective in some children with autism by decreasing their stereotypic or bizarre behaviors, as well as their self-destructive repetitive activities (Cohen & Young, 1977; Fish, 1976). Chlorpromazine has been shown to have a sedative effect. Other tranquilizers, such as trifluoperazine, haloperidol, thiothixene, and molindone have been found to be less effective than chlorpromazine (Fish, 1976). Imipramine has been studied in these children with equivocal results: Campbell and co-workers (1971) report that imipramine has some stimulating and some sedative effects; but, in general, is felt to be a poor drug for this population.

Stimulants such as amphetamines and methylphenidate usually increase symptomatology in children with autism and exaggerate their psychotic disturbances (Fish, 1971). Some children, however, who did not respond to neuroleptics improved markedly with amphetamines (Fish, 1976). A study by Campbell et al. (1971) using triiodothyronine reported that all but three of 20 children included in this study improved. More recent studies on a hyperserotonemic subgroup of children with autism are available (Geller et al., 1982; Ritvo et al., 1984), which show ameliorative effects of fenfluramine.

Subsequent to these preliminary observations, a multicenter study was initiated to further investigate the effects of fenfluramine on the behavior of children with autism. Several studies have been completed by groups of investigators who participated in the multicenter study (August et al., 1985; Klykylo et al., 1985; Groden et al., submitted for publication). These studies reported clinical improvement in some children in some areas after fenfluramine administration, primarily relating to activity level, attention, motor function, and social awareness. The final results of the multicenter study will provide more information on various effects fenfluramine has on children with autism.

If carried out appropriately, drug treatment can be a valuable adjunct to the total management of the child with autism. Yet the risk and toxicity should be weighed against the possible therapeutic gain. Close follow-up of children on medication is mandatory since some drugs are known to have side effects. The efficiency and dosage of a given medication need to be reevaluated periodically. It is understood that if a child does not improve, is regressing or interfering side effects are observed, the medication that initially was thought to be of benefit to the child should be discontinued. If a child receives medication, this should be made known to the private physician, educational staff, and other professionals involved in the care of the child.

As mentioned, children with autism who have overt seizures or behaviors that resemble a seizure-like disorder or who have markedly abnormal EEGs will often be helped by anticonvulsive therapy. Regular follow-up by a pediatric neurologist and periodic reassessment of the effectiveness of the specific seizure medication are essential. The team can provide the physician with specific feedback on the effects of prescribed medications, including early recognition (if they are trained) of deleterious side effects.

Vitamin/Metabolic Therapies

There have been other approaches to the treatment of children with autism. Anecdotal reports of the administration of megavitamins indicate some improvement in this population (Rimland, 1973); however, no controlled study as yet has demonstrated a marked benefit from megavitamin therapy (Greenbaum, 1970). Various other drugs used with these children have been discussed in recent reviews by Fish (1971) and Campbell (1978).

Special diets and exclusion of certain foods from the diet have been recommended methods of treatment. Although certain nutrients do impact on the metabolic function of the central nervous system, there are no well-controlled studies that show that a particular nutrient (amino acid or vitamin) resulted in a significant improvement of the overall function and behavior of these children.

General Health Care

Since the medical consultant does not provide primary medical care, the child will need a private pediatrician who will provide medical care of acute illnesses, give immunizations, and offer general well-child care. Beyond the general health maintenance, it is important that the child with autism be seen regularly by a dentist. Many of these children have poor dental hygiene, dental caries, and other intraoral disorders. Therefore dental examinations should be carried out at regular intervals. If a child is uncooperative, premedications can be given by the attending physician.

Often the provision of general health care requires well-thought-out collaborative arrangements among the caring professionals. Compliance with routine (e.g., dental evaluation, opthomologist exam, blood tests, EEG, etc.) and specialized (e.g., allergy evaluation, gynecological examinations, CAT scan) evaluation procedures may leave much to be desired in children with communication deficits. An alternative to foregoing the exam or performing it under sedation—especially if the procedure requires a series of, or repeated measures—is for the physician and behavioral specialist to work cooperatively to prepare the child. For example, if a child is fearful of doctors and dentists, desensitization to these fears by gradual exposure to medical settings and procedures can be carried out by a treatment team member, with the physician's cooperation. In such a situation, the physician may decide what tests need to be done immediately and which can await the proper preparation activities. Sometimes a child's perceptual and communication deficits require the use of unique and adapted vision-evaluation procedures such as suggested by Newsom and Simon (1982).

CONCLUSIONS

Medical evaluation and management are an integral part of the overall comprehensive assessment and long-term care of the child with autism. Although the consulting physician will be primarily involved in obtaining the medical history, providing physical and neurological examinations, and focusing on treatment aspects, a knowledge of neuroscience will be a major contribution to the overall integrated assessment of the child. In caring for a child with autism, the physician's role is to minimize the handicap and thus facilitate the efforts of the other professionals involved. As a result of caring for a number of children with autism, the physician can generate and test hypotheses about the neurologic, biochemical, or biobehavioral nature of autism. By working collaboratively with parents and professionals on a team, the physician can play a vital role in a partnership that not only is beneficial to the child but can also contribute to our greater understanding of the medical issues in autism.

REFERENCES

August, G. J., Raz, N. & Davis-Baird, T. (1985). Brief report: Effects of fenfluramine on behavioral, cognitive, and affective disturbances in autistic children. *Journal of Autism and Developmental Disorders, 15,* 97–107.

Bender, L. (1973). The life course of children with schizophrenia. *American Journal of Psychiatry, 130,* 783–786.

Bender, L. & Faretra, G. (1961). Pregnancy and birth histories of children with psychiatric problems. *Proceedings of the Third World Congress of Psychiatry, 2,* 1329–1333.

Berlin, I. N. & Szurek, S. A. (1973). Psychosis of childhood retrospect and prospect. In S. A. Szurek and I. N. Berlin (Eds.), *Clinical studies in childhood psychosis.* New York: Brunner/Mazel.

Campbell, M. (1978). Pharmacotherapy. In M. Rutter and E. Schopler (Eds.), *Autism, a reappraisal of concepts and treatment.* New York and London: Plenum Press, pp 337–355.

Campbell, M., Fish, B., Shapiro, T. & Floyd, A. (1971). Imipramine in preschool autistic and schizophrenic children. *Journal of Autism and Childhood Schizophrenia, 3,* 267–282.

Cohen, D. J. & Young, J. G. (1977). Neurochemistry and children's psychiatry. *Journal of American Academic Child Psychiatry, 16,* 353–411.

Coleman, M. & Blass, J. P. (1985). Autism and lactic acidosis. *Journal of Autism and Developmental Disorders, 15,* 1–8.

Fish, B. (1976). Pharmacotherapy for autistic and schizophrenic children. In E. Ritvo, B. Freeman, E. Ornitz, and P. Tanguay (Eds.), *Autism: Diagnosis, current research and management.*

Fish, B. (1971). The "one child, one drug" myth of stimulants in hyperkinesis. Importance of diagnostic categories in evaluating treatment. *Archives of General Psychiatry, 25,* 193–203.

Folstein, S. & Rutter, M. (1978). A twin study of individuals with infantile autism. In M. Rutter and E. Schopler (Eds.), *Autism, a reappraisal of concepts and treatment.* New York and London: Plenum Press, pp 219–241.

Geller, E., Ritvo, E. R. & Freeman, B. J. (1982). Preliminary observations on the effect of fenfluramine on blood serotonin and symptoms in three autistic boys. *New England Journal of Medicine, 307,* 165–169.

Gillberg, C. (1983). Identical triplets with infantile autism and the fragile-x syndrome. *British Journal of Psychiatry, 143,* 256–260.

Gittleman, M. & Birch, H. G. (1967). Childhood schizophrenia. *Archives of General Psychiatry, 17,* 16–25.

Greenbaum, G. H. (1970). An evaluation of niacinamide in the treatment of childhood schizophrenia. *American Journal of Psychiatry, 127,* 129–132.

Groden, G., Pueschel, S. F., Groden, J., Dondey, M., Zane, T. & Veliceur, W. (1987). Effects of fenfluramine on the behavior of autistic individuals. (Research In Developmental Disorders, 8(2).)

Hanson, D. R. & Gottesman, I. I. (1976). The genetics, if any, of infantile autism and childhood schizophrenia. *Journal of Autism and Childhood Schizophrenia, 6,* 52–66.

Hinton, G. G. (1963). Childhood psychosis or mental retardation: A diagnostic dilemma. *Canadian Medical Association Journal, 89,* 1020–1024.

Hutt, C., Hutt, S. J., Lee, D. & Ounsted, C. (1965). A behavioral and electroencephalographic study of autistic children. *Journal of Psychiatry. 3,* 181–197.

Klykylo, W. M., Feldis, D., O'Grady, D., Ross, D. L. & Halloran, C. (1985). Brief report: Clinical effects of fenfluramine in ten autistic subjects. *Journal of Autism and Developmental Disorders, 15,* 417–423.

Kolvin, I., Ounstead, C. & Roth, N. (1971). Six studies in the childhood psychosis V. Cerebral dysfunction and childhood psychosis. *British Journal of Psychiatry, 118,* 407–414.

Lelord, G., Laffort, F., Jusseaume, P. & Stephant, J. L. (1973). Comparative study of conditioning of averaged evoked responses by coupling sound and light in normal and autistic children. *Psychophysiology, 10,* 415–425.

Lobascher, M. E., Kingerlee, P. E. & Gubbay, S. S. (1970). Childhood autism: An investigation of aetiological factors in twenty-five cases. *British Journal of Psychiatry, 117,* 525–529.

Lowe, T. L., Tanaka, K., Seashore, M. R., Young, J. G. & Cohen, D. J. (1980). Detection of phenylketonuria in autistic and psychiatric children. *Journal of the American Medical Association, 243,* 126–128.

Meryash, D. L., Szymanski, L. S. & Gerald, P. S. (1982). Infantile autism associated with the fragile X syndrome. *Journal of Autism and Developmental Disorders, 12,* 245–301.

Newsom, C. D. & Simon, K. M. (1982). Vision testing. In R. L. Koegel, A. Rincover, and A. L. Egel (Eds.), *Educating and understanding autistic children.* San Diego, Calif.: College Hill, pp. 52–63.

Ornitz, E. M. (1978). Biological homogeneity or heterogeneity. In M. Rutter and E. Schopler (Eds.), *Autism, a reappraisal of concepts and treatment.* New York and London: Plenum Press, pp. 243–250.

Ornitz, E. M. (1978). Neurophysiological studies. In M. Rutter and E. Schopler (Eds.), *Autism, a reappraisal of concepts and treatment.* New York and London: Plenum Press, pp 117–139.

Ornitz, E. M., Ritvo, E. R., Brown, M. B., LaFranco, S., Parmelee, T. & Walter, R. D. (1969). The EEG and rapid eye movement during REM sleep in normal and autistic children. *Electroencephography and Clinical Neurophysiology, 26,* 167–175.

Pollack, M. & Woerner, M. G. (1966). Pre- and perinatal complications and "childhood schizophrenia": A comparison of five controlled studies. *Journal of Child Psychology and Psychiatry and Allied Disciplines, 7,* 235–242.

Pueschel, S. M., Herman, R. & Groden, G. (1985). Brief report: Screening children with autism for fragile-X syndrome and phenylketonuria. *Journal of Autism and Developmental Disorders, 15,* 335–338.

Rimland, B. (1973). High dosage levels of certain vitamins in the treatment of children with severe mental disorders. In D. Hawkins and L. Pauling (Eds.), *Orthomolecular psychiatry.* San Francisco: W. H. Freeman.

Ritvo, E. R. & Freeman, B. J. (1984). A medical model of autism: Etiology, pathology, and treatment. *Pediatric Annals, 13*(4), 298–305.

Ritvo, E. R., Freeman, B. T. & Geller, E. (1984). Effects of fenfluramine on 14 autistic outpatients. *Journal of the American Academy of Child Psychiatry, 22,*(6), 549–558.

Ritvo, E. R., Ritvo, E. C. & Brothers, A. M. (1982). Genetic and immenohematologic factors in autism. *Journal of Autism and Childhood Schizophrenia, 12,* 109–114.

Rutter, M. (1978). Etiology and treatment: Cause and cure. In M. Rutter and E. Schopler (Eds.), *Autism, a reappraisal of concepts and treatment.* New York and London: Plenum Press, pp. 327–335.

Small, J. G. (1975). EEG and neurophysiological studies of early infantile autism. *Biological Psychiatry, 10,* 385–398.

Taft, L. T. & Goldfarb, W. (1964). Prenatal and perinatal factors in childhood schizophrenia. *Developmental Medical and Child Neurology, 6,* 32–43.

Torrey, E. F., Hirsch, S. P. & McCabe, K. D. (1975). Early childhood psychosis and bleeding during pregnancy. *Journal of Autism and Childhood Schizophrenia, 5,* 287–297.

CHAPTER

7

Parent and Family Involvement

Gerald Groden, Ph.D.
Dale Domingue, M.S.

Literature Survey of Behavioral Parent
    Training
    Childhood Problems
    Content
    Individual Versus Group Training
    Settings
    Techniques
    Parent Cooperation
    Autism

A Model for Maximizing Family
    Competence
    Goals of the Model
    Elements of the Model
Conclusions
References

PARENT INVOLVEMENT IN THE TREATment and education of severely disturbed children developed as a result of difficulties encountered in the traditional approach to parent and family therapy. Within the psychoanalytic model, several intervention strategies have been commonly employed—either singly or in combination. Foremost among these is counseling that focuses on the parents and their feelings toward themselves, their child, and their parental roles. Often there is little or no direct intervention with the child. Sometimes individual counseling or play therapy for the child parallels psychotherapy for the parent(s). These approaches have been generally based on the assumption that pathology in the parents is at the root of the child's difficulties. Klebanoff (1959) revealed the difficulties of this assumption in his study that showed that the parental attitudes of mothers of schizophrenic children did not differ from those of mothers of children with organic brain disorders. Such approaches are quite time consuming and less appropriate for families in which the child's problems do not result from parental psychopathology.

With such children, without intervention to alter the child's behavioral problems, progress through counseling for the parents regarding their own feelings and roles may proceed very slowly, if at all. As Tymchuk (1979) has pointed out, "The parent, after having seen the therapist, must still return home to face a screaming child. . . ." (p. 18), and, in general, the adverse effect of children with autism on their families can be considerable (Schopler & Mesibov, 1984; DeMyer, 1979).

From problems with traditional approaches to parent–child intervention evolved the training of parents to act as therapists or direct-change agents for their children's behavioral difficulties. Several advantages of parent training have been noted (O'Dell, 1974; Weathers & Liberman, 1978). The most obvious is that because the child spends much time in the home with one or more of the parents, he receives direct intervention for much of each day instead of for one or two hours a week during therapy (Tharp & Wetzel, 1969). Conversely, many more children can be reached instead of just those who can be seen individually by a therapist. Another very important advantage of parent involvement is its preventive aspect. Training builds confidence and skills in parents, who then may be able to prevent future problems in the target child or in their other children. Since parents have primary influence on their children, particularly during the early years, they are in a key position to prevent behavioral and emotional problems. Finally, having parents as direct change agents leads to efforts to resolve difficulties within the natural environment, thus eliminating or reducing problems of generalization from an artificial therapy setting to the natural home setting.

There are two basic counseling models that are used in parent training: reflective and behavioral (Tavormina, 1974). Reflective counseling emphasizes such factors as parental awareness, understanding, and acceptance of children's feelings. Content areas vary. In some programs emphasis is placed on sharpening parents' communication skills (Gordon, 1970). In others emphasis may be placed on improving the parents' insight into their own and their children's behaviors and interactions (MacNamara, 1963). The second counseling model, behavioral, has emphasized observable behavior, both of the child and of the parents. The importance of environmental factors, including the parents' interactions with the child, is given primary attention. Content centers around behavioral management principles and techniques. Parents are taught to alter the children's environment, including their own behavioral responses toward their children, in order to effect changes in their children's behavior.

Emphasis in this chapter will be on the behavioral approach to parent training. O'Dell (1974), in his discussion of this approach, compiled the following list of its advantages (p. 419):

a. the ability for persons unskilled in sophisticated therapy techniques to learn the principles of behavior modification;
b. behavior modification is based on empirically derived theory;
c. many persons can be taught at one time;
d. a short training period is required;
e. a minimum of professional staff can have more treatment impact than in one-to-one treatment models;
f. many parents like a treatment model that does not assume "sick" behavior based on the medical model;
g. many childhood problems consist of rather well-defined behaviors that are conducive to behavioral treatment;
h. the applicability of behavior modification in dealing with problems in the natural environment.

The following will present a survey of the behavioral parent-training literature. It is included to provide the reader with some information on the history of significant topics in behaviorial parent training and is not intended to be exhaustive.

LITERATURE SURVEY OF BEHAVIORAL PARENT TRAINING

One of the earliest accounts of using parents to implement formal behavior management programs within the home was that by Williams (1959). Williams assisted the parents of a youngster to reduce his bedtime tantrums by using extinction. Circumstances led to a period of discontinuation of extinction procedures because the child temporarily had another caretaker. Tantrums increased during this time, but decreased again when the extinction program was reintroduced by the parents. The results clearly demonstrated the usefulness of training parents to implement behavioral programs to reduce child problem behaviors. In addition, Ayllon and Michael (1959) demonstrated that an unskilled individual in the home could be taught to alter children's behaviors effectively by manipulation of reinforcement contingencies.

Over the past 20 years, there has been a continuing and broadening investigation into the training and use of parents as behavioral change agents. Much of this investigation has been in the form of single-case studies that demonstrate the effectiveness of parent involvement.

Recently more studies have been conducted to compare different parent training approaches and techniques (e.g., Kovitz, 1976; O'Dell, et al., 1979; Flanagan, et al., 1979). Success rates for improving children's behavior through parent training programs using a behavioral approach have been encouraging. Weathers and Liberman, in a 1978 review of the literature, reported a 40-100 percent success rate, depending on the criteria used. There is great variability among studies in the quality of experimental design, variables employed, inclusion of follow-up measures, and generalizability. Nevertheless, spurred on by the successes of investigators and clinicians, significant advances have been made in parent training programs. Programs have been implemented across a wide range of parameters, including parental backgrounds, types of child behavior problems, content areas of training, training approaches (e.g., individualized versus group), settings (e.g., clinic versus home), and training techniques (e.g., didactic, modeling, role playing). We will now look more closely at some of these variables and their effects, alone as well as in combination, on parent training programs.

Childhood Problems

Behaviorally oriented programs have been used with parents faced with a wide variety of childhood difficulties. A sampling of these includes tantrums (Williams, 1959; Boardman, 1962), noncompliance (Peed et al., 1977, Breiner & Beck, 1984), hyperactivity (Duley et al., 1983), school phobias (Patterson, 1965; Tahmisian & McReynolds, 1971), and overdependence (Wahler et al., 1965). Parents have also been used to increase appropriate verbal behavior in children with speech or language dysfunctions (Hewett, 1965; Risley & Wolf, 1968; Lovaas, 1977; Harris et al., 1982).

Some clinicians have specialized in the treatment of particular behavior problems. Patterson (1971), for example, has concentrated on helping parents to reduce aggressive behavior in their children. In addition to developmentally normal children, much has been done with multiproblem developmentally disabled children and their parents (Tymchuk, 1979) and retarded children (Watson & Bassinger, 1974), as well as children diagnosed as autistic (Kozloff, 1973; Kaufman et al., 1979). Work with autistic children and their families will be covered in detail later.

Content

With regard to the content of parent training programs, clinicians differ in the emphasis they give. Some, such as Lindsley (1966), avoid instruction in general behavioral principles, whereas others emphasize this, or at least include it in their programs. For example, both Patterson and Kaufman and their colleagues include training in general principles as part of their parent training programs. To investigate the desirability of offering training in general behavioral principles, O'Dell and co-workers (1977) compared parents attending a workshop in parent training who received general principles training prior to the workshop with those who did not receive such prior training. Comparisons were made across several variables, ranging, from behavior modification skills to attendance and attitudes toward the training to reported use of procedures at follow-up. In all cases general principles training in combination with the workshop failed to reflect advantages over the workshop alone. Hudson (1982) has reported similar findings. On the other hand, Koegel and colleagues (1978) and McMahon, and co-workers (1981) have reported advantages of teaching general principles for generalization of training skills.

Other trainers have found through their experiences that specific content areas are of particular importance. For example, Weathers and Liberman (1978) noted that the parents with whom they worked were already using punishment and deprivation, generally incorrectly, but often with good results. As a result they concentrated on, and required parents to work on, a positive behavioral program during their training. Patterson (1971) emphasized what he felt were the two most critical steps for parents: careful observation-recording techniques and correct use of positive reinforcement. O'Dell, and colleagues (1982) also emphasize the importance of reinforcement. Time out from reinforcement has received much attention in the literature, probably because it is a punishing consequence that does not necessarily involve aversive physical or verbal interaction. Forehand (1977) includes that consequence as a regular part of his program for increasing compliance, and Bean and Roberts (1981) and Roberts, and colleagues (1981) have provided information on effects of different time-out release contingencies and child resistance to time out respectively. In addition to these child-oriented procedures, the added advantage of teaching parents self-management procedures and problem-solving strategies has also been reported (Sanders, 1982; Sanders & Christensen, 1985).

Individual versus Group Training

Another variable in parent training programs is the use of an individual versus a group format. Group presentation has the advantages of more efficient use of professional time and provision for supportive parent interaction. These advantages appear to depend, however, on a number of factors, including the purpose of the training program or its intended content, the severity of the children's or families' difficulties, and the variability in background of the parents. Group training programs have demonstrated decreases in targeted child behavior problems (Rose, 1974; Kaufman et al., 1977), as well as in changes in parental attitude and confidence (Kaufman et al., 1977; Tavormina, 1974). However, literature reviews (O'Dell, 1974; Tavormina, 1974) have pointed out that individual consultation may be more effective in many cases, especially when the identified behavioral difficulties involve complex behavioral chains. There have been conflicting reports as to the relative efficiency of the two formats. Mira (1970) compared individual versus group intervention formats in the families of 82 children with a wide range of behavioral difficulties. It was found that it took almost twice as much professional time per family to effect behavioral change in the group setting than with individual counseling. On the other hand, other researchers (Kovitz, 1976; Christensen et al., 1980;

Pevsner, 1982) have compared both methods and found the group approach to be more time efficient and as effective as individual approaches.

Successful integration of individual counseling with group training has been achieved by several clinicians (Patterson et al., 1975; Miller, 1975). Patterson and his associates, for example, begin intervention with individual baseline observation. Parents are given reading material as well as individual sessions to instruct them in the basics of behavior modification. Groups are then established in which they are assisted in setting up and carrying out home behavioral change programs. This is followed by individual follow-up.

Settings

In planning parent training programs, consideration must be given to the setting in addition to deciding whether sessions will be individual, group, or both. Usually the choice of setting is among a classroom, agency or other clinical location and the home. There are, of course, advantages to both. The clinical setting offers an absence of extraneous stimuli and economy of professional time. Groups are typically more conveniently handled in this setting. Parent observation in the classroom, combined with videotaping and direct feedback, has been shown to be particularly successful for some parents (Baker and McCurry, 1984). Sessions in the home allow the clinician to observe directly the individual aspects of the home and parent–child interaction in this setting. The home setting also reduces the need for generalization to the home of skills learned by the parents in a clinic (Mash et al., 1976). Studies have been conducted that demonstrate the advantages of using signaling and immediate feedback (discussed in the next section), and these techniques have been used in the home successfully (Zeilberger et al., 1968; Johnson & Brown, 1969). However, it is often the case that forms of these techniques that allow the removal of the trainer from parent–child interactions (e.g., one-way mirrors, especially in conjunction with electronic signaling devices) can be utilized only in the clinic. Clinic and home settings, of course, have been employed in combination (Patterson, 1971). Further research on the advantages of utilizing home as compared to clinical settings is needed (Sulzer-Azaroff & Pollack, 1982).

Techniques

The choice of teaching or training technique is yet another consideration in the implementation of a parent training program. Some of the more common methods include the use of reading materials, the didactic presentation of material, modeling, and role playing, as well as the use of signaling and/or immediate feedback during in vivo training sessions. All have advantages and combinations are usually quite successful.

The market abounds with behavior management texts and program packages for parents (e.g., Patterson, 1976; Baker et al., 1976; Rettig, 1973). Most are written in an interesting manner and save the clinician considerable preparation time. Patterson (1971) found that providing parents with reading material alone did not result in desired changes in child behaviors. Kaufman and his associates (1977) discovered that the use of a text (Kozloff, 1974) alone did result in improvement in parents' teaching skills, but this was inferior to use of the text in conjunction with group training sessions. In their recent review of self-help manuals, McMahon and Forehand (1980) stated that there is some evidence to indicate that such manuals can be helpful without additional therapeutic assistance for some populations and some behaviors. Hansen and coworkers (1984) reported that text and audiotapes were helpful for a large percent, but not all, of mothers with whom they worked.

Modeling and role playing and behavioral rehearsal with feedback are very successful techniques. Weathers and Liberman (1978) suggest the use of didactic training as an initial, efficient means of teaching general behavioral principles, followed by modeling and behavioral rehearsal to train parents in specific skills and techniques. They list cost effectiveness and the ability to employ less highly skilled staff as advantages of didactic teaching, especially when prepared leader's guides and audiovisual aids are utilized. Several investigators (Webster-Stratton, 1981; O'Dell et al., 1982) have also reported videotape modeling to be effective. Webster-Stratton (1982) found maintenance of most changes reported earlier at a one-year follow-up. O'Dell (1974) has pointed out that although these techniques are costly, they produce rapid changes and reduce communication problems. Numerous intervention procedures for various problems have, of course, appeared in the literature. Parental attitudes toward these procedures must be taken into consideration, in addition to their efficiency (Frentz & Kelley, 1986).

Parent Cooperation

Investigators have reported some difficulties with parent cooperation in attendance and in carrying out procedures, and have addressed some of these difficulties. Patterson and colleagues (1967) subtracted from clinic fees for documented parental use of positive reinforcement, while Mira (1970) made admittance to sessions contingent on parents collecting data. Eyeberg and Johnson (1974) made return of initial deposits contingent on completion of assignments, and Muir and Milan (1982) reported that they made lottery tickets contingent on child progress.

Cooperation, for many reasons, may vary inversely with the number and degree of problems within a family. Griest and co-workers (1982) state, not surprisingly, that their findings suggest that a positive outcome of parent training is adversely affected by parental personal, marital, and extramarital adjustment. Wahler (1980) has provided considerable insight into the difficulties that isolated, or "insular," parents might have in successfully participating in parent training attempts and has made suggestions for assisting them. Self-efficacy has been described as a potent concept to aid in understanding and modifying a person's degree of involvement in difficult or feared activities (Bandura, 1977). In light of this, Groden has suggested the utilization of parents' perceived self-efficacy, for both predicting parent involvement in working with their children and for enhancing such involvement. He has developed and is field testing a Parenting Self-Efficacy Scale for these purposes (Groden & Barrera, 1985). The successful application of parent training technology with especially problematic families and the effects of such variables as self-efficacy, stress and social support will probably soon be a primary focus in the parent training literature. Professionals must also keep in mind, of course, that a perceived lack of cooperation may reflect an ineffective approach on their part (Donnellan, 1984).

Autism

Parent training has played a particularly significant role in the field of autism. Parents of these children, who often show severe emotional, interpersonal, and learning problems, have perhaps benefited most from programs that help them to understand and deal with their highly perplexing children better. But this has not always been the case. As a result of the writings of such professionals as Kanner (1943), Ferster (1961), and Bettelheim (1967), parents were viewed as having played a causal role in the development of autism in their children and were not entrusted with therapeutic responsibility. This view has gradually changed as a result of a lack of hard evidence to support it, as well as increased evidence of organic dysfunctioning in children with autism. Impetus was given to this theoretical switch by a report by Klebenoff (1959), who found that parents of children with organic brain damage did not differ from parents of severely disturbed children on personality factors. This was interpreted to indicate that whatever difficulties the latter did manifest could just as easily be a result of the day-to-day difficulties and frustrations that parents of these children must face.

Wolf and colleagues (1964) were among the first to demonstrate the effectiveness of behavior therapy techniques with severely behaviorally disturbed children and the added impact of parent involvement. These authors taught both ward personnel and the parents of a 3½ year-old boy with autism how to deal with the child's severe behavioral problems while he was still institutionalized and then during a transition process to his own home. Problems that were reduced or eliminated included severe self-injury, refusal to sleep, and lengthy temper tantrums, as well as throwing his glasses, which he needed in order to see adequately. Six months after his return home, his mother reported no problems in these areas and that he was a "new source of joy" to his family. This pioneering report was followed by other successful efforts to teach parents of children with autism behavioral techniques they could apply in their own homes. Among these were reports by Wetzel and co-workers (1966) on temper tantrums; by Nordquist and Wahler (1973) on ritualism, crying and whining and compliance problems; by Johnson and co-workers (1978), also on compliance difficulties; and by Moore and Bailey (1973) and Wildman and Simon (1978) on increasing social interaction. Also, in a recent report Groden and colleagues (1983) described the successful application of behavioral parent training in an early intervention program for infants and very young children with autism.

Because of the pervasiveness of communication problems in these children, a number of workers have utilized parents as collaborators or primary change agents in this area, including Casey (1977), Goldstein and Lanyon (1971), and Wolf and colleagues (1964). Harris and Milch (1981) recently reviewed this area.

The critical importance of close parental involvement in

therapeutic endeavors was highlighted by Lovaas and colleagues (1973), who noted a deterioration in the behavior of the children with whom they had worked following treatment, when parents and caretakers had not received training, in contrast to the continued progress of children whose parents or caregivers had received training. They perceived the problem to be, at least partially, one of stimulus generalization, possibly based in turn on extreme overselectivity. The deterioration problem was largely avoided by having parents carry out therapy techniques in the posttreatment environment. The utilization of parents as treatment allies is now widely endorsed and practiced (O'Dell, 1974; Schopler, 1976; Schopler & Reichler, 1971). Added research support for this position has been provided by Schreibman & Britten (1984). These authors compared the benefits of direct treatment for children with autism without parent training with parent training only. They reported as much initial and more lasting improvement in the children whose parents had received training. Various materials have been developed to facilitate the process of parent training with and without trainers (Hemsley et al., 1978; Kozloff, 1974; Watson & Bassinger, 1974. A study by Kaufman et al. (1977) of Kozloff's procedures suggests that they may be effective. Similarly Hemsley et al. (1978) have reported positive findings with their program. Marcus and co-workers (1978) evaluated the parents as cotherapist model (TEACCH) and reported positive changes in parent overall teaching effectiveness, as well as in the children's compliance. A later review of five studies using this model (Schopler et al., 1982) further supported its effectiveness.

There is no doubt that providing parents of children with autism the necessary knowledge and encouragement to further their children's developmental potential has been an important step toward both maintaining family equilibrium and improving the likelihood that the children will lead productive and dignified lives. As Helm & Kozloff (1986) point out, however much additional work needs to be done to clarify the relative importance of different treatment variables and in general to improve research in this area. The following section will describe a parent training model designed to facilitate the parents' competence in developing their children's potential.

A MODEL FOR MAXIMIZING FAMILY COMPETENCE

Goals of the Model

The model has three main goals:

1. To teach parents techniques designed to help them function more effectively as parents and teachers. (Throughout this section, the word "parents" should be understood to include additional family members who could also profit from activities intended for parents.)
2. To provide support to families in meeting the challenges of having a behaviorally disturbed child.
3. To provide parents with information that will help them in advocating for their child on state and national levels.

Elements of the Model

In accordance with the model, these goals are accomplished through such activities as pre-entry meetings with parents to discuss center and family roles to facilitate positive attitudes and expectancies; post entry informing interviews to convey to parents the center's findings regarding their child's diagnosis, assets and particular problems and the center's feelings regarding causative factors, remedial approaches and prognosis; parent training workshops; parent participation in day programs; home and community based training programs; individual, family, and group therapy and counseling; group education meetings; respite services and sibling programs; and availability and circulation of written instructional materials on topics ranging from advocacy to home-based behavioral procedures through a parent/family library.

As is so wisely urged by Cutler and Kosloff (1987) and Donnellan and Mirenda (1984), parents of the children are regarded as partners with the staff and invited to share their unique experiences and knowlege to help their children overcome their disabilities and to live as independently and productively as possible in their environment. The staff members share their knowledge and skills with them throughout the child's enrollment. As parents and other family members are provided this responsibility and respect, a productive relationship develops that is especially advantageous for the children.

INTRODUCTORY WORKSHOPS

Workshops should begin shortly after children are admitted to a program, and held weekly for four weeks. These sessions are best held in the evening when parents are more likely to be available and ideally should last for approximately 1½ hours. They are designed to introduce the parents and other appropriate family members to those basic principles and procedures of behavior therapy that will help them to understand some of the reasons for their children's behaviors, as well as techniques for altering them. They are also geared toward providing parents with the necessary background to benefit from staff home visits, which begin after the final workshop meeting.

Group membership can be initially, but not solely, determined on the basis of when a child enters the program. Those parents whose children begin the program within a given time interval are often grouped together. Groups are generally limited to three to five sets of parents as a larger number does not allow for each parent to participate sufficiently. Conversely, if the group is initially too small, absences may render the number too few for fruitful group discussion. It is important to have parents of somewhat similar intellectual levels, as the group can be unnecessarily hampered by one who has difficulty in understanding the content, and may be intimidated and suffer loss in self-esteem by a parent who is excessively knowledgeable or talkative. Also, it is often wiser not to include parents who appear to be very angry or excessively discouraged as they can impair the motivation of other group members. Individual sessions, at least initially, are preferable for these parents.

Every effort should be made to ensure the presence of group members from the first meeting on. Parents of disturbed children, especially older and more disruptive children, sometimes feel that they have already devoted sufficient time to the children and owe it to themselves and their families to transfer those responsibilities to others. An attempt can be made to assure attendance by preadmission contacts with the parents during which the importance of parent participation is stressed, by rediscussion of this as necessary, by telephone contacts prior to meetings, and by making the meetings as rewarding as possible through such activities as informal pre- and postmeeting conversation, refreshments, and reinforcement of verbal participation.

Content. The following topics should be covered in the workshops:

1. General introduction to, and background of, behavior therapy.
2. Influences of specific antecedents and consequences (e.g., frustration, inconsistency, positive reinforcement, extinction, punishment) upon behavior.

3. Behavioral analysis.

4. Steps in program implementation; that is, pinpointing, measurement, behavioral analysis, intervention, and measurement.

5. Self-management procedures for parents and other appropriate family members. This includes some discussion of Schacter and Singer's (1962) findings on factors influencing how one interprets events, and in turn the influence of interpretations of events on one's emotions and behaviors. Self-control and relaxation procedures are also introduced.

Principles and techniques are taught primarily through discussion, live and videotape modeling, and role playing with feedback. Didactic teaching should be kept to a minimum as parents appear to respond least favorably to this format. Modeling and role playing are heavily relied upon in light of the studies indicating their importance.

The first part of an initial meeting is quite informal, and is devoted to helping families become acquainted and comfortable with one another as well as with center staff. They introduce themselves in turn, and tell the group something about themselves and their problems. Thus the parents soon recognize the similarity of their problems and frustrations, a process that appears to be therapeutic in itself, and also helps develop cohesiveness. During this phase group members often interrupt a speaker to agree that much of what is being described applies also to their children, and to offer suggestions that have proved useful. Many minor problems are often alleviated in this fashion, and the parents experience a sense of relief and a feeling of competence by sharing experiences, frustrations, and solutions.

Following this, a rationale for parent involvement should be presented that include Lovaas and colleagues' (1973) data on the outcome of the interventions with and without follow-up and Koegel and coworkers' (1982) findings of the differential effects of parent-only and clinic-only interventions mentioned earlier. Special emphasis should be played on an additional finding reported by the later authors that parent-training-only parents had considerably more leisure time following training than did child-training-only parents. It has also proved helpful at this point to have a parent whose child has entered the program earlier and who has successfully used the techniques to be discussed attend this first meeting and share these successes with the group. The formal sessions should end at the specified time. If the group continues beyond that time, some parents are hesitant to leave even though they may wish to do so. Parents are, of course, welcome to continue informal discussions after the sessions. Data should be obtained on how well workshop objectives are accomplished through such methods as written pre- post-assessments of the parents' knowledge of behavioral principles, as well as performance pre- post-assessments of the parents' ability to utilize the behavioral interventions taught. Parent attitudes toward workshop components should also be assessed.

HOME/COMMUNITY PROGRAMS

Once exposed to the basic principles and techniques of behavior management, parents are ready to contribute maximally to the family/staff team in alleviating specific problems concerning their child. Home visits serve the purposes of extending the children's programs to their homes and communities and of obtaining any information that might be useful in the children's day programs. The parents are generally appreciative of these visits, and see this outreach as a sign of personal concern for them and the family. Home visits should be carried out, as far as possible, by the same staff persons who work with the children daily. In contrast to staff utilized in many other models, such staff members are already familiar with the children's programs, and, in most cases, well acquainted with their parents. Notebooks serve to familiarize each with the other, as well as convey important information on the child's behavior in both home and class situations. Instruction to further enhance parents' skills in behavior therapy is an integral part of these home visits. The teaching is competency based and is accomplished through modeling, role playing, and verbal and written (Groden & Cautela, 1981) materials. The staff receives special instruction in this aspect of the work, including relationship-enhancing and behavioral analysis and intervention skills, before beginning home visits, and is supervised throughout.

The treatment model is a triadic one that consists of supervisor, home visitor, and family, as described by Tharp and Wetzel (1969). In addition to contacts between family members and the home visitor, supervisors also meet with the family, when necessary, either at the center or in the home. Care should be taken to ensure that parents are aware that their home visitors are members of a team with considerable combined experience and a commitment to helping them with any problems, small or large. Supervision is carried out through both individual and group meetings. It was originally planned in the model for each family to be visited twice a month on the average. Experience has shown, however, that some families require more frequent visits while others need or want less. Parents often request assistance in reducing a child's problematic behaviors at home and in the community, especially when the child is relatively new to the center. Also we find that we must help new parents understand that it is wiser to apply newly learned approaches to small problems before attempting their use with major ones. As in the day program, positive procedures are always preferred and attempts are always made to teach or increase alternative adaptive behaviors when decreasing maladaptive ones. Whenever feasible, parents are first taught and then carry out interventions in the day program before doing so at home. Teaching typically involves verbal instruction, modeling, rehearsal, and implementation feedback. Home visitors keep a notebook for the family, which is organized to provide materials utilized on the home visits, such as program planning, data, note taking, and report forms, in the order in which they will be needed. Parents are given, and encouraged to use, a similar notebook to help provide structure to staff–family meetings and to help them organize their material and program-related activities.

When a home visit is arranged for a particular family, the visitor fills out a card indicating the date and time of visit. This card is then placed on a large, wall-mounted monthly calendar over the date on which the visit is to be made. Within three days following the visit, the visitor should complete a brief questionnaire concerning the nature and outcome of the meeting, to be given to the supervisor. The card on the calendar is checked off as a visit completed and given to the coordinator. If home visit cards remain on the calendar more than three days following a visit, the staff member responsible receives a reminder from the coordinator.

To help ensure that the assistance provided to families is sufficient and appropriate, twice a year the supervisor and the home visitor working with a particular family indicate their judgment of the type and intensity (rated from a high of 3 to a low of 1) of assistance needed. At the same time, the family is sent a questionnaire on which they are asked to indicate the extent to which their child has progressed in the areas in which they have been receiving assistance and whether any new concerns have arisen with which they would like assistance. They are also asked if they would like more or less help than they are receiving, or are satisfied with the current level of assistance. These are also given ratings of 3 to 1. Additional space is left on the questionnaire for elaboration of responses. When this questionnaire is returned, it can be analyzed along with the staff judgments. Both sources of information can then be utilized in planning future visits. These two types of ratings should be placed opposite the family's name on a wall chart, an example of which is shown in Figure 7-1. On the same row and to the right, the dates of future visits can be plotted. In this way a quick look at the wall

UNIT   Senior   YEAR   1985-86

NAME	Need Rating		Contact						
	Parent 9/85	Staff 9/85	9/1	9/8	9/15	9/22	9/29	10/6	10/13
Warren	2	2							
White	3	2							
Allen	1	1							
Roberts	1	2							
Murray	3	3							
Dolan	1	1							

Figure 7-1
Parent/Family Program
Contact Overview Sheet

chart will indicate the match between estimated need and actual dates of visits to center families.

SIBLING PROGRAM

Siblings of handicapped children have special difficulties, as has been commented upon by other writers in the field. Unlike their parents, however, they lack the experience and knowledge that would help them to deal with the issue. Until recently little was written about their special problems, and they had little help. Fortunately this situation has been changing (Colletti & Harris, 1977). In light of the needs of siblings in the areas of understanding the problems of their handicapped brother or sister and in dealing with the resulting intra- and extrafamilial situations, a sibling program is offered as a part of the model. Siblings attend group meeetings at which these problems are discussed and information and coping strategies are provided, and also get together at social events, which their families attend. They visit the classroom periodically, as well, to help carry out programs with both nonrelated children and their siblings. In this way they improve their ability, and thus their confidence in their efforts, to help with their siblings at home.

DAY PROGRAM PARTICIPATION

One of the most obvious and cost-efficient ways of familiarizing parents with their children's program is for them to visit their child's day program periodically to observe and participate in the various therapeutic and teaching activities. Such observation and participation are especially advantageous in that they provide the parents with the opportunity to see how their children act in structured settings outside of the home and to attempt to apply procedures within that setting. Parents are strongly encouraged to attend as their schedules permit; mothers have been found to do so more than fathers. In some instances, when it has been particularly inconvenient for parents to visit, videotapes of programs have been taken to their homes. Some parents are able to visit the day program weekly, sometimes meeting in groups to discuss the day's activities or other matters, while others visit on an irregular basis.

PARENT/FAMILY GROUPS

Participation in the initial four workshop meetings is expected of all parents. In addition to the support provided by the group and the group leader, parents are motivated by the progress the other members report with their children and they learn from the group's experiences and combined knowledge. Other group meetings, or series of meetings, for such purposes as improving communication skills or increasing supportive interactions between spouses, are held throughout the year and are attended by those parents who desire to do so.

Other parent and family activities, such as picnics and holiday parties, should be held periodically. These functions encourage parents to participate in pleasurable activities and often involve siblings and friends.

INDIVIDUAL AND FAMILY COUNSELING

Counseling is offered as needed. Self-control procedures mentioned or taught during the workshops, as well as other approaches, are often utilized more extensively during counseling sessions. When there are problems that involve the whole family, an attempt should be made to meet with the family as a unit. This is seen to be a much more productive way of helping families solve problems than individual meetings, and the families often seem to prefer this approach. When marital difficulties surface as a part of the overall problem, it is often better also to meet with the married partners in the absence of other family members. Family members can be seen individually as needed. Sometimes it is necessary to refer families to agencies in their communities for counseling, if that is more convenient for them, or if the presenting problems are peripheral to their children.

Parent counseling frequently involves encouraging and assisting parents to utilize the techniques taught to them in the initial workshops and on home visits. Some parents, for example, express attitudes toward their children, which, they say, make it very difficult for them to shape and reinforce targeted behavior. These attitudes, in turn, sometimes result from their interpretations of the reasons for their children's bothersome behaviors. For instance, they may feel their child purposefully upsets them and takes pleasure in doing so. These parents then develop negative feelings toward their children. To enable such parents to be more effective with their children, they must be helped to reduce or eliminate these negative feelings. Procedures used to accomplish this objective, as well as to help resolve other difficulties interfering with facilitative parent–child relationships, include cognitive restructuring, relaxation, and imagery techniques, (the last was dealt with in detail in Chapter 3). With regard to cognitive restructuring, parents may be shown that several interpretations of the reason for a child's behavior are possible, one apparently as valid as another. It can also be pointed out that while one interpretation might result in their feeling negatively toward their child, another might result in a positive feeling. Therefore, it makes sense to choose an interpretation that does not needlessly upset the parents, and that allows them to react constructively. For example, the child may be acting in a bothersome manner not purposefully to upset them, but because that is the only way the child has learned to react to a particular situation. If he knew a more appropriate way to react, the child would react in that way.

Relaxation is used with the rationale that there will always be events in our lives with the potential to upset us, and that this skill will help us confront such events and remain calm. Imagery techniques such as covert conditioning (Cautela & Kearney, 1986) are used frequently and are very helpful. Covert reinforcement, one of the covert conditioning techniques, can be used as an additional procedure—for example, with the parent who feels negatively toward a child when a particular behavior occurs and who states that this negative feeling makes appropriate responding difficult. With this procedure the parent imagines the child engaging in the behavior, then imagines himself reacting to that behavior calmly and appropriately, and finally imagines being reinforced. This technique (which also has a desensitizing effect), if carried out a number of times in imagery, will help the parent to respond calmly and appropriately. Other covert conditioning procedures include covert modeling, covert negative reinforcement, and covert extinction. These are described by Cautela and Kearney. Further discussion of helpful procedures in working with families of developmentally disabled children can be found in such sources as Harris (1983) and Tymchuk (1979).

Parents sometimes can be just as helpful to other parents as staff members, and even more so for some purposes. For example, parents of newly admitted children find it very reassuring to discuss the center with a parent of a child who has been attending the center, as well as with staff. Sometimes parents can be asked to contact parents who are considering enrolling their child in the center, if it is thought that this would help them in their decision making. Parents may feel that other parents are unbiased and can view situations from their own perspective. A parent can also be called upon to assist another parent who is having difficulties with his child with problems similar to those the first parent has experienced and overcome. This aspect has shown much promise and will be expanded in the future.

RESPITE SERVICES

All parents need respite from their parental duties. This applies especially to parents of severely behaviorally disturbed children. Without time for themselves, free from the minute-to-minute duties that go along with rearing their children, many parents would find coping extremely difficult, if not impossible. For this reason a respite program is also offered to parents, which provides care for their child for periods of several hours to two weeks. Children are cared for both in and out of their homes, depending on parental desires and requirements. Whenever possible, staff members who provide such respite are those who work with the children during the day. Thus special familiarization activities are unnecessary and consistency of care is assured.

PARENT LIBRARY

Finally, a very important part of the parent–family program model is the parent–family library, which should be supplied with books, journals, pamphlets, and tapes concerning all areas felt to be of use and interest to family members. Topics covered by the literature should include behavior management, developmental and educational facilitation, sexual development, developmental disabilities, and information such as can be found in Cutler's helpful book (1981) describing how parents cut through bureaucracy to effectively advocate for their children. Parents assist in selecting material for the library, as well as in running it. It is recommended that material be kept on open shelves to encourage browsing and that the library be open during the day and in the evening when parent meetings and other evening functions are taking place.

CONCLUSIONS

The preceding sections have outlined a model for the provision of services to families of children with autism and other behavioral disorders. The model can be characterized by a sensitivity to the many needs of these families, and the provision of a spectrum of services to meet them. It is an outgrowth of, reflects and, it is hoped, contributes to current empirical findings in the literature; it also contains an evaluation component to help ensure that it accomplishes its goals while increasing its effectiveness.

Methods to evaluate the effectiveness of initial workshops were discussed earlier. The model also contains procedures for additional parent program evaluation procedures, including parent statements of the extent of child change in designated areas, extent of actual change based on parent-collected data, and parents' overall satisfaction with the amount and quality of services supplied.

Although it is intended that the parent–family program be sufficiently structured to be sensitive to and respond to family needs, it also must be fluid enough to change over time as new needs are discovered or as better ways are found to meet existing needs. Families will always play a role in such changes.

REFERENCES

Ayllon, T. & Michael, J. (1959). The psychiatric nurse as a behavioral engineer. *Journal of the Experimental Analysis of Behavior*, 323–334.

Baker, B. L. & McCurry, M. C. (1984). School-based parent training: An alternative for parents predicted to demonstrate low teaching proficiency following group training. *Education and Training of the Mentally Retarded*, 19(4), 261–267.

Baker, B. L., Brightman, A. J., Heifetz, L. J. & Murphy, D. M. (1976). *Behavior problems*. Champaign, Ill.: Research Press.

Bandura, A. (1977). Self-efficacy: Toward a unifying theory of behavioral change. *Psychological Review*, 84, 191–215.

Bean, A. W. & Roberts, M. W. (1981). The effect of time-out release contingencies on changes in child noncompliance. *Journal of Abnormal Child Psychology*, 9, 95–105.

Bettleheim, B. (1967). *The empty fortress—Infantile autism and the birth of the self.* New York: Free Press.

Boardman, W. R. (1962). A brief behavior disorder. *Journal of Consulting Psychology*, 26, 293–297.

Breiner, J. & Beck, S. (1984). Parents as change agents in the management of their developmentally delayed children's noncompliant behaviors: A critical review. *Applied Research in Mental Retardation*, 5, 259–278.

Casey, L. (1977). Development of communicative behavior in autistic children: A parent program using signed speech. *Devereux Forum*, 12(1), 1–15.

Cautela, J. R. & Kearney, A. J. (1986). (The covert conditioning handbook.) New York: Springer Press.

Christensen, A., Johnson, S. M., Phillips, S. & Glasgow, R. E. (1980). Cost effectiveness in behavioral family theraphy. *Behavior Therapy*, 11, 208–226.

Cohen, D. J. & Donnellan, A. M. (Eds.) (1987). *Handbook of autism and disorders of atypical development*. New York: Wiley Press.

Colletti, G. & Harris, S. L. (1977). Behavior modification in the home: Siblings as behavior modifiers, parents as observers. *Journal of Abnormal Child Psychology*, 5(1), 21–30.

Cutler, B. C. (1981). *Unraveling the special education maze*. Chicago: Research Press.

Cutler, B.C. & Kozloff, M. A. (1987). Living with autism: Effects on families and family needs. In D. J. Cohen, and A. M. Donnellan, (Eds.) *Handbook of autism and disorders of atypical development*. New York: Wiley Press.

DeMyer, M. K. (1979). *Parents and children in autism*. New York: Wiley & Sons.

Donnellan, A. M. (1984). The criterion of the least dangerous assumption. *Behavioral Disorders*, 9(2), 141–150.

Donnellan, A. M. & Mirenda, P. L. (1984). Issues related to professional involvement with families of individuals with autism and other severe handicaps. *TASH Journal*, 9, 16–25.

Dubey, D. R., O'Leary, S. G. & Kaufman, K. F. (1983). Training parents of hyperactive children in child management: A comparative outcome study. *Journal of Child Psychology*, 11(2), 229–246.

Eyeberg, S. M. & Johnson, S. M. (1974). Multiple assessment of behavior modification with families: Effects of contingency contracting and order of treated problems. *Journal of Consulting and Clinical Psychology*, 42, 594–606.

Ferster, C. B. (1961). Positive reinforcement and behavioral deficits of autistic children. *Child Development*, 32, 437–456.

Flanagan, S., Adams, H. E. & Forehand, R. (1979). A comparison of four instructional techniques for teaching parents to use time-out. *Behavior Therapy*, 10, 94–102.

Forehand, R. (1977). Child non-compliance to parent commands. Behavioral analysis and treatment. In M. Hersen, R. M. Eisler, and P. M. Miller (Eds.), *Progress in behavior modification* (Vol. 5). New York: Academic Press.

Frentz, C. & Kelley, M. L. (1986). Parents' acceptance of reductive treatment methods: The influence of problem severity and perception of child behavior. *Behavior Therapy*, 17(1), 75–81.

Goldstein, S. B. & Lanyon, R. I. (1971). Parent-clinicians in the language training of an autistic child. *Journal of Speech and Hearing Disorders*, 36(4), 552–560.

Gordon, T. (1970). *Parent effectiveness training*. New York: Peter H. Wyden.

Griest, D. L., Douglas, L. & Forehand, R. (1982). Effects of parent enhancement therapy on the treatment outcome and generalization of a parent training program. *Behavior Research and Therapy*, 20, 429–436.

Groden, G. & Barrera, R. D. (1985). Parent training: Getting parents more involved. Problems and potential solutions. Unpublished paper presented at Association for Behavior Analysis Conference, Columbus, Ohio, May, 1985.

Groden, G. & Cautela, J. R. (1981). Behavior therapy: A survey of Procedures for counselors. *The Personnel and Guidance Journal*, 175–180.

Groden, G., Domingue, D., Chesnick, M., Groden, J. & Baron, G. (1983). Early intervention with autistic children: A case presentation with pre-program, program and follow-up data. *Psychological Reports*, 53, 715–722.

Hansen, D. J., Tisdelle, D. A. & O'Dell, S. L. (1984). Teaching parents time out with media materials: The importance of observation and feedback. *Journal of Child and Adolescent Psychology*, 1(1), 20–25.

Harris, S. L. (1983). *Families of the developmentally disabled: A guide to behavioral intervention*. New York: Pergamon Press.

Harris, S. L. & Milch, R. E. (1981). Training parents as behavior therapists for their autistic children. *Clinical Psychology Review*, 1, 49–63.

Harris, S. L., Wolchik, S. A. & Milch, R. E. (1982). Changing the speech of autistic children and their parents. *Child and Family Behavior Therapy*, 4, 151–173.

Helm, D. T. & Kozloff, M. A. (1986). Research on parent training: Shortcomings and remedies. *Journal of Autism and Developmental Disorders*, 16(1), 1–22.

Hemsley, R., Howlin, P., Berger, M., Hersou, L., Holbrook, D., Rutter, M. & Yule, W. (1978). Treating autistic children in a family context. In M. Rutter and E. Schopler, (Eds.), *Autism: A Reappraisal of concepts and treatment*. New York: Plenum Press.

Hewett, F. (1965). Teaching speech to an autistic child through operant conditioning. *American Journal of Orthopsychiatry*, 34, 927–936.

Hudson, A. M. (1982). Training parents of developmentally handicapped children: A component analysis. *Behavior Therapy*, 13, 325–333.

Johnson, S. A. & Brown, R. A. (1969). Producing behavior change in parents of disturbed children. *Journal of Child Psychology and Psychiatry*, 10, 107–121.

Johnson, M. B., Whitman, T. I. & Barloon-Noble, R. (1978). A home-based program for a preschool behaviorally disturbed child with parents as therapists. *Journal of Behavior Therapy and Experimental Psychiatry*, 9(1), 65–70.

Kanner, L. (1943). Autistic disturbances of affective contact. *Nervous Child*, 2, 217–250.

Kaufman, K. F., Tyson-Stoehr, R. & Bakalor, J. (1979). *Developing family training programs for parents of autistic adolescents*. Paper presented at the meeting of the American Psychological Association, New York, N.Y.

Kaufman, K. F., Villani, T. V., Takalor, J., Price, G. H., Prinz, R. J., Paradise, B. & Tyson, R. (1977). *Systematic evaluation of comprehensive training for parents of autistic children.* Presented at American Psychological Association Annual Convention, New York, N.Y.

Klebanoff, L. (1959). Parental attitudes of mothers of schizophrenic, brain injured and retarded and normal children. *American Journal of Orthopsychiatry, 29*(3), 445–454.

Koegel, R. L., Shreibman, L., Britten, K., Burke, J. & O'Niell, R. (1982). A comparison of parent training to direct child treatment. In R. Koegel, A. Rincover, and A. Egel (Eds.), *Educating and understanding autistic children.* San Diego, Calif.: College Hill Press.

Koegel, R. L., Glahn, R. L. & Nieminen, G. S. (1978). Generalization of parent training results. *Journal of Applied Behavior Analysis, 11,* 95–109.

Kovitz, K. E. (1976). Comparing group and individual methods for training parents in child management techniques. In E. J. Mash, L. C. Handy, and L. A. Hamerlynch (Eds.), *Behavior modification approaches to parenting.* New York: Brunner/Mazel.

Kozloff, M. A. (1974). *Educating children with learning and behavior problems.* New York: Wiley.

Kozloff, M. A. (1973). *Reaching the autistic child: A parent training program.* Champaign, Ill.: Research Press.

Lindsley, O. R. (1966). Teaching parents to modify their children's behavior. In E. Arnold (Ed.), *Helping parents help their children.* New York, Bruner/Mazel.

Lovaas, I. (1977). *The autistic child—language development through behavior modification.* New York: Irvington.

Lovaas, O. I., Koegel, R., Simmons, J. Q. & Long, J. S. (1973). Some generalization and follow-up measures on autistic children in behavior therapy. *Journal of Applied Behavior Analysis, 6,* 131–166.

MacNamara, M. (1963). Helping children through their mother. *Journal of Psychology and Psychiatry, 4,* 29–46.

Marcus, L. M., Lansing, M., Andrews, M. & Schopler, C. B. (1978). Improvement of teaching effectiveness in parents of autistic children. *Journal of the American Academy of Child Psychiatry, 17*(4), 625–639.

Mash, E. J., Handy, L. C. & Hamerlynck, L. A. (Eds.) (1976). *Behavior modification approaches to parenting.* New York: Brunner/Mazel.

McMahon, R. J. & Forehand, R. (1980). Self-help behavior therapies in parent training. In B. B. Lahey and A. E. Kazdin (Eds.), *Advances in clinical child psychology* (Vol. 3). New York: Plenum.

McMahon, R J., Forehand, R. & Griest, D. L. (1981). Effects of knowledge of social learning principles on enhancing treatment outcome and generalization in parent training program. *Journal of Consulting and Clinical Psychology, 49,* 526–532.

Miller, W. H. (1975). *Systematic parent training: Procedures, cases and issues.* Champaign, Ill.: Research Press.

Mira, M. (1970). Results of a behavior modification training program for parents and teachers. *Behavior Research and Therapy, 8,* 309–311.

Moore, B. L. & Bailey, J. S. (1973). Social punishment in the modification of a preschool child's "autistic-like" behavior with a mother as a therapist. *Journal of Applied Behavior Analysis, 6,* 497–507.

Muir, K. A. & Milan, M. A. (1982). Parent reinforcement for child achievement: The use of a lottery to maximize parent training effects. *Journal of Applied Behavior Analysis, 15*, 455–460.

Nordquist, V. M. & Wahler, R. G. (1973). Naturalistic treatment of an autistic child. *Journal of Applied Behavior Analysis,* 6(1), 79–87.

O'Dell, S. L. (1974). Training parents in behavior modification: A review, *Psychological Bulletin, 81*, 418–433.

O'Dell, S. L., Flynn, J. M. & Benlolo, L. T. (1977). A comparison of parent training techniques in child behavior modification. *Journal of Behavior Therapy and Experimental Psychiatry, 8*, 261–268.

O'Dell, S. L., Mahoney, N. D., Horton, W. G. & Turner, P. E. (1979). Media-assisted parent-training: Alternative models. *Behavior Therapy, 10*, 103–110.

O'Dell, S. L., O'Quinn, J., Alford, B. A., O'Briant, A. L., Brodlyn, A. S. & Riebenhain, J. E. (1982). Predicting the acquisition of parenting skills via four training methods. *Behavior Therapy, 13*, 194–208.

Patterson, G. R. (1965). A learning theory approach to the treatment of the school phobic child. In L. P. Ullman and L. Krasner (Eds.), *Case studies in behavior modification.* New York: Holt, Rinehart Winston.

Patterson, G. R. (1971). *Families: Applications of social learning to family life.* Champaign, Ill.: Research Press.

Patterson, G. R. (1976). *Living with children: New methods for parents and teachers.* Champaign, Ill.: Research Press.

Patterson, G. R., McNeal, S., Hawkins, N. & Phelps, R. (1967). Reprogramming the social environment. *Journal of Child Psychology and Psychiatry, 8*, 181–195.

Patterson, G. R., Neid, J. B., Jones, R. R. & Conger, R. E. (1975). *A social learning approach to family intervention. Volume 1: Families with aggressive children.* Eugene, Ore.: Castalia.

Peed, S., Roberts, M. & Forehand, R. (1977). Evaluation of the effectiveness of a standardized parent training program in altering the interaction of mothers and their non-compliant children. *Behavior Modification, 1*, 323–350.

Pevsner, R. (1982). Group parent training versus individual family therapy: An outcome study. *Journal of Behavior Therapy and Experimental Psychiatry, 13*, 119–122.

Rettig, E. B. (1973). *ABC's for parents—An educational workshop in behavior modification.* Champaign, Ill.: Research Press.

Risley, T. & Wolf, M. (1968). Experimental manipulation of autistic behaviors and generalization into the home. In R. Ulrich, T. Stachnik, and J. Mabry (Eds.), *Control of human behavior.* Glenview, Ill.: Scott, Foresman.

Roberts, M. W., Hatzenbuehler, L. C. & Bean, A. (1981). The effects of differential attention and timeout on child non-compliance. *Behavior Therapy, 12*, 93–99.

Rose, S. D. (1974). Training parents in groups as behavior modifiers of their mentally retarded children. *Journal of Behavior Therapy and Experimental Psychiatry, 5*, 135–140.

Sanders, M. R. (1982). The generalization of parent responding to community settings: The effects of instructions, plus feedback, and self-management training, *Behavioral Psychotherapy, 10*, 273–287.

Sanders, M. R. & Christensen, A. P. (1985). A comparison of the effects of child

management and planned activities training in five parenting environments. *Journal of Abnormal Child Psychology, 13*(1), 101–118.
Schachter, S. & Singer, J. E. (1962). Cognitive, social and physiological determinants of emotional state. *Psychological Review,* 69, 379–399.
Schopler, E. (1976). Toward reducing behavior problems in autistic children. *Journal of Autism and Childhood Schizophrenia,* 6(1), 1–13.
Schopler, E. & Mesibov, G. (1984). *The effects of Autism on the Family.* New York: Plenum Press.
Schopler, E., Mesibov, G. & Baker, A. (1982). Evaluation of treatment for autistic children and their parents. *Journal of the American Academy of Child Psychiatry,* 21, 226–267.
Schopler, E. & Reichler, R. J. (1971). Parents as co-therapists in the treatment of psychotic children. *Journal of Autism and childhood Schizophrenia,* 1(1), 87–102.
Schreibman, L. & Britten, K. R. (1984). Training parents as therapists for autistic children: Rationale, techniques and results. In W. P. Christian, G. T. Hannah, and T. J. Glahn, (Eds.) *Programming effective human services.* New York: Plenum Press.
Sulzer-Azaroff, B. & Pollack, M. J. (1982). The modification of child behavior problems in the home. In A. S. Bellack, M. Hersen and A. E. Kazdin (Eds.), *International handbook of behavior modification and therapy.* New York: Plenum Press.
Tahmisian, J. & McReynolds, W. (1971). Use of parents as behavioral engineers in the treatment of a school-phobic girl. *Journal of Counseling Psychology,* 18, 225–228.
Tavormina, J. B. (1974). Basic models of parent counseling: A critical review. *Psychological Bulletin,* 81, 827–835.
Tharp, R. & Wetzel, R. (1969). *Behavior modification in the natural environment.* New York, Academic Press.
Tymchuk, A. (1979). *Parent and family therapy.* New York: S. P. Medical and Scientific Books.
Wahler, R. G. (1980). The insular mother: Her problems in parent-child treatment. *Journal of Applied Behavior Analysis,* 13, 207–219.
Wahler, R. G., Winkel, G. H., Peterson, R. F. & Morrison, D. C. (1965). Mothers as behavior therapists for their own children. *Behavior Research and Therapy,* 3, 113–124.
Watson, L. S. & Bassinger, J. F. (1974). Parent training technology: A potential service delivery system. *Mental Retardation,* 12(5) 3–10.
Weathers, L. R. & Liberman, R. P. (1978). Modification of family behavior. *Child Behavior Therapy.* New York: Gardner Press.
Webster-Stratton, C. (1981). The long-term effects of a videotape modeling parent-training program: Comparison of immediate and 1-year follow-up results. *Behavior Therapy,* 13, 702–714.
Webster-Stratton, C. (1981). Videotape modeling: A method of education, *Journal of Clinical Child Psychology,* 10, 93–98.
Wetzel, R. J., Baker, J., Roney, M. & Martin, M. (1966). Outpatient treatment of autistic behavior. *Behavior Research and Therapy,* 4, 169–177.
Wildman, R. W. & Simon, S. J. (1978). An indirect method for increasing the rate of social interaction in an autistic child. *Journal of Clinical Psychology,* 34(1), 144–149.

Williams C. G. (1959). The elimination of tantrum behavior by extinction procedures. *Journal of Abnormal and Social Psychology, 59,* 269.

Wolf, M. M., Risley, T. R. & Mees, H. (1964). Application of operant conditioning procedures to the behavior problems of an autistic child. *Behavior Research and Therapy, 1,* 305–312.

Zeilberger, J., Sampen, S. E., & Sloane, H. N., Jr. (1968). Modification of a child's problem behaviors in the home with the mother as therapist. *Journal of Applied Behavior Analysis, 1,* 47–53.

CHAPTER

8

Teaching for Performance
A GUIDE FOR PREPARING CLINICIANS AND TEACHERS OF THE SEVERELY HANDICAPPED

Grace Baron, Ph.D.
Susan E. Stevenson, M.Ed.

Personnel Preparation: Current Status
Teaching for Performance Model: A
    Conceptual Base
The Field/Service Setting
The Trainee
The Program Philosophy

Personnel Instruction Program (PIP)
    Description
    Application
    Summary
References

PERSONNEL PREPARATION: CURRENT STATUS

THE CURRENT LEGISLATIVE MANDATES to provide education and treatment services to all handicapped individuals, coupled with the increased sophistication and militancy of parents and advocacy groups, have in recent years forced the relatively rapid creation of service systems for autistic and severely disturbed children and youth. These demands have merged productively with efforts of behaviorally oriented clinicians and educators to refocus their energies from laboratory-based investigations to interventions in applied settings. In recent years, instructors responsible for personnel preparation in clinical and educational fields have generated a variety of instructional conceptualizations, training sequences, and demonstration materials designed to pass on knowledge and skills to persons who work with children with autism and severe behavior disorders.

It remains a regrettable fact, however, that in many areas of our country too few people are graduating from teacher- and clinician-preparation programs with the necessary skills or experience for effectively carrying out behavioral treatment and instruction. Though notable efforts are being made in universities and colleges to prepare and certify teachers and clinicians to work responsibly and effectively with severely disturbed children within a behavioral framework, preservice and inservice education remain the primary learning strategy and site for the majority of individuals who work, or will work, with persons with autism. Furthermore, in both academic and field settings, personnel preparation remains synonymous with classroom-based, didactic instruction and paper-and-pencil evaluations (Marshall & Marks, 1981). "School never really prepared me for this" is the all-too-common complaint of the new employee. As he becomes part of the "real world" of the field setting, the new employee correctly senses discontinuities between the classroom and the field. These include a shift from:

1. The relatively "passive," detached learning style of the classroom to the more "active," involved, hands-on requirement of the work site.

2. Classroom evaluation based on what one knows (e.g., written tests) to evaluation based on what one can do (e.g., effectively managing a behavior problem).

It is no wonder that so many employees respond to this situation with negative scanning of the field itself and of their own abilities.

TEACHING FOR PERFORMANCE MODEL: A CONCEPTUAL BASE

The model outlined in this chapter evolved from its authors' day-to-day experiences in developing clinician- and teacher-preparation programs in a range of field service settings. Whether this setting was a school for retarded children, a state hospital ward, a rehabilitative vocational center, or a treatment center for children with autism, the personnel-preparation task was always explicitly the same: *to provide a relatively naive group of individuals with the competencies to work effectively and happily with behaviorally disordered clients.* Our response to this task has been to develop a field-based personnel-preparation program that is guided by the principle of "teaching for performance." In order to equip a person best to work successfully with individuals with severe handicaps, it is recommended that the individual's training be designed with his intended performance goals in mind. Rather than primarily targeting broad competencies or abstract goals (e.g., sensitivity or awareness to the educational needs of persons with handicaps), it is best to teach first those specific tasks the individual will be expected to perform. Instead of giving instruction only in classrooms physically separate from the setting where performance will be expected and measured, an emphasis should be placed on instruction given in the clinician/teacher's functioning environment. Instead of assuming that there is a single skill constellation that will adequately prepare each clinician/teacher to work with individuals with severe handicaps, it is assumed that the unique features, needs, and expectations of each employee require an individualized approach to personnel preparation. There is no single, best approach to personnel preparation. A strategy is proposed here for designing and carrying out a training program to suit the needs of any learning or therapeutic environment.

The conceptual base of this model includes an assessment and appreciation of (1) salient features of the field setting itself and (2) the variable characteristics of employees in the field setting. Furthermore, this model has emerged from, and is congruent with, developmental, ecological, and behavioral perspectives in human service delivery. Though this program was developed in the context of a small, private, nonprofit treatment and education center, the authors anticipate that many of its aspects may be applicable to a range of service settings.

The Field/Service Setting

Though field settings often vary significantly in size, client/service-provider ratio, administrative structure, geographical location, and so on, there are some salient features common to most service settings. Such features, either implicitly or explicitly, shape an individual's role in a work environment, and therefore warrant a closer examination.

1. *The field/service setting is a dynamic, changing system.* In most treatment centers and classrooms, changes occur routinely, and sometimes unexpectedly, at various levels (e.g., classroom structure and setting, lines of supervision, interpersonal ties, program targets, intake and transition of clients, and perceptions and attitudes of funding agents and support groups). Teachers and therapists may be prepared by academic training for the change inherent in client behavior and learning, but rarely are treatment teachers prepared for the social and environmental changes they will experience, nor do they expect that such changes will require new skills for effective performance. Training needs to give the trainee an expectation of the changes that can occur, and personal and professional strategies to deal with a dynamic system.

2. *The field/service setting primarily emphasizes product, not preparation.* The service setting usually cannot give the trainer and trainee very much "release time" from their responsibilities with clients. Here training is done primarily on site (i.e., in the classroom, workshop, home, or community environments, and during times the clients are present and engaged in programming). As a result, while a training program should be structured and ideally should occur *before* actual service is required of the employee, it is often necessary that an employee learn by doing. Furthermore, in many service programs, trainees do NOT begin at the same time, nor do they have a homogeneous blend of education and abilities. In a service- and product-oriented setting, training efforts are often required to be flexible in schedule and implementation strategies.

3. *The field/service setting emphasizes both individual responsibility and team performance.* While a trainee can be prepared with principles and decision models, in real life he may not always have the luxuries of referring to the literature, calling in experts, or following the ideal decision model when making a clinical decision. A training program has to stress the importance of using substantiated methods and team corroboration, but also what to do when one does not have the guidance of literature or experience, when it is too impractical or impossible

to follow a prescribed sequence, and when a treatment team is not available.

4. *The field/service setting is a network of processes.* Each particular treatment or teaching setting is an individualized network of processes such as program administration, public relations, program development, team treatment, parent work, evaluation, and program implementation. Trainees have to know about, appreciate, effectively interrelate with, and even help develop many of the processes beyond their primary responsibility of treatment implementation. Staff members are valued not only in terms of how well they do their job, but also how they support others in doing their jobs. If one does not have this "social sense," the training should include efforts to develop an awareness of the effects of one's own behavior on other crucial elements of the service system and the social impact of one's actions or inactions on others.

The Trainee

Foxx (1980), in a recent attempt to identify the characteristics of an effective teacher, underscores the importance of a genuine attitude of caring, eternal optimism, a strong will, a sensitivity toward subtle behavior changes, a willingness to take risks, and so on. Though conspicuous by their absence in most competency-based curricula, such characteristics are often the features according to which teacher/clinicians are selected and evaluated. Personnel-preparation efforts might well benefit by a more detailed examination of such personal and social skills. Identifying a constellation of attributes of an effective worker can lead to operational definitions and procedures for measuring the existence and acquisition of these skills, and perhaps even procedures for teaching these more subtle aspects of effective performance. Furthermore, an assessment of teacher characteristics can help pinpoint (1) the contribution an individual can make to a treatment program and (2) the rewards anticipated by that individual in return (Castetter, 1976).

1. *The trainee works for a variety of personal and professional goals.* The treatment and educational system provides the opportunity for individuals to attain such goals as first-hand experience prior to formal educational training, experience that will assist in making career decisions, allows the application of learned theory and knowledge, and extends knowledge into new realms. Personal goals may involve the

family and economic security, recognition, and a social network. Any of these goals will influence one's attitude and approach toward personnel preparation.

2. *The trainee is motivated by a variety of features of the work setting.* These include wanting to help others, getting personal satisfaction from clients' growth, social enrichment among co-workers, professional enrichment through working with knowledgeable staff and supervisors, personal creativity, advancement in the employment hierarchy, and financial gain. Obviously there is seldom a single motivating factor that influences the performance of an individual, but rather a combination of many. Determining a staff member's primary motivation is central to planning and shaping a trainee's program of instruction and employment.

3. *Trainees differ in social stimulus value.* The various verbal and nonverbal messages a person communicates to clients and colleagues alike will have an effect on both performance and others in the environment. Service-agency personnel often place a high degree of importance on social skills (Zane et al., 1982). Recent social perception research (Schiff, 1980) identifies several clusters of nonverbal behaviors that influence the quality of social interaction. These include (a) kinesics (i.e., behaviors such as facial expression, eye contact, and gestures); (b) proxemics (i.e., the use of space and the organization of behavior within space); and (c) paralinquistics (i.e., nonverbal but vocal or speech-related behaviors such as intonation, rhythm, loudness, speed rate, articulation, and quality). The ability of individuals to utilize these phenomena can have an impact on establishing stimulus control with a client and setting up a successful learning situation. Similarly the ability to read and evaluate the verbal and nonverbal cues of clients and colleagues affects the appropriateness of the social response.

4. *Trainees respond to others in a variety of interaction styles.* For example, individuals vary in their general use of reinforcement, punishment, and extinction to affect the behavior of others. Some may employ a broad repertoire of reinforcement styles and easily adapt to working with a broad range of clients, while some work more effectively with one response style (e.g., social reinforcement), or with one type of client. Moreover, these variable interaction styles influence the type of learning opportunities the individual provides for the client. For example, some may be excellent at providing a large number of learning trials in a given period of time, and others may more readily extend the learning trial to new cues and reinforcers and make it relevant to the client.

5. *Trainees enter the service setting with variable skills.* Differences in the extent and nature of preservice education and experience result in an unevenness of staff preparation and abilities (Castetter, 1976). Moreover, staff members are typically grouped for training purposes by either (a) job title (i.e., a label such as unit supervisor, special-education teacher, treatment teacher) or (b) preservice training/degree (i.e., number of years and type of experience). Such groupings may facilitate instruction, but do not guarantee that individuals will gain the necessary knowledge to learn effectively. It would be more appropriate for training to focus on maximizing existing skills and preparing staff with skills necessary for effectively carrying out responsibilities within a particular position.

Current models guiding efforts at personnel preparation have not, at least explicitly, emphasized the full range of knowledge and skills required for effective performance in the field. In planning an effective personnel-preparation program, one should examine the real-life setting in which the teacher/clinician will work, pinpoint and analyze the broad range of skills necessary for effective performance in that setting, and teach those skills.

The Program Philosophy

The same developmental, ecological, and behavioral principles that generate and direct treatment and teaching efforts can also provide a guide to the implementation of a personnel preparation program.

1. *The developmental perspective is reflected in both the timing and the sequence of personnel preparation.* The training program can be conceptualized as a series of critical periods during which particular learning experiences must take place. A trainee, for example, should experience early in the training program the significant impact of effectively shaping a response into a client's repertoire if one is ever to believe that the contingencies one delivers will make a difference. Also, a training program should present material at the appropriate time and place, and in an appropriate sequence. No matter how well the content of a personnel-preparation program is planned, it will be of little impact if the staff does not have an adequate experiential base on which to assimilate the information. To this end personnel preparation should be structured as a "hands-on" effort that requires the systematic introduction of con-

cepts and the presentation and integration of those concepts with concrete experience.

2. *The ecological perspective shapes three important aspects of the personnel-preparation program.* The first of these is the identification of training targets. There is growing concensus that programs for special-needs children should be functional; that is, tied to increasing skills the client needs to operate successfully in the real-world environment (Brown et al., 1976; Johnson & Koegel, 1982). It is suggested that this same principle be extended to personnel preparation. That is, the attitudes and skills that are taught must be relevant to and useful in the field/service setting. Skills that the trainee acquires should not be taught in isolation, but should be woven into the total fabric of experiences and the competencies required by the program.

Second, the ecological perspective influences where the training experiences should occur. The traditional preservice, or in-service model relies heavily, if not exclusively, on didactic instructions in a setting physically removed from the "booming, buzzing confusion" of the classroom. The field-based, service-oriented instructional approach relies on the real-world environment as the site for the trainee's learning experience. It is necessary to assess the environmental conditions in which the trainee must operate and determine how these will interact with the information being presented. More diverse methods of instructions, such as media presentation, workshops, lectures, participatory discussions, and analog practice sessions, can help prepare a base for, or perhaps extend, the experience a trainee has in the classroom, workshop, community, home settings, or wherever the hands-on learning takes place.

3. *Perhaps the most salient aspect of this model is its dependence on a behavioral climate.* This influences the core curriculum of informational and performance competencies the trainee is expected to learn. The literature surrounding autism and behavior disorders identifies the primary skills needed by service providers for this population as behavioral intervention strategies (Smith, 1979; Zane et al., 1982). This behavioral perspective provides not only the primary content of personnel preparation, but also the methods by which personnel preparation and the supervision process are carried out. Just as it is expected that trainees become competent in certain behavioral procedures (i.e., behavioral assessment of antecedent, response, consequent variable; task analyses; measurement procedures; positive intervention procedures; and data-based decision making), it is also expected that the same behavioral principles apply in choosing, executing, and evaluating a

training program (Kazdin, 1975). This growing technology emphasizes the effectiveness of using procedures such as modeling, role playing, feedback, social reinforcement (i.e., praise, approval, and attention), tangible rewards or special privileges, and token reinforcement. There is perhaps no better way for a trainee to comprehend the essential features of behavioral intervention principles than to experience the application of the same principles during the day-to-day training activities.

In summary the conceptual framework of a field-based, service-oriented model includes these key elements:

• Training must be dynamic and adapted to the requirements of the field/service setting and should primarily take place on site.
• Each trainee should be perceived as an individual with needs, styles, and competencies that influence his performance.
• Training not only should teach, but also should exemplify a program philosophy of (1) functional goal setting, (2) organized learning experiences, and (3) a focus on behavioral intervention strategies.

This training program is one that is guided by the general, pragmatic principle of "teaching for performance." That is, to prepare a person to work successfully in a service-oriented, field setting, the training should begin with the specific skills (rather than broad competencies) required by the work site. The Personnel Instruction Program (PIP), presented in the remainder of this chapter, exemplifies this principle.

PERSONNEL INSTRUCTION PROGRAM (PIP)

Description

An assumption of most behavioral training programs is that, in order to give the trainee generalizable skills, one must train clinicians and teachers in general behavior modification principles and general competencies (Horner, 1977; Koegel et al., 1982; Zane et al., 1982). As discussed earlier, however, the scheduling, funding, supervision, and program needs in a field/service setting may leave very little time or resources for such complete and general training to take place. The Personnel Instruction Program (PIP) is a pragmatic system of on-line personnel preparation that serves the dynamic and service-oriented needs of the field setting. It does this by first teaching the trainee specific functional skills, and then expanding these skills into broader, generalizable competencies. Furthermore, the PIP is a personalized training program that produces a PIP plan (see Figure 8-1) to direct the training of each employee. Since no two trainees are alike, no two PIP plans are alike. However, the principle of teaching for performance is reflected in the following features common to all PIP plans.

1. *The training plan expresses the competencies required, and specifies the objectives and instructional methods for learning these competencies, and the evaluation methods to measure the effectiveness of the training.* Much like a client's Individual Education Plan (IEP), a trainee's PIP plan allows for an individualized set of training goals, interventions, and assessments. The trainee's individuality in terms of skill level, personal or professional goals, and interaction style can be reflected in the overall plan. Each PIP plan also reflects the individuality of the training site, client goals, available instructional materials, and scheduling requirements. Also, each plan produces a functional training program that teaches those skills the trainee needs to perform effectively in the work site. Furthermore, the specificity of PIP targets, procedures, and scheduling clarifies the expectations the field/service setting has for the trainee during the training period and provides a record of training goals that have been met. Finally, the specific, task-oriented, data-based nature of the PIP plan gives the trainee an opportunity to learn, through personal experience, an application of behavioral, ecological and developmental philosophy and methodology that integrates the clients' IEPs.

2. *The training plan includes a personalized combination of formal instruction and hands-on practice.* Each trainee's plan reflects a variety of instructional strategies, often carried out in a range of training environments by a variety of trainers. The primary learning site is the employee's work area. Generally training is given via procedures such as *modeling* by a trainer, then *rehearsal* by the trainee, and finally *feedback* from the trainer. This instructional strategy is also central to other behaviorally oriented programs for training clinicians and teachers (Donnellan, 1980; Kazdin, 1975; Koegel et al., 1982). Whenever possible, groups of trainees are instructed in didactic or workshop settings in core competencies (e.g., human rights model, program philosophy, essential program systems, the rationale and procedures of relaxation therapy). Lessons are given via verbal instruction, readings, a personalized system of instruction, video instruction, or demonstration and practice. (See Table 8-1 for a listing of possible instructional arrange-

Trainee _____ Unit/Placement _____
Title _____   Supervisor _____

List below any individual or group programs, activities, unit procedures, administrative tasks, or relevant principles that will be included in the trainee's orientation. This should be a guide for the supervisors in preparing PIP's and checking for completion of training areas.

P	Competency Area	Readings	D.S.	Verbal	D.S.	Video Tapes	D.S.	Demos	D.S.	Comp.
1	General Unit Goals	Orientation Manual	9/6							9/16
2	General Unit Procedures	Orientation Proc. Manual	9/6							9/23
3	Implementing Clients'IPPs	IPPs & Task Obj. Sheets	9/6	weekly team meetings	9/13			with team	9/7	9/23
4	Implementing Behavioral interventions on the IPOs	Intervention Descriptions	9/6	weekly team meetings	9/13			with team	9/7	9/23
5	Effective Communication w Colleagues Treatment Team	Castetter Book Chapter	9/12	meetings w/ supervisor	9/15					10/28
6	Coordinating Interns and Volunteers	BDC Policy	9/12							9/23
7	Observing, Describing & Recording Behavior	E. Reese Handout	9/19	weekly team meetings	9/22	group training tape	9/30			9/30
8	Methods of Collecting Raw Data	S./Azaroff bk.chapter	9/19	weekly team meetings	9/21			recording reliability	10/83	11/4
9	General Coordinator Responsibilities	Staff Proc. Manual	9/12	meetings w/ supervisor	9/15					9/30
10	Effective Leadership	Castetter Book Chapter	9/26	weekly team meetings	9/26			in meetings	9/28	11/25
11	Scheduling			meeting w/ supervisor	9/26			w/supervisor	9/26	10/24
12	Charting Goals	SBC Manual	9/26	program review	10/3			with team	10/83	11/16

Code: "P" - Priority   "D.S." - Date Scheduled

**Figure 8-1
PIP Planning Form**

Table 8-1
Instructional Alternatives for Staff Training

Modes of Instruction	Components	Training Site Unit	Training Lab
Verbal instruction	1. Inservice (large-group) presentation		X
	2. Small-group instruction	X	X
	3. Individual verbal instruction	X	X
Readings	1. Journals, texts		X
	2. Groden Center materials	X	X
Video instruction	1. Published tape series		X
	2. Center-prepared videotapes		X
Demonstration (on line—do, observe, give feedback)	1. Weekly unit demonstration with director	X	
	2. Individual instructional demo by trainer	X	X
	3. On-line program analysis of trainee with assigned client(s) and programs	X	

ments.) However, the core of the training sequence is always that specific set of behavioral and program competencies required by the staff member to function effectively with the clients assigned. This core is imbedded in a general list of competencies (see Table 8-2) and training targets. This list was initially generated by discussion among program planners and by review and analysis of curricula and training programs for teachers and clinicians of the severely handicapped (e.g., Fredericks et al., 1979; Horner, 1977; Sulzer-Azaroff et al., 1975; Christie et al., 1977; Wilcox, 1977). Periodically the competency list has been revised in line with changing or expanding program requirements.

3. *The training plan reflects the wide range of training targets necessary for effective work in the field/service setting.* Individuals often need instruction not only in the "hard" competencies of behavioral management and curriculum skills, but also in what are often perceived as the "softer" (i.e., harder to define) competencies of fitting into the general program or work site, learning new (e.g., administrative) competencies, and professional growth. Though few field/service settings can require

such a broad range of competencies in new employees, there is some advantage to the trainee to see the range of possible training targets that might be achieved. Objectifying both the hard and soft competencies also equates them in importance and gives the trainee the expectation that even these softer support skills can be learned.

There are some other advantages of a personnel instruction program built on the preceding features. First, it is broad and flexible enough to structure training programs for supervisory staff, direct service staff, interns, and volunteers. Second, though certain supervisory level employees are generally designated and prepared to be trainers, any staff member with existing skills can function as a trainer in a PIP plan. Third, because of the flexibility and individuality of the PIP plan, it adapts easily to a treatment program's needs to hire employees individually or at irregular (and sometimes unpredicted) times during the year. Since group instruction is a secondary instructional strategy, employees need not all begin training simultaneously. Finally, PIP plans produce a staff with variable, rather than homogeneous, competencies. This is advantageous for a multidimensional treatment program designed to serve clients with a range of needs. The heterogeneity in staff skill repertoires reinforces the heterogeneity of intervention strategies required to provide individualized and effective treatment.

Application

This final section describes the systematic use of PIP plans to orient new employees. It includes administrative guidelines to facilitate applications.

STAFF ORIENTATION SEQUENCE (SOS).

The first weeks of employment are a "critical period" in personnel preparation. Skills and attitudes not acquired during this period may be more difficult, and in some instances impossible, to develop later in employment. A PIP plan for a new employee is termed an SOS to highlight the importance of giving good instruction quickly to each beginning trainee. The SOS covers and includes five phases:

1. Introduction of trainee to program.
2. Development and implementation of training plan.
3. Review of training status.
4. Analysis of training.
5. Evaluation of trainee.

Table 8-2
Competency Areas

I. Agency overview
   A. Autism, behavioral disorders, and related handicaps
   B. Agency philosophy
      1. Ecological, developmental and behavioral programming
      2. Principles of normalization and functionality
      3. Curriculum design and integration
   C. Agency structure and interdisciplinary services
      1. Organizational design and service responsibility
      2. General unit/Speciality goals
   D. Personnel concerns
      1. General agency procedures
      2. General unit procedures
   E. Medical concerns
      1. Emergency medical procedures
      2. Basic first-aid procedures
      3. Physical control techniques for protection

II. *Behavior therapy principles*
   A. Observing, describing, and recording behavior
   B. Components of effective behavioral programming
   C. Behavioral strategies to accelerate behaviors and skills
      1. Environmental and curriculum change
      2. Reinforcement—positive and negative
      3. Token systems, contingency contracting, and other secondary reinforcers
      4. Shaping, fading, prompting, chaining, modeling, and graduated guidance
   D. Behavioral strategies to decelerate behaviors
      1. DRO, DRI, DRL
      2. Extinction
      3. Time out—nonexclusionary and exclusionary
      4. Punishment—overcorrection, aversive stimuli, response—cost, and restitution
      5. Physical restraint—manual and mechanical; partial and full
   E. Self-control procedures
      1. Relaxation
      2. Imagery and covert conditioning

III. *Individualized programming: planning, implementation, and evaluation*
   A. Multidisciplinary assessment
      1. Conducting an initial behavioral evaluation
      2. Conducting an educational evaluation
      3. Conducting a speech and language evaluation
   B. Curriculum area descriptions
      1. Sensorimotor
      2. Communication
      3. Independent home living skills
      4. Socialization
      5. Independent vocational skills

        6. Leisure
- C. Individual Program Plans (IPP)
   1. Planning IPPs
   2. Implementing IPPs
- D. Human rights in behavioral programming
   1. Planning behavioral interventions
   2. Implementing behavioral interventions
- E. Teaching strategies for acquisition, maintenance, and generalization of skills
   1. Discrete trial learning
   2. Instructional arrangements
   3. Schedules of reinforcement
- F. Preparation and utilization of instructional environment, materials, and activities
- G. Planning and implementing home programs
- H. Evaluating client progress
   1. Principles of precision teaching
   2. Methods of collecting raw data
   3. Setting up charts
   4. Charting goals
   5. Quarterly intersect evaluation

V. *Administrative concerns*

- A. Professional development
- B. Effective communication skills
   1. Colleagues and treatment team
   2. Parents
   3. Professionals outside the agency
   4. Community relationships
   5. Report writing
- C. Effective leadership skills
- D. Effective program coordination
   1. General coordinator responsibilities
   2. Scheduling
   3. Interns and volunteers
- E. Effective program supervision
   1. General supervisory responsibilities
   2. Coordination of IPP and IPO development
   3. Monitoring of IPP and IPO implementation
   4. Evaluation of client's IPP and IPO progress
- F. Supervising personnel
   1. Interviewing and hiring
   2. Staff training
   3. Staff evaluation
- G. State and federal legislation
- H. Planning, implementing, and evaluating research

Each step in these phases is depicted in Figure 8-2, the SOS procedural detail flowchart.

Phase 1. Introduction of Trainee to Program. This phase serves to acquaint the trainee with the work site and training program. During this phase it is important for the training supervisor to be a personal guide and resource to the new employee. Prior to training the trainee has completed a written survey that provides the training supervisor with a sample of the trainee's knowledge, problem-solving ability, and written communication skills. On the first day of SOS training, the employee reads about and discusses with the training supervisor the program philosophy and procedures, observes the work site, and meets other employees. Prior to the first day of training, the supervisor has reviewed and coordinated information obtained from (1) previous interviews with the trainee; (2) the trainee's performance on a competency survey, and (3) the needs and resources of the trainee's work and training site. With this information the supervisor writes a PIP plan and shares this with the employee. The supervisor also prepares a memo for all staff members that introduces the trainee and describes the trainee's background.

Phase 2. Development and Implementation of PIP Plan. This phase begins when the supervisor outlines the trainee's PIP plan (see Figure 8-1). This plan lists the specific programs that the trainee will learn to carry out (e.g., mobility program, relaxation training, group data taking, Distar Reading Level 1); essential program systems (e.g., human rights model, communication with families); and some larger competency areas (e.g., use of positive reinforcement, behavioral observation strategies, language and communication programs). For each of these programs, the supervisor prepares a Competency Area Plan (CAP) (see Figure 8-3), which includes short-term objectives with criteria and target dates, instructional methodology, trainer(s) and training site(s), and method of evaluation of training. These CAPs are prioritized and scheduled, and training begins (usually on day 2).

As the trainee learns the CAPs, the supervisor and trainer(s) observe the programs and provide verbal and written critiques of the trainee's performance, using a Program Analysis procedure as described in Chapter 9 (Figure 9-8). This method provides immediate feedback to the trainee, identifies specific competencies, and establishes a record of growth. At the end of each day, the trainee gives an SOS Daily Report (see Figure 8-4) to the training supervisor. This report provides the trainee with an opportunity to review the activities of the day, scan for successes and problems, and ask for clarification or help as needed.

Phase 3. Review of Training Status. After two to three weeks of train-

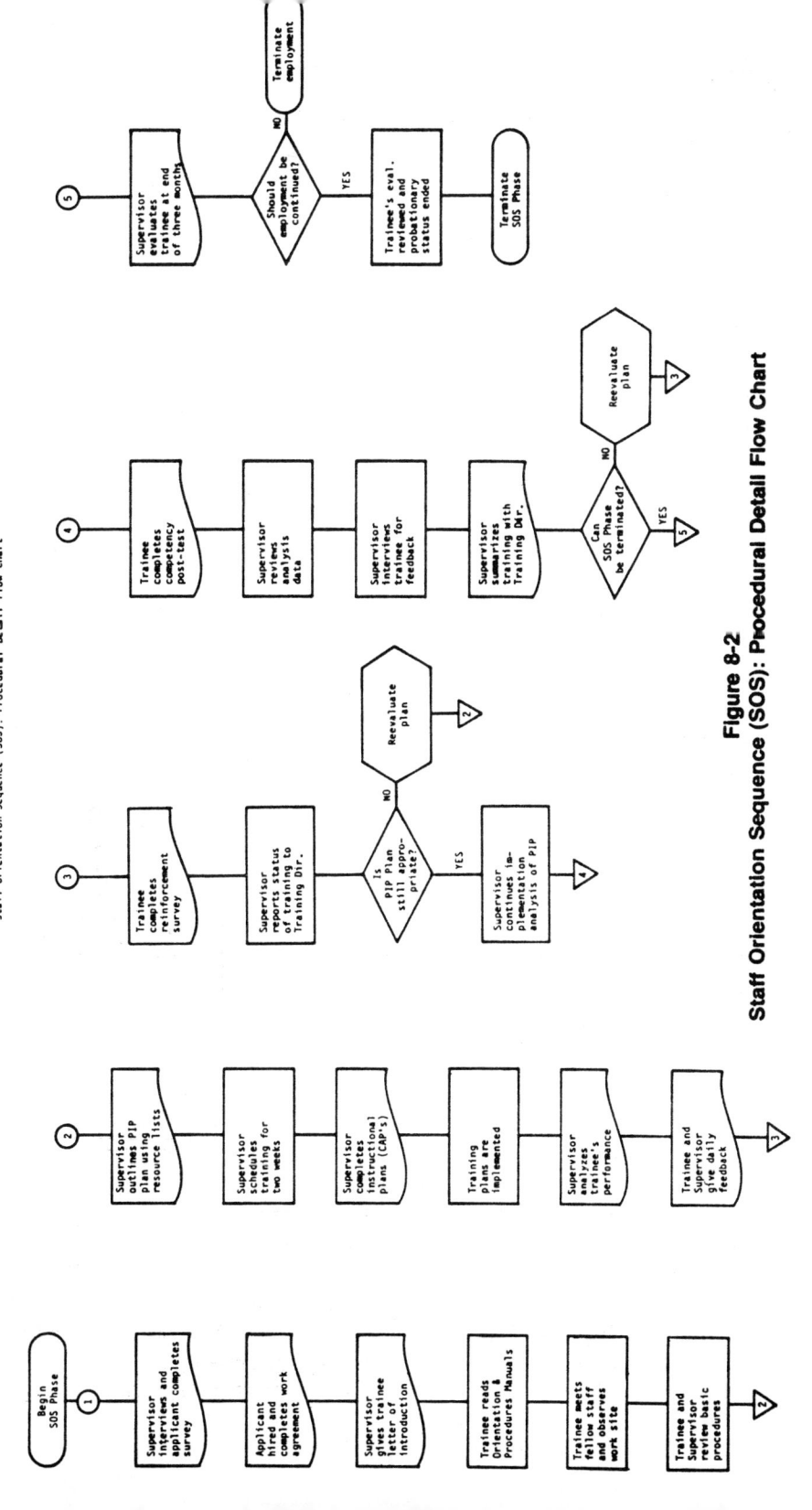

Figure 8-2
Staff Orientation Sequence (SOS): Procedural Detail Flow Chart

**Figure 8-2
Staff Orientation Sequence (SOS): Procedural Detail Flow Chart**

Trainee:	Competency: III. Individualized Programming	Present Date:
Supervisor/Trainer:	Skill: D. Human Rights in Behavioral Programming 2. Implementing Behavioral Interventions on the IPO	Review Date(s): ___ ___
Training Site(s):		___ ___

SHORT-TERM OBJECTIVES (including target dates)	DATE MET	INSTRUCTIONAL PLAN	METHOD OF EVALUATION
1. Trainee will describe the IPP behavioral targets, their corresponding IPO acceleration and deleleration pairs, and their interventions. Client: Target Date:		1. -Read clients IPP Behavioral Area Plans, IPO, and the Intervention Description Forms. -Discuss with Supervisor and Treatment Team	1. Correct identification of information demonstrated through -listing IPP goal, target pairs, and intervention names -verbally describing IDP procedures
2. Trainee will describe the rationale for using the particular interventions with the client and the methods of collecting data. Target Date:		2. -Discuss with Supervisor and Treatment Team -Review past charts	2. -Verbal description of information
3. Trainee will carryout the interventions, using the appropriate procedures with the appropriate timing and data collection techniques. Target Date:		3. -Supervisor/Trainer demonstration of intervention -Supervisor/Trainer observation of of trainer carrying out procedures	3. Program Analyses
4. Trainee will use charts to plot the data and monitor client progress. Target Date:		4. -Meetings with Supervisor and treatment team	4. Review charts and Weekly Program Cover Sheets.

Competency Area Plan (CAP)

Trainee:	Competency: IV. Administrative Concerns	Present Date:
Supervisor/Trainer:	Skill: C. Effective Leadership Skills.	Review Date(s): ___ ___
Training Site(s):		___ ___

SHORT-TERM OBJECTIVES (including target dates)	DATE MET	INSTRUCTIONAL PLAN	METHOD OF EVALUATION
1. Trainee demonstrates effective communication with both subordinate and supervisory staff. Target Date:		1. -Reading: "How to be a Successful Supervisor through Leadership and Human Dynamics" -Weekly Meetings to discuss guidelines and unit info -Demonstration -Observation	1. -Review of procedures established for channeling information -Staff feedback & satisfaction -Program Analyses -Written quiz -Lack of Problems -Programming innovation -general performance of staff (review staff evaluations.
2. Trainee demonstrates knowledge of individual and group dynamics through employing appropriate supervisory strategies. Target Date:			
3. Trainee demonstrates ability to effectively reinforce and criticize staff. Target Date:		2.-5. Same as above	2.-5. Same as above
4. Trainee will demonstrate ability to motivate staff to accept and promote change. Target Date:			
5. Trainee will demonstrate ability to anticipate problems and intervene early. Target Date:			

Figure 8-3
Competency Area Plan (CAP)

ing, when the employee has sampled the work site and its requirements, the supervisor and trainee both complete surveys designed to facilitate communication between the supervisor and the employee on personal goals, motivators, social stimulus value, and interaction style. The **trainee** rates preferences for instructional arrangements, age and cognitive levels of clients, teaching particular skills, types of intervention strategies, special projects, amount of supervision, motivators, and goals. The supervisor describes the trainee's goals; what seems to motivate the trainee; whether he works well with a team, is adaptable, and is a problem solver; how nonverbal communication is employed at the work site; and what typifies the trainee's interaction style with clients

```
Trainee: _____        Date: _____

Supervisor: _____        Supervisor Check when Reviewed ____
```

List below the activities you performed today:

Unit Programs	Readings	Video-viewing	Other

What did you enjoy about work today?

_____
_____
_____
_____

Did anything happen today that you found difficult to understand, was unpleasant for you, or that you did not enjoy?

_____
_____
_____
_____

Return this form to your Training Supervisor (Unit Supervisor).

**Figure 8-4
SOS Daily Report**

and colleagues. Identifying these attributes assists in making the most effective matches between program and employee needs, and this ultimately benefits the overall program goals.

A review of the survey information and program analysis forms helps to determine whether the original PIP plan is still appropriate. If changes are needed, new CAPs are prepared, scheduled, and implemented. If the original PIP plan is still appropriate, it continues to be implemented with additional program analyses conducted by the supervisor and/or trainer(s).

Phase 4. Analysis of Training. At the end of the six weeks (30 days) of training, the supervisor administers the competency survey posttest to the trainee; reviews the evaluative data from program analyses done on CAPs; and interviews the trainee to discuss progress, satisfaction, and concerns of both the trainee and the supervisor. A determination is made as to whether the intensive training phase can be terminated. If it cannot, the information is reevaluated and appropriate alterations are made. If the trainee has progressed satisfactorily, phase 5 begins with the trainee continuing to carry out his responsibilities, and receiving feedback from the supervisor.

Phase 5. Evaluation of Trainee. When the trainee has completed three months of employment, the supervisor completes an evaluation rating the trainee's performance. If it is satisfactory, future personnel goals are discussed with the trainee, and the SOS training is terminated.

At this point a trainee has been evaluated and given feedback not only on the ability to *understand* a client population and a body of knowledge required for effective intervention, but also (and perhaps more important) the ability to *perform* the tasks and programs required for changing a client's behavior. A trainee equiped with such feedback is better prepared to judge the appropriateness and value of the work site. A field/service setting in which new employees display a reasonable level of competency is better able to serve its clients.

OTHER USES AND FEATURES OF PIP.

By no means is an employee's training completed with the end of SOS training. Personnel preparation is best seen as an ongoing process that is adapted to the growing and changing needs of employees throughout their tenure with a field/service setting.

Ongoing Staff Training. While the entire SOS is not necessary for ongoing personnel-instruction programs, its essential features are appropriate for all staff members, including experienced persons going on to new positions, staff members increasing their expertise (e.g., learning to be a supervisor or a specialized resource person), substitute staff, and volunteers and interns with a shorter tenure in the field/service setting. Individualized PIP plans can be written for the trainee that also include prioritized CAPs, on-line observation and feedback, and attention to variable needs of the trainee and the field/service setting.

CAP Bank. Writing individual CAPs for each trainee can be a time-consuming task for trainers. One can make available a file of all previously written CAPs, categorized by PIP competencies (see Table 8-2). Supervisors then can examine models of similar CAPs and use some or all of the objectives, instructional strategies, and evaluation procedures as necessary.

Competency Bank. The PIP plan can be entered into an employee's personnel file where it provides a handy summary for a supervisor of that person's existing skill repertoire. However, a field/service setting may want to organize all employees' completed PIP plans into a master competency bank. This file would list all employees with training in each of the program competencies. Reference to such a bank should inform and expedite decisions about which employees would be more appropriate for certain new clients or programs. For example, if a program required a new group-oriented classroom, all employees with training (and certified competency) in group-instructional strategies could be considered.

Summary

Field/service settings present program supervisors with the often difficult task of training new employees with as little disturbance as possible to the flow of program services to their clients. Employees often begin a job with the hope that their best skills will be recognized and utilized by the employer and with the expectation of quickly learning new skills. The Personnel Instruction Program (PIP), as outlined in this chapter, emphasizes the importance of meeting these employer and employee needs. It suggests that a pragmatic strategy of "teaching for performance," or quickly giving a trainee on-line skills in relevant work settings, can prepare employees to contribute in a most positive way to the program services. Furthermore, it suggests that these early functional skills can be the core of a training program that provides the employee with a broad and complete repertoire of competencies.

The PIP model underscores the notion that there is no "standard" employee. The goal of training is not to produce homogeneous or minimally prepared employees, but to allow each employee to become and remain an individual within a work site. This approach to personnel preparation also includes a clear delineation of responsibility, both to the trainee to learn new skills and trainer, to provide the learning opportunities.

The PIP model has grown from the environmental demands and resources of a program dedicated to giving the best possible service to autistic and severely disturbed clients. The authors anticipate that the philosophy and operations of the PIP model may be helpful to others who are charged with personnel preparation in similar human-service settings.

REFERENCES

Brown, L., Nietupski, J. & Hamre-Nietupski, S. (1976). The criterion of ultimate functioning and public school services for severely handicapped students. In M. A. Thomas (Ed.), *Hey, don't forget about me!* Reston, Va.: Council for Exceptional Children.

Castetter, W. B. (1976). *The personnel function in educational administration.* New York: Macmillan.

Christie, L. S., Williams, W., Edelman, S., Hill, M. G., Fox, T. J., Fox, W. L., Sousie, S. P. & York, R. (1977). *A master's level training program to prepare teachers serving learners in need of intensive special education.* Burlington, Vt.: University of Vermont.

Donnellan, A. M. (1980). An educational perspective of autism: Implication for curriculum development and personnel development. In B. Wilcox and A. Thompson (Eds.), *Critical issues in educating autistic children and youth.* Washington: U.S. Department of Education, Office of Special Education, pp. 53–88.

Foxx, R. M. (1980). *The highly disruptive client: Legal, clinical, and administrative issues in developing and implementing behavior modification programs.* Workshop presentation, Toledo, Ohio.

Fredericks, H. D., Anderson, R. & Baldwin, V. (1979). Identifying competency indicators of teachers of the severely handicapped. *AAESPH Review,* 4, 81–95.

Horner, R. D. (1977). A competency-based approach to preparing teachers of the severely and profoundly handicapped. In E. Sontag, J. Smith & N. Certo (Eds.), *Educational programming for the severely/profoundly handicapped.* Reston, Va.: Council for Exceptional Children, 430–444.

Johnson, J. & Koegel, R. L. (1982). Behavioral assessment and curriculum development. In R. L. Koegel, A. Rincover, and A. L. Egel (Eds.), *Educating and understanding autistic children.* San Diego, Calif.: College-Hill Press, pp. 1–32.

Kazdin, A. E. (1975). *Behavior modification in applied settings.* Homewoods, Ill.: Dorsey Press.

Koegel, R. L., Russo, D. C., Rincover, A. & Schreibman, L. (1982). Assessing and training teachers. In R. L. Koegel, A. Rincover, and A. L. Egel (Eds.), *Educating and understanding autistic children.* San Diego, Calif.: College-Hill Press.

Marshall, A. M. & Marks, H. (1981). Implementation of "zero reject" training in an institutional setting. *Analysis and intervention in developmental disabilities, 1,* 23–36.

Schiff, W. (1980). *Perception: An applied approach.* Boston: Houghton-Mifflin.

Smith, M. (1979). *The development and study of competencies needed by teachers of students with autistic characteristics.* Unpublished doctoral dissertation, Michigan State University.

Sulzer-Azaroff, B., Thaw, J. & Thomas, C. (1975). Behavioral competencies for the evaluation of behavioral modifiers. In S. W. Wood (Ed.), *Issues in evaluating behavior modification.* Champaign, Ill.: Research Press.

Wilcox, B. (1977). A competency-based approach to preparing teachers of the severely and profoundly handicapped: Perspective I. In E. Sontag, J. Smith, and N. Certo (Eds.), *Educational programming for the severely and profoundly handicapped.* Reston, Va.: Council for Exceptional Children.

Zane, T., Sulzer-Azaroff, B., Handen, B. L. & Fox, C. (1982). Validation of a competency-based training program in developmental disabilities. *Journal of the Association for the Severely Handicapped, 7,* 27–31.

CHAPTER

9

A Systems Approach for Educators and Clinicians Working with Persons with Autism: Putting It All Together

June Groden, Ph.D.
Grace Baron, Ph.D.
Anne Pentecost, M.Ed.
Susan Stevenson, M.Ed.

Assessment
   Comparison of Functional and Traditional Assessment
   Sources of Data for Functional Assessment
   Summary of Assessment
Plan Development
   The Spectrum: A Model for Integrating Personalized Plans
   Designation of Plan Components
   Summary

Implementation
   Relationship Between Planners and Implementors
   Environmental Design
   Scheduling Concerns
   Intervention Strategies
   Documentation Procedures
Ongoing Data Analysis
   Analysis and Review Procedures
   Considerations in Program Change
   Summary of Ongoing Data Analysis
Summary of Chapter
References

> We must resist complacency. We must reject the perpetuation in our education system of familiar practices with unproven results. We must, instead, reassess, reconsider, redesign, and redirect our strategies to resolve multiple needs.—R. Paul Thompson (1980)

"FAMILIAR PRACTICES" IN ANY EDUCATIONAL or treatment system have a way of resisting change. Curricula, programs, and procedures that have worked well in the past comfort and direct us as we undertake new ventures. This chapter argues, as does Thompson, that fully to meet the multiple educational and programming needs of children with autism and other severe disorders, we must resist the urge to do only that which has worked well in the past. Rather, an organization designed to meet the needs of such children must develop strategies to foster change, and must include incremental and self-evaluative methods of deriving new and sanctioned practices. Furthermore, developing such change-making strategies can support an organization's extended survival (Campbell et al., 1977).

This chapter is a joint effort by educational and clinical specialists, as well as program administrators, to present an approach to resisting complacency and maximizing program effectiveness while educating and treating children with severe behavior disorders. It is hoped that it will serve the dual purposes of:

1. Providing a curriculum model and a practical foundation for the educational specialist who must design, implement, and evaluate an Individual Educational Plan (IEP) for a child with a severe behavior disorder.

2. Introducing educators, clinicians, and administrators to a model for defining and integrating the range of services as required in programs for children with severe behavior disorders. This model is called the Feedback Loop System (FLS).

Systems analysis and systems theory present a helpful conceptual base for the difficult task of designing dynamic learning environments and effective human services (Frederiksen, 1982; Christian, 1984; Churchman, 1968; Foster, 1978; Liao & Miller, 1977). A typical systems analysis of an educational or human-service organization includes the following segments:

- *System goals:* What is to be achieved
- *System environments and resources:* Where it will be and what will be used to accomplish goals
- *System management:* Who will be responsible for which elements
- *System activities:* How the goals will be implemented

- *System evaluation:*   How goal achievement will be measured

Typically the *goals* and *activities* for individuals in an educational or human service organization are organized around an IEP or a personalized life plan that (1) works toward meeting the client's needs, and (2) meets federal and state regulations concerning education and treatment. Also, a chosen plan usually reflects the expectations of the primary funding agency and the service setting. Often such plans are not comprehensive. For example, a school system may generate a plan that includes academic goals exclusively or a vocational setting may target work adjustment skills primarily. On the other hand, a plan or curriculum designed to meet the multiple life needs of a child with a severe disorder must include a broader range of program goals and activities and can more appropriately be called an IPP, or Individualized Program Plan. Furthermore, programs may vary in the environments and resources as well as management and evaluation procedures chosen, but usually require the combination of many disciplines (e.g., education, psychology, psychiatry) working in a range of physical environments.

While segments of a systems analysis function autonomously, the synthesis of each is achieved primarily through the institution of an organized structure of administration. Meals (1977) argues that the design and implementation of educational and therapeutic systems should not be seen as events, but as a process that includes a repeating series of decision-making activities that are highly interdependent. The process of educating and treating children with autism or other severe impairments may typically include the decision-making activities or (1) assessment, (2) plan development, (3) program implementation, and (4) ongoing data analysis. One aim of this chapter is to provide for the special educator or clinician an organizational system that defines and integrates these four activities. Each activity or phase of the system "feeds back" information, which is then used in the next phase. The process does not end with the fourth phase, data analysis, but returns to the first assessment phase and repeats each activity, continuing to "loop" around through all phases. The model called the Feedback Loop System is depicted in Figure 9-1 and will be described in detail throughout the remainder of this chapter.

ASSESSMENT

The first phase of the Feedback Loop System is assessment. The type of information received from assessment is critical to developing a comprehensive and functional program for an individual. Assessment must be linked to therapeutic ends and focus on those variables particularly relevant for treatment. For this reason the more traditional approaches to assessment may not result in realistic treatment plans that are specific enough for evaluating a client's progress, workable within the resources and realities of the environment, and relevant to the client's survival.

Comparison of Functional and Traditional Assessment

A *functional* assessment differs in significant ways from a *traditional* assessment. (See Table 9-1).

The most central difference is that a functional assessment is integrally tied to an implementation plan. That is, assessments are conducted with the intent that the findings and recommendations will be

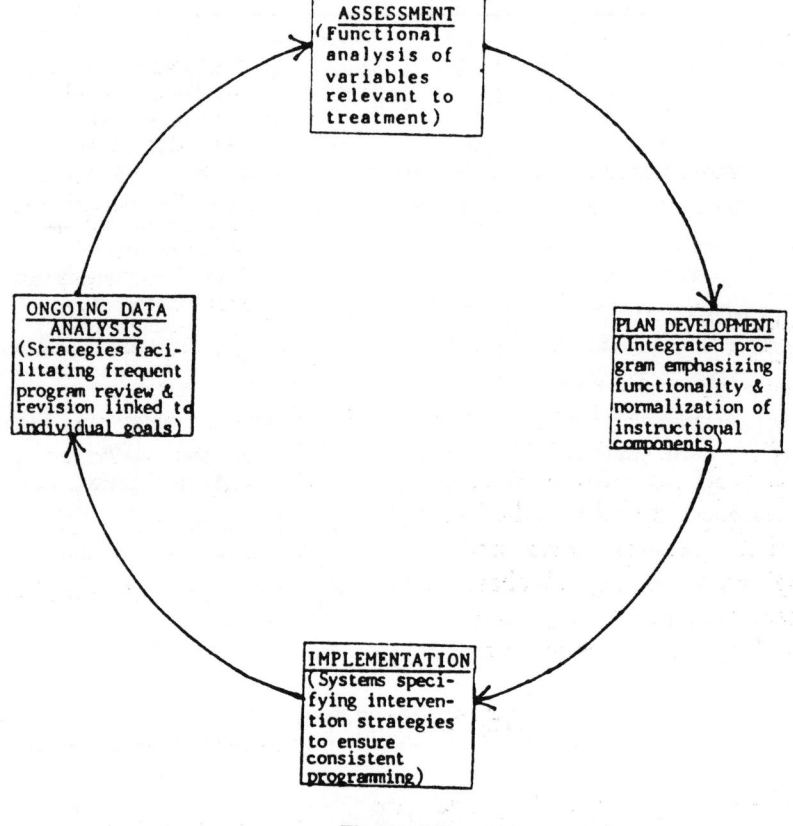

Figure 9-1
Feedback Loop Model

Table 9-1
Comparison of Functional and Traditional Assessment

	Traditional Evaluations	Functional Assessment
Length/goal	Short-term assessment isolated from treatment	Long-term (i.e., four to six weeks) assessment tied to treatment and implementation
Setting	Assessments conducted primarily in one setting that is foreign to the client	Multiple observation in different settings familiar to the client (i.e., home, school)
Test data employed	Emphasis placed on standardized tests	Focus on functional analyses that describe relevant antecedent and consequent events
Client reactivity	Assessment possibly influenced by client's fear or shyness with an unfamiliar evaluator in an unfamiliar environment	Assessment beneficially influenced by the client's positive relationships with evaluators and familiarity with environments
Data sample used	Usually one observation, making it difficult to determine the client's rate of learning to set goals	Several observations over time to assess the client's rate of learning in order to set realistic goals
Learning channel analysis	Learning channel or modes are not usually highlighted	Appropriate learning channels (e.g., visual, auditory, tactile) selected so that instructional styles will best suit the client's preferred mode of learning

put to immediate use, and future evaluation will provide accountability for the recommendations. This is in contrast to traditional assessments, which may be isolated conceptually as well as physically from treatment, and may often result in recommendations that are never implemented. Chapter 2 in this volume details many features of a functional evaluation. A teacher/therapist may gather data for a functional evaluation from a number of sources.

Sources of Data for Functional Assessment

The term "assessment" can include a screening prior to placement, the initial assessment (when the client enters a program), and periodic evaluation in all areas of the client's development. These components are discussed in the following, and include descriptions of types of assessments utilized and involvement of evaluators, environments, and time.

1. *Screening.* A preadmission screening provides an opportunity for record review and an abbreviated assessment of the client's cognitive, gross motor, perceptual motor, readiness, academic, and speech and language skills. Parents and other care givers provide information on their expectations, concerns, skills, and resources. This screening information is then used as part of the criteria for acceptance into a program and for temporary placement of a child for further assessment.

2. *Initial assessment.* An initial assessment phase should continue for a period of four to six weeks. A thorough behavioral evaluation, detailed in Chapter 2, is one portion of an initial assessment. This is complemented by determination of developmental and educational skill levels, as well as learning style and rate, and a functional analysis of the family and its network. See Chapters 4, 5 and 6 for an in-depth discussion of some portions of this interdisciplinary evaluation. A teacher/therapist who remains with the client for the full assessment period can provide data about a client's functioning level and program needs from four different sources.

a. *Observation in the natural environment.* Often overlooked are observations in the various environments in which a client functions. We encourage the evaluator to observe and record all aspects of the client's behavioral repetoire in "natural" classroom scenarios, often without interruption for extended periods of time. This provides data relevant to some existing contingencies governing a client's behavior. Observations in the home provide information on the nature and degree of the client's interaction with family members, potential reinforcers, and skills and deficits. They also assist in determining whether help or guidance is needed by the family. Community-based observations (e.g., McDonalds, grocery store, parks) help evaluate the client's independent functioning, social skills, self-control, behavioral deficiencies and excesses, and general affective development within the community.

Natural environments provide a rich source of information about a client. It is especially important to have good observational systems to collect reliable data. Interaction analysis systems, such as that described by Ragland and colleagues (1978), provide needed information for future program planning. These systems are methods of directly observing a client as he interacts with peers, adults, or the environment, and of recording the frequency, duration, or other measures in order to analyze these interactions.

b. *Standardized tests and diagnostic inventories.* Information from standardized tests is incorporated into the assessment process whenever applicable. These tests may include the Key Math Diagnostic Arithmetic Test (American Guidance Service, 1976); the Peabody Individual Achievement Test (American Guidance Service, 1976); the Woodcock Reading Mastery Test (American Guidance Service, 1970); the Slosson Oral Reading Test (Slosson Educational Publications, 1963); and Brigance Diagnostic Inventories (Brigance, 1978). Since these tests are standardized or norm referenced, they also provide a valuable tool for reassessment so that growth can be measured over time or in comparison with a normal population.

c. *Criterion-referenced tests.* Criterion-referenced tests that incorporate prescriptive teaching programs are an invaluable aid.

As White (1977) points out:

Criterion-referenced assessment is one in which the child's performance is compared against that level of performance required to be successful in a task. Unlike norm-referenced assessment, with criterion-referenced assessment all children could presumably fail to reach a criterion or all children could pass. (p. 734)

The Teaching Research Infant and Child Curriculum (Ferdericks, 1976) is an example of a curriculum that incorporates criterion-referenced assessment and accompanying prescriptive programs. In the initial (start-up) phases of developing a program for clients with special needs, packaged assessments and prescriptive programs can be of invaluable aid. They allow the staff the freedom to design substructures to a program, such as training criteria, scheduling, and forms, while providing clients with individualized programs. They can also furnish the springboard from which more personalized functional programs can be developed. In other words, during the formative stage of a new program, the use of criterion-referenced programs is suggested. Then, as the program evolves, more personalized prescriptions appropriate to client and program needs can be written.

The "precision teaching" model (Lindsley, 1971) of assessment and continued evaluation can be used to turn almost any curricular guidelines into a criterion-referenced assessment with instructional prescription. An example of this is the reading of functional words. After developing a list of important reading words such as "poison" and "stop," the client is assessed on the number of words read correctly, read incorrectly, or skipped during a one-minute test. A teaching program is then designed on the basis of the client's responses. New words are added as mastery of previously learned ones is achieved. Reassessment on a daily or weekly basis using the one-minute timing test furnishes the assessment and evaluation information.

d. *Interviews and family systems analysis.* The teacher/therapist may also have many opportunities to interact with other family members. These interviews and less formal interactions are a rich source of data about the functional role the client plays in the family system, the strengths and deficits of the family, and the amount of involvement the family can have in a client's individualized program plan. As Chapter 7 emphasizes, any service provider should try to look at a broad picture of the whole family and its network, and to establish a harmonious plan to meet both the cilent's needs and those of the family.

5. *Reassessment.* Teacher/therapists are generally involved in overall program reassessment which is mandated to occur on an annual basis. At this time all of the client's programs are evaluated simultaneously so that goals can be reviewed and prioritized and new annual individualized plans prepared. Evaluations (i.e., educational, medical, physical and occupational therapy, psychological, psychiatric, speech and language, and social history) are readministered every three years according to federal regulations, or more often if needed. A progress report is written regarding the attainment of individual objectives. These new assessments and data are used to evaluate individual program goals and select new targets.

Teacher/therapists also play a vital role in reassessing client progress on a more regular, if not daily, basis. This topic is discussed later in the chapter.

Summary of Assessment

Assessments are critical to the Feedback Loop System through providing the foundation upon which all treatment and educational plans are built. They must elicit information that is specific and focused on therapeutic ends. This comprehensive assessment process leads into the next activity of the system, which involves the organization of the information into a plan for reaching the client's goals.

PLAN DEVELOPMENT

Recommendations from all of the assessments must be integrated and prioritized. This integration provides the basis for the second phase of the feedback loop, plan development. Plan development is the process through which a comprehensive program (referrred to here as a personalized plan) is formulated for an individual. The asssessment recommendations are identified within the framework of a curriculum that is organized by skill areas across expanding environments. The recommendations are then expressed as annual goals, and further delineated into short-term objectives that specify measurable behaviors, criterion levels, and projected dates for attainment.

This section will present considerations that enter into the plan development process of integrating and prioritizing recommendations and in designing specific skill area plans. A curriculum model, referred to as the Spectrum, is described here, and examples of the application of this model in the plan development process are presented.

The Spectrum: A Model for Integrating Personalized Plans

When developing programs for special-needs individuals, it is beneficial to have a framework that indicates the scope of the program's content, and as such is identified as the curriculum (Zais, 1976). For several years educators have been describing curricula for individuals with special needs in terms of outcome statements. These statements usually reflect the philosophy of a particular agency or beliefs held by the general society as to what knowledge and skills are important in the education of special-needs individuals. Typically the outcome statements are categorized into domains that potentially can encompass any and all skills, or limit, by their very detail, various other opportunities provided for learning.

The curriculum model referred to as the Spectrum is based on a philosophy that integrates developmental, behavioral, and ecological principles. The scope and content of this curriculum are defined as those skills and knowledge that are necessary for an individual to function as independently and productively as possible in a socially acceptable fashion. This philosophy is supported throughout much of the more recent literature for the severely handicapped (Nirje, 1969;

Baumgart et al., 1982), and considers the concept of functionality, normalization, and partial participation. Each of these concepts is discussed later in this section.

The Spectrum as depicted in Figure 9-2 identifies six major skill areas: sensorimotor, communication, socialization, independent home living, independent vocational skills, and leisure. Each of these areas or domains is further broken down into more specific competencies. Additionally the Spectrum reflects the concept of functional programming in

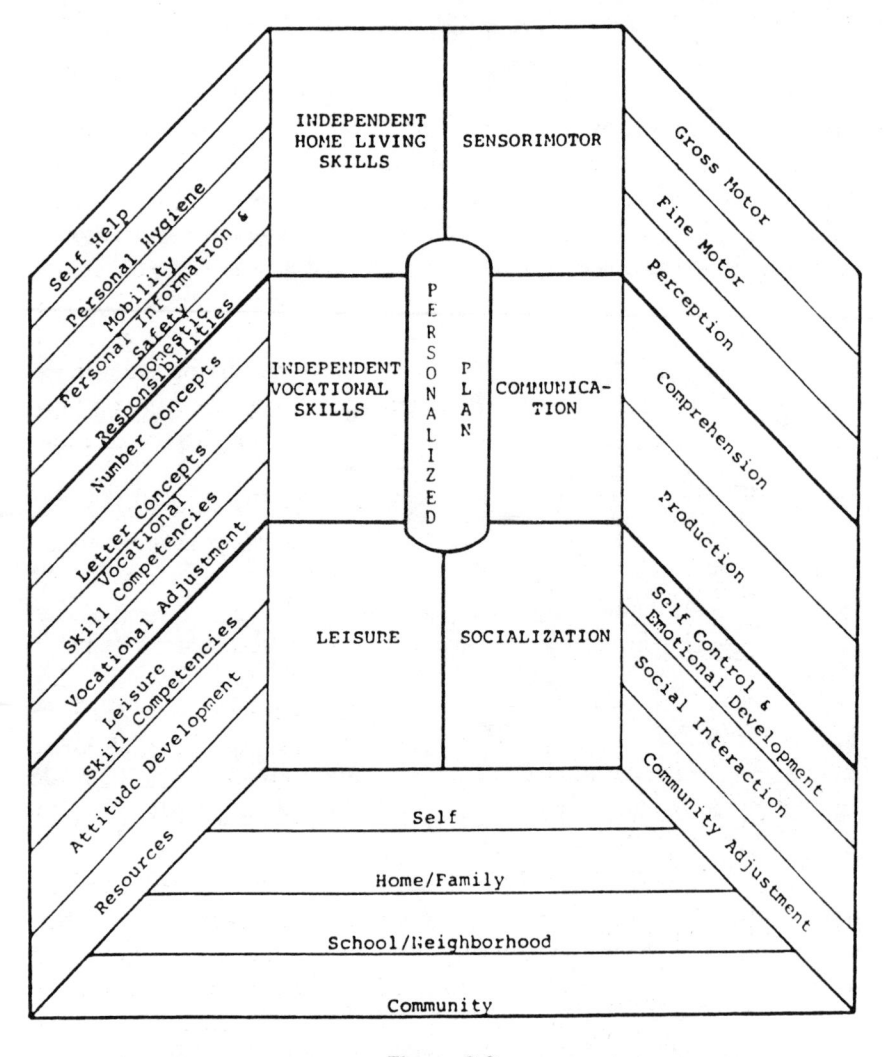

Figure 9-2
The Groden Center Spectrum:
A Model for Integrating Personalized Life Plans

expanding environments, including the self, home and family, school and neighborhood, and community (Goldstein, 1972; Zuckerman, 1978). Because different competencies and skill levels are required in different settings, and because skills become more complex as environments become more intricate, curriculum areas must always be identified within the context of these expanding environments.

The Spectrum model provides the framework within which personalized plans can be developed. However, before developing specific objectives, assessment information and recommendations must be integrated and prioritized.

1. *Prioritization.* In organizing an individual's personalized plan, a number of decisions must be made regarding which recommendations should be more heavily emphasized. These decisions are critical ones, and ultimately affect a person's level of productivity and independence in life. Input into this decision-making process is provided by individuals and their family, by the staff and consultants, and by professional research literature. It should be emphasized that each client's program is planned on an individual basis and reflects that individual's personal interests and needs in both current and projected living situations. Considerations that influence the prioritization component of the program planning process include the concepts of functionality, normalization, and partial participation.

a. *Functionality.* The concept of functional skills is most aptly labeled by Brown and colleagues (1976) as the criterion of ultimate functioning: If an individual cannot perform a task and someone else has to do it for that individual, then the task is functional to the needs of the individual. The functional necessity of a given program is its primary justification for inclusion in an individual's personalized plan. In developing a program, useful, efficient skills that will maximize independence and productivity must be targeted. For example, a traditional mathematics program might teach a child to verbalize rote addition sums to 20. A more functional program is to teach that client to total prices, using a calculator, in making store purchases.

Similarly, a traditional telling-time program may involve identification of the times to the hour. A more functional approach teaches identification of those times during the day that are meaningful to a particular client (such as lunchtime at 12:00 and bus time at 2:30). In evaluating the functionality of any goal, it must be examined for its current and future use in an individual's life. Teaching clients to identify times in association with events ultimately leads those individuals to learn to follow schedules independently. Whether those clients can verbalize clock time whenever asked is not nearly as important as whether they can read their own schedule and be where they should be at appointed times.

b. *Normalization.* The concept of normalization (Nirje, 1969) refers to minimizing discrepancies between handicapped individuals and their nonhandicapped peers. Not only must handicapped individuals be taught the most efficient, useful skills possible, but they also must be taught these skills in ways that promote dignity, self-respect, and confidence. Objectives in a personalized plan should reflect skills and materials that are age appropriate, and should be carried out in the least restrictive "natural" environment. A handicapped adolescent, for example, may have severely delayed fine motor skills that have been targeted for improvement. Rather than having this individual put pegs into a pegboard, more functional, age-appropriate, and "normalized" tasks can be specified. For instance, in the area of vocational education, this individual can perform a number of tasks that are useful and practical, and will help develop fine motor skills. For example, he can sort parts, using a pincer grasp to transfer the pieces from one container to another; assemble items from simple nuts and bolts to complex parts; fold collated materials; or carry out woodworking tasks. Likewise, it is not very age appropriate (or efficient in the long term) for a 14-year-old individual to work on handwriting by repeatedly completing a dotted alphabet. It would be much more useful and suitable to work on comparable skills in the context of learning personal data. In this way the client not only will learn to write the specified information, but also to respond to the written cues of "name," "address," "telephone number" with the appropriate written information.

Examples of the normalization of traditional programs are plentiful and can be applied to every program area. Each objective must be weighed for its appropriateness in terms of age, interest, and ability level, and individualized programs that meet a client's specific needs within a normal context must be developed.

c. *Partial participation.* This concepts refers to the modifications in materials or procedures that allow handicapped individuals to participate, at least partially, in appropriate activities and enironments (Baumgart et al., 1982). Professionals cannot predetermine limits on the basis of a person's handicaps or functioning level, but must provide for the greatest degree of involvement possible.

Individuals with very different abilities and skill levels may be involved in a food-preparation program. One client may be able to read and follow the steps of a recipe, while another may carry out the steps by following a sequence of picture cards. Even though the second client does not have the skills needed to follow a recipe, he still can participate very appropriately in the program, with a small modification in procedure and materials.

It should also be noted that any modification must be functional. An adaptation that is not practical, and does not truly increase an individual's independence, should not be pursued.

2. *Integration.* The ultimate goal of the plan development process is to design a cohesive and comprehensive program. It is the responsibility of the program planners to review all assessments, summarize their recommendations, and identify the environments in which the recommendations are applicable. See Figure 9-3 for an example of a Consultant Recommendations chart.

Each recommendation must also be examined to identify the various curriculum areas that contribute to the component skills of that recommendation. Specific objectives can then be developed and organized within curriculum areas and environments. This integration process not only provides a more comprehensive and coordinated program, but it also ensures more successful acquisition and generalization of skills.

Following is an example of the integration of a specific program recommendation within a number of different curriculum areas. A general goal might be for a client to prepare a meal independently. The client may need to recognize food item words and to categorize the items into food groups. The learner can practice writing skills when making a shopping list, and subsequently practice actual visits to the grocery store. After locating the specified items, the individual must go to the cashier and pay for them. These items can then be used to prepare a lunch. Within this single goal, skills in reading, language, community mobility, independent living, math, behavioral management, and socialization have all been incorporated into a single program.

In laying the groundwork for a personalized plan, each recommendation must be examined in terms of its application in as many domains as appropriate. Organizing a program within the framework of the Spectrum model provides unity to the resulting personalized plan.

Designation of Plan Components

By establishing priority areas of emphasis, and by organizing and integrating all of the assessment information, the goals that will be

Systems Approach

Consultant Recommendations Chart

Client's Name: Paul Smith Evaluation: Psychological
Unit: Junior Consultant: _____, M.S.
Supervisor: _____ Date of Evaluation: 3/86

The unit supervisor will complete this form when reviewing a client's psychological, psychiatric, social history, medical, physical therapy, and occupational therapy evaluations. The information is to be reviewed by the unit director and then used in developing the IPP.

Summary Findings: very sociable - enjoys conversation - has made progress in controlling interfering behaviors [since entry eval 2 yrs. ago] - during present eval., exhibited following problematic behaviors: irrelevant verbalizations and attentional deficits, poor task focus, poor organizational skills in approach to presented tasks; inability to plan -

Recommendations	Follow-up (parent notification, IPP plan, referral, meeting, etc.)	Date
- focus on language development - organization & sequencing elements	Referral to BDC Speech and Lang. specialist and IPP plan	4/86

- focus on attentional deficits	1) Behavioral program
	2) Program plans -
	  - Relaxation & Imagery Therapy
	  - Independent Work
		3/86

Reviewed by Unit Director: _____
Date: _____

**Figure 9-3
Consultant Recommendations Chart**

included in the personalized plan of an individual are targeted. *Annual and short-term objectives* in a specific program area are specified in measurable terms, with criteria and projected dates of achievement. Examples of several program area plans are shown in Figure 9-4.

In addition to specifying annual and short-term objectives, each area plan should also delineate information regarding instructional arrangements, materials, scheduling, and methods of evaluation for that

Individual's Name: Gerry	Area: Functional Academic/Voc. Prep		Present Date: March, 1983
Prepared By:	Program: Number Concepts - Money/Calculator		Review Date: May, 1984
ENTRY LEVEL Date: February, 1981 Level: names coins; counts pennies	**PRESENT LEVEL** Gerry counts out the exact change for an item, using a combination of coins and bills, with verbal prompting.	**ANNUAL GOAL** Gerry will independently add the cost of 3 items, using his calculator, and count out the indicated amount using assorted coins and bills, with 90% accuracy (up to $5.00)	**UNIT PLACEMENT**
SHORT TERM OBJECTIVES (Including target date) 1) Gerry will independently count out the exact price of one specified item, 90% accuracy by 6/83. 2) Gerry will add the prices of two items and count out the specified amount, 90% accuracy, by 9/83. 3) Gerry will add the prices of 3 items and count out the correct amount, 90% accuracy, by 12/83.	**DATE MET**	**RESOURCES** MATERIALS: - Money - Price labels SESSIONS AND INSTRUCTIONAL ARRANGEMENTS: 3 times per week 25 minutes per session small group And on unit field trip, and throughout the day.	**METHOD OF EVALUATION** - Data Sheet - Anecdotal Records

Individual's Name: Gerry	Area: Vocational		Present Date: March, 1983
Prepared By:	Program: Contract Work - Rate building		Review Date: March, 1984
ENTRY LEVEL Date: 3/82 Level: Readiness	**PRESENT LEVEL** Gerry currently works at 45% of industrial rate on Leviton contract work.	**ANNUAL GOAL** Gerry will work at 85% of industrial rate on all Leviton contract work	**UNIT PLACEMENT**
SHORT TERM OBJECTIVES (Including target date) 1) Gerry will work at 55% of industrial rate on all Leviton contract work by 6/83. 2) Gerry will work at 65% of industrial rate on all Leviton contract work by 9/83. 3) Gerry will work at 75% of industrial rate on all Leviton contract work by 12/83. 4) Gerry will work at 85% of industrial rate on all Leviton contract work by 3/84.	**DATE MET**	**RESOURCES** MATERIALS: Leviton contract work Sorting bins Clippers SESSIONS AND INSTRUCTIONAL ARRANGEMENTS: - One hour sessions - 3 sessions weekly	**METHOD OF EVALUATION** - BDC production sheet

Figure 9-4
Examples of Program Area Plans

particular program. Following is a brief description of each component and of the factors involved in the determination of each.

The *materials* to be used in implementing given objectives are specified on each area plan, and the curriculum or program sequence that is to be used is clearly stated. Options must be carefully evaluated on the basis of individual needs. Some standard curricula that have been successfully implemented with individuals with autism include the Direct Instruction Program (Englemann & Bruner, 1974), the Edmark Reading Program (Edmark Associates, 1977), and the Teaching Research Curriculum (Fredericks, 1976).

Often, due to the absence of appropriate purchasable materials or the specific nature of an individual's programming needs, a task analysis or skill sequence must be generated. A task analysis is the breaking down of a task into its smallest component parts. A skill sequence is the logical arrangement of a number of related task analyses. When necessary a specific skill sequence is designated as the appropriate curriculum to follow.

The term *instructional arrangements* refers to the ratio of client(s) to staff, as well as to the type and location of instructional practice. There are a number of options regarding instructional arrangements, including one to one sessions, small group sessions of two or three clients, or larger group arrangements of more than three individuals with one treatment teacher.

One-to-one instruction is preferable when severe attentional deficits or behavioral excesses require the systematic introduction of environmental and instructional variables. Acquisition of skills previously absent from a client's repertoire frequently takes place in a one-to-one setting. Once skills are performed correctly under these circumstances, they can be transferred to and maintained in other instructional arrangements. A one-to-one arrangement is also advantageous when a program is first conducted in the natural environments, such as using banking skills in a bank rather than a classroom.

Group arrangements may be composed of other clients who have also mastered a given skill and may range from small groups to increasingly larger ones. In addition to involving greater numbers of clients, practice situations should also gradually encompass more complex situations and settings.

The *schedule* of a particular program indicates the number of times it should occur each week, as well as the length of each session. The primary criterion in determining these conditions should be the priority that program has in the total goals of the individual's personalized plan, as well as the skill level of that individual. Attentional deficits of some clients dictate the benefit of shorter, more frequent sessions, spaced throughout the day. Other clients may respond best to longer sessions of less frequency.

The *method of evaluation* indicates the way in which the objectives will be documented and evaluated. These evaluation methods may include the recording of raw data (frequency, duration, speed tests, time samples), charting, mastery tests included in standard curricula, anecodotal notes, and samples of work.

Summary

The result of the plan development process is a personalized plan that is comprised of programs from a number of curriculum areas. Throughout the process a comprehensive plan that identifies the significant needs of an individual and that provides an integrated and functional program is designed. The development of the personalized plan provides the basis for the next phase of system implementation of the goals.

IMPLEMENTATION

After assessment has been completed and the personalized plan has been written, the next phase is implementation. Implementation, or the carrying out of the specific plan, is, unfortunately, the step at which systems often break down. Clients with special needs have multiple evaluation and individual program plans over the years, but many of these programs never reach the stage where they are put to practical use. This description of the implementation phase offers suggestions to ensure that the personalized plan becomes the "working" instruction tool.

A number of system features influence the successful implementation of individual goals. These include (1) the relationship between the "planners" and the "implementors," (2) the design of the instructional environments, (3) the schedule, (4) the intervention strategies, and (5) the procedures used to integrate the system features.

Relationship Between Planners and Implementors

Where a program is carried out and the people by whom it is carried out and supervised are crucial "setting events" that influence the ability to implement any program. There are three types of arrangements available to service providers, each with some advantages.

In a *single-agency team approach,* the assessment is carried out within a single agency by a multidisciplinary treatment team, which must include the person who will be the educational or therapeutic direct-service provider (e.g., teacher/therapist). The team has continuous involvement with the client throughout the assessment, planning, implementation, and evaluation process (Groden et al., 1984). In large agencies such as a local education system, there is often a school psychologist who conducts the assessment, a prescriptive teacher who writes the individual plans, and a teacher who carries out the plans. A teacher who has no input into a plan, and may, in fact, disagree with it, may not carry it out properly. If the psychologist and prescriptive teacher have little contact with the client throughout the year, important priorities, behaviors, and instructional strategies may be missed. Therefore, in a single-agency team approach, it is critical that there be continued involvement and interaction of all the team members.

An example of a *multiagency cooperative approach* is an evaluation or diagnostic clinic that conducts the assessment and makes recommendations directly to a school or treatment center in which the client is placed. Both agencies participate in the program planning process. This can be a workable arrangement if the agencies share similar philosophies, interact regularly, and include the "implementor" in the input and planning activities.

In a *multiagency nonparticipatory approach,* an evaluation clinic writes recommendations, but has no formal arrangements with the primary service provider for the client. In this case the evaluations and recommendations often are not used for instructional purposes. This is probably the least desirable arrangement.

The authors of the Feedback Loop System suggest the use of the single-agency team approach because of its obvious advantages in providing an opportunity for a high degree of interaction among team members. Additionally the client is more accessible to all team members, which helps to establish familiarity with the client's needs and ongoing evaluation. It is also suggested that the direct service providers, the implementors, work on treatment teams that also include supervisors and specialists. This allows for a greater range of input into a client's program, and also facilitates the development of a strong support system for the staff and generalization opportunities for the clients.

Environmental Design

To implement a variety of programs with differing formats (one to one, small groups, large groups), it is important to design instructional environments that are flexible and functional with regard to the program plans. Rooms should be designed with furniture that is easily moveable and versatile. Instructional areas can be partitioned for one-to-one training, small group activities, and independent work. Inside each of these partitions, there should be shelves that contain the necessary instructional materials for the various needs of the clients. This eases the task of frequently gathering together curricula, reinforcers, data sheets, and so on. Furthermore, the instructional environment should be designed to resemble natural environmental setups, which will assist in the transition of the client's skills to those natural environments. As often as possible, instruction should actually take place in the environment in which the behavior is expected to be performed.

Scheduling Concerns

It is important to design a daily schedule that integrates each client's programs with time and staffing variables. This is often an arduous task. However, that amount of specificity (i.e., that a program is to take place for 20 minutes, five days a week, on an one-to-one basis) is necessary to ensure implementation. Furthermore, a program schedule should account for all time. In addition to instructional periods, lunch and recreational time, and arrivals and departures, all time should be utilized to implement client programs. Staff members should be responsible for specific clients at these times. There should be no "dead time" in a client's program.

Since children with special needs may have shorter attention spans or be more active, it is preferable to alternate activities. For example, sessions may last for 20 to 25 minutes, followed by five to ten minutes of physical or recreational time for the clients. This brief interval of time affords the clients a break and gives the staff the opportunity to schedule reinforcing events, record data, and prepare for the next instructional session. It is also beneficial to alternate activities such as reading with active ones such as grooming.

A schedule must remain flexible. As discussed earlier, a service setting is a dynamic system that has to accommodate staff and client absences, program changes, behavioral difficulties, parent visits, and so forth. Designing the schedule in a manner that allows this flexibility will make it easier for staff members to adjust their expectations to the realities of situations.

Intervention Strategies

It is not within the scope of this chapter to describe specific intervention procedures. For more in-depth discussion, the following books are suggested: *Teaching Developmentally Disabled Children: The Me Book* (Lovaas, 1981); *Applying Behavior Analysis Procedures with Children and Youth* (Sulzer-Azaroff & Mayer, 1977); *Teaching Makes a Difference: A Teacher's Manual* (Donnellan, 1976); and *Educating and Understanding Autistic Children* (Koegel et al., 1982). These books detail the myriad of variables one must consider when choosing instructional and intervention strategies for a particular client within a particular program.

In all cases, however, the teacher/therapist must always decide whether the target program is to be concerned with the acquisition of new skills, generalization of acquired skills, or maintenance of existing skills.

The intervention variables can be categorized in several ways to organize the instructional plan better. The authors have found the following four categories useful.

The *number of trials delivered* to the learner probably will have a direct relationship to the interaction opportunities available between the therapist and client. The lower the client–therapist ratio, the more frequently can instructional trials occur, which facilitates acquisition of new skills. The *instructional stimuli* include considerations of the setting, materials, and teacher. By keeping these variables consistent, or by varying them within a program, skills can be newly learned or generalized. The chosen *instructional techniques* (such as prompting, chaining, shaping, fading, modeling, stimulus delay, graduated guidance, massed or distributed trials) may vary according to whether one is teaching for acquisition, generalization, or maintenance. Table 9-2 summarizes some of the instructional options that are appropriate when teaching for acquisition, generalization, and maintenance. Finally, the *schedule and type of reinforcement* will be critical to learning. One must choose among a continuous, variable, or naturally occurring schedule of reinforcement, and among primary, secondary, or naturally occurring types of reinforcers. Each of these four categories intervention must be considered when planning a specific intervention strategy.

Documentation Procedures

The best-designed programs may break down at the implementation phase if they are not properly communicated to or by the direct service provider. In addition the lack of record-keeping procedures of program implementation may result in poor or inadequate decision making. Procedures are important that specify, in writing, *what* is being taught, *where* it is carried out, the *materials* needed, and *how* to teach the program. By detailing this information, more consistent implementation of a program can take place across treatment staff, and better program analysis can be conducted according to the program variables. Documentation of when, for how long, and by whom each program was carried out, and information on the client's responses during a particular session, are equally important in providing accountability. The following system is one that successfully addresses these needs.

Each client's personalized plan can be broken down into the individual program areas (e.g., peer interaction, mobility, calculator skills) that specify objectives and criteria, instructional arrangements, materials, and method of evaluation. From this information a description can be written of *how* to carry out the objectives. Figure 9-5 is an example of a completed task objective sheet. The materials and setting are identified and the instructional cues specified. These include verbal and nonverbal instructions, prompts and procedures for fading prompts, correction procedures, a reinforcement schedule, a method of recording data, and procedures for generalizing the skill. Each time a client achieves an objective, a new Task Objective Sheet must be completed that describes procedures for implementing the next objective in that program area.

Along with the Area Plan and Task Objective Sheet, a record should be kept of each time the program is implemented. Figure 9-6 shows a Skill Area Face Sheet on which are recorded the number of minutes spent each week on a program, the name of the staff member

Acquisition	Generalization	Maintenance
1) Large number of instructional trials delivered within low ratio client: therapist arrangement (one to one, two to one)	1) Spaced instructional practice delivered in low to medium ratio client: therapist arrangements (two to one, small group)	1) Naturally-occurring number of practice opportunities in incidental client: therapist interactions
2) Stimulus consistency (i.e., teacher, materials and environment)	2) Variable stimuli a) multiple teachers b) multiple materials c) multiple environments	2) Naturally-occurring stimuli (i.e. time, people, environments)
3) More prompts and shaping techniques	3) Fading of prompts and varying of instructional cues	3) Naturally-occurring instructional/environmental cues
4) Continuous schedule of reinforcement with more primary reinforcers	4) Variable schedule of reinforcement with more secondary reinforcers	4) Naturally-occurring reinforcers (internal and external)

Table 9-2
Instructional Variables in Teaching for Acquisition, Generalization and Maintenance

Child: Gerald   IEP Area: __Number Concepts (Money)__

Teacher: _____   Date Started: __3/85__   Date Completed: _____
....

Objective: __To independently add the cost of three items using a calculator and count out the__
__indicated amount using assorted coins and bills up to five dollars.__

Materials/Setting: __Money, price labels.__

Method of Recording: __Data sheet, anecdotal records__

Instructions/Cues:
Verbal: __"Gerry, please add these items on the table with your calculator."__
__"Now count out the money to pay for the item(s)."__

Non-Verbal: __Modeling__

Incorrect Response: __"No, Gerry let's try again." Begin problem again and proceed more slowly,__
__model correct response if necessary.__

Criterion Level of Acceptable Behavior: __90%__

Schedule of Reinforcement: __CRF, using praise__

Suggested Activities: __Store settings inside BDC and progressing to community settings.__
(for stimulus
variation and
generalization)

Figure 9-5
Task Objective Sheet

who carried out the program, a general rating of the client's performance, and any comment or anecdotal record about the session. When evaluating a program, one can refer to this information to determine if there are patterns of problems on particular days or with particular staff, if the program is being implemented as often as necessary, or if there are behaviors that interfere with learning.

All of this information, along with raw-data sheets, task analysis or skill sequences, and charts, can be organized in a "file box" or notebook system, where each program has its own folder or section. This system allows the teacher/therapist to have the information on hand at all times and provides easy access to the information for the fourth phase of the feedback loop, ongoing data analysis.

ONGOING DATA ANALYSIS

The aspect of the Feedback Loop System that provides a unique strength is the dynamic and continuous nature of the fourth phase, the evaluation component. Ongoing data analysis refers to the process of tracking and reviewing a client's performance in each program. This analysis is not made up of isolated events at periodic intervals, but is a continuous process that takes place daily and is tied to the instructional objectives and procedures. This allows a treatment team to make immediate decisions about a program according to data on the client's progress.

Some individual curricular programs have built-in methods of evaluation. Many standard curricula, such as DISTAR (Englemann & Bruner, 1974) include regular or intermittent mastery tests. Speed tests and time sampling of behavior and responses can be incorporated into many programs using the precision teaching strategies of Lindsley (1971) mentioned earlier. Other data analysis methods include task analysis "step" charting and various observational systems appropriate to certain programs. However, these methods are useful only when they are embedded in procedures that ensure systematic and repetitive analysis.

Analysis and Review Procedures

Each objective for a client has a specified criterion level, projected achievement date, and evaluation method. It is important to collect

Child's Name: Gerry
Program Area: Money Skills
Program Coordinator: _____

Code:
M = minutes
I = teacher's initials
R = rating 1-5; 5 high
N.O. = no opportunity
ABS = absent

WEEK OF	MONDAY M	I	R	Anecdote	TUESDAY M	I	R	Anecdote	WEDNESDAY M	I	R	Anecdote	THURSDAY M	I	R	Anecdote	FRIDAY M	I	R	Anecdote	Total M
3/29					10	JM	4+		10	JM	4+		10	JM	5						
4/19					20	JM	3+		15	JM	4+					Interfering behavior					
4/26					20	JM	5						10	JM	5						
5/4					20	GJ	4						10	JM	5						
5/10					15	JM	4+		15	JM	5+										

Figure 9-6
Skill Area Face Sheet

227

data and review each of these programs at least weekly, keeping the analysis up to date and concise. Data should also be reviewed by the entire treatment team and decisions made based on these data. Three procedures for conducting ongoing data analyses are described here.

1. *Standard Celeration Charts.* One of the most pragmatic methods of evaluating performance for a given program objective is through the use of Standard Celeration Charts. These charts, developed by Lindsley (1971), reflect five months of program movement on a daily basis, and are designed to display behavior change data proportionally rather than in absolute figures. Individual behaviors or responses can be charted according to either frequency or duration. The charts monitor not only performance (a single data point), but also changes in performance in terms of acceleration, deceleration, or maintenance of a behavior. By targeting a goal on the chart at this achievement level and projected date, programmatic decisions can be made based on the progression of the data toward that targeted goal.

Since data are charted daily or weekly, the charts should be reviewed continuously. If the performance data are not moving acceptably toward a goal, this triggers the treatment team to investigate the possible reasons for the problem. All the program data are then carefully analyzed prior to making any changes in an individual's program. It should be noted that other kinds of charts can be utilized in a similar fashion, but may not yield as much information.

2. *Summaries of weekly program review.* The program review is a method in which data are analyzed and summarized for each client on a weekly basis. Figure 9-7 is an example of a strategy for summarizing program information, which can then be communicated to the treatment team. This Weekly Program Cover Sheet has space for listing each of a client's academic, therapeutic, and behavioral programs, along with the frequency with which each program is to be implemented. At the end of each week, the teacher/therapist should complete the form, indicating how many times a program was actually carried out, reasons why programs were missed, any goals met, whether a program is progressing satisfactorily or unsatisfactorily, and general comments or concerns. This information is routed through the treatment team weekly and alerts the supervisor to any problems with scheduling or programming, and changes can be made immediately when necessary.

3. *Program analysis.* Program analysis is an ongoing observational method of analyzing both client and teacher performance within a given program area. The observer provides written and oral feedback to the teacher during or following the observation. Other teachers can also

Name: Gerry Week Of: _____

Program Coordinator: _____ Unit: _____

Program Areas	no. sche.	no. comp.	Reason Missed	IPP S/U	Goal Met	Comments
Self Control- Relax. Therapy	5x10					
Social-Sexual Development	2x30					
Store Exchange	1x30					
Riding Bus	2x30					
Food Prep.	1x30					
Table Manners	3x30					
Hygiene	5x15					
No. Concepts: Money	2x30					
No. Concepts: Calculator	3x30					
Letter Concepts Sight Vocab.	3x30					
Letter Concepts Writing	2x30					
Sp. & Lang.: Relating Events	4x20					
Physical Educ.	3x30					
Voc. Educ.: Skill Develop.	5x45					
Voc. Educ.: Work Adjustmt.	5x15					

*Chart: A = accelerated; D = decelerated; S = stable

Behaviors to Accelerate	Cht.	*Goal Met	IPP S/U	Comments	Behaviors to Decelerate	Cht.	*Goal Met	IPP S/U	Comments
Verbalizing Emotions					Tantrums				
Initiated Greetings					Non-Compliance				
Independent Work									

**Figure 9-7
Weekly Program Cover Sheet**

observe, thereby providing training opportunities for a number of people simultaneously. The program analysis is thus a training and evaluation tool whereby a supervisor or specialist observes in the instructional environment (classroom, home, community, etc.) and analyzes teacher characteristics (e.g., use of social learning principles such as prompting or reinforcement), environmental design, appropriateness of materials, intervention strategies, and also learner characteristics (e.g., motivation, interest, attention). Figure 9-8 provides a format for this kind of analysis. The program is described, the date observed indicated, a general rating given, and various recommendations made.

A follow-up date should also be noted on which observations are to be repeated to see if the program recommendations were implemented and to determine the impact of the recommendations on the individual. In this way the program analysis provides another checkpoint for analyzing data on a continuous basis and feeding back information into the system.

Considerations in Program Change

A programmatic change may be indicated in several instances. When an individual meets all projected annual objectives prior to the yearly review date, a decision must be made regarding whether to extend programming in that specific area for further skill acquisition or to focus on generalization, maintenance, and independent production of current skills. If data reflect little or no change in a program, or movement in the wrong direction, a change is also necessary. Decisions regarding programmatic changes are made by an individual's treatment team after a careful analysis of data, records, materials, and procedures. The following variables must be carefully examined when considering modification or expansion of existing programs.

1. *Schedule requirements.* The treatment team must determine whether an adequate number of sessions for instruction and practice are specified in the individual program area plan, and whether these scheduling requirements are actually being met. The number and length of sessions carried out on a day-to-day basis should correspond to the specifications in the individual area plan. If it is concluded that the scheduling requirements need to be changed, then an individual's overall program schedule must be examined to determine where the modifications can be made in terms of time requirements.

Name(s): Gerry   Program: Number Concepts-Money
Staff: Jean   Observer: _____
Rating Code: Outstanding(5) Very Good(4) Satisfactory(3) Needs Improving(2) Unsatisfactory(1)

Program Description: Gerry is working on adding three prices of different items on a calculator. He then has to count out the correct amount of money using assorted bills and coins up to five dollars.

DATE	Analysis:
4/26	Jean, you're doing a nice job of reinforcing Gerry following each time he correctly enters a price into the calculator. Begin fading the prompt of color-coding the addition key on the calculator and have Gerry verbalize each step as he carries it out. Gerry seems to be randomly counting out the coins, causing him some confusion. Spend an additional five minutes each instructional period having him practice identifying larger and smaller denominations and counting out various amounts always beginning with the largest denomination indicated. Keep up the good work; he's on target for his goal.

5
4
3
2
1

DATE	Analysis:

5
4
3
2
1

DATE	Analysis:

5
4
3
2
1

**Figure 9-8
Program Analysis**

2. *Program consistency.* A second variable that the treatment team must consider is whether the specified procedures and consequences are being consistently administered. A primary reason for delineating implementation procedures so clearly is to facilitate replicability across sessions and across personnel. Structured and consistent interventions are essential to learning and behavior change. If a program is not being carried out consistently, the Task Objective Sheet may need to be reevaluated for clarity.

3. *Interfering behaviors.* At times inappropriate and problem behaviors are clearly the inhibiting elements when a program is not moving in the desired direction. This may indicate the need for structuring the environment somewhat differently, for modifying existing behavior management programs, or for developing new behavior management programs for specific problem behaviors.

4. *Instructional strategies.* If procedures are being carried out consistently as described, it may be that the strategies need to be modified. Methodologies and instructional procedures that should be examined include the clarity of directions, the client–teacher ratio, needed cues and prompts, the arrangement of materials and their presentation, the structuring of the environment, the manipulation of consequences and antecedents, and the schedule of reinforcement (continuous, intermittent, ratio, interval, etc.).

5. *Program content.* One of the most important variables that must be analyzed is the appropriateness of the program content itself. When an individual is not progressing in a skill, reevaluation may be necessary. Content modifications may involve a change in curriculum materials, a finer breakdown of task analysis steps, or a reevaluation of priority objectives.

6. *Variety of program options.*

Both staff and clients must be aware of, and have reasonable access to, alternatives and real choices in program options. For example, when a change or expansion is required in vocational services, options at the center in which this model was developed and is operative include:

- *Community job sites.* The vocational program provides both center-based and community-based instruction. The center-based component includes assessment activities, sub-contracted factory work, and preplacement skill acquisition to prepare clients for specific jobs in community work sites (Paine, Bellamy, & Wilcox (Eds.), 1984). Community-based work sites include a number of departments at local hospitals, hotels, and restaurants. In the

various sites, clients are introduced to jobs such as indoor and outdoor maintenance, clerical and office skills, laundry services, food services, materials handling, child care, and patient transportation.
- *Supervised training and supported employment.* Following thorough evaluation and preparation, clients begin working at a job site which is carefully selected, based upon client aptitude and interest, and specific job characteristics (Wehman, 1981). The center's community-based vocational training programs include volunteer work experiences as well as paid employment. The work schedule and the level of continued supervision are determined on an individual basis. In establishing paying job positions, center personnel work with potential employers to ensure that the employer benefits from available tax credits and reimbursement.
- *Work Adjustment.* Throughout all vocational programs there is a strong emphasis on work adjustment skills (Lynch, Kiernan, & Stark (Eds.), 1982). "Work adjustment" refers to program areas such as general job behaviors (rate, independence, interview skills); socialization (self-control, interaction skills); functional letter concepts (recognition of essential vocabulary, completion of application forms); functional number concepts (adherence to work schedule, use of money with vending machines); communication (social greetings, ability to communicate needs); and independent living skills (personal appearance and grooming, use of public transportation).

An individual's revised program should include an opportunity to sample and perhaps combine creatively from such a rich range of choices. In our experience the more opportunity both staff and clients have to actively participate in real program choices, the more functional, creative, and effective are the programs they generate and implement.

Summary of Ongoing Data Analysis

The significance of the data analysis component of the Feedback Loop System is that program modifications can be made immediately, as soon as the need is indicated. The data are collected and analyzed in accordance with the clients' objectives and provide information for making program decisions. Through the constant examination of programs, data, instructional strategies, and behavioral interventions, it is possible to monitor the appropriateness and effectiveness of programs on a continual basis and to provide a high quality personalized plan more efficiently.

CHAPTER SUMMARY

In review, the systems and procedures of the Feedback Loop System facilitate the appropriate assessment, planning, implementation, and evaluation of each individual's personalized plan. The Feedback Loop System is an organizational behavioral management approach that may be applicable in a number of human-service programs. It is sensitive to the multiple needs of clients and their families, and at the same time it integrates the diverse features of a complex service system. The value of the system lies in its adaptability, accountability, and organizational structure.

This approach to functional programming ensures that what is written as the personalized plan for each client is in fact carried out and continuously monitored to allow each client to develop and reach his maximum potential. The Feedback Loop System provides a means to design and implement programs within the context of the Spectrum model. Together they provide the unique integrated structure that ultimately strengthens comprehensive educational and clinical programming.

REFERENCES

American Guidance Service (1976). *Key Math Diagnostic Arithmetic Test.* Circle Pines, Minn.
American Guidance Service (1976). *Peabody Individual Achievement Test.* Circle Pines, Minn.
American Guidance Service (1970). *Woodcock Reading Mastery Test.* Circle Pines, Minn.
Baumgart, D., Brown, L., Pumpian, I., Nisbet, J., Ford, A., Sweet, M., Messine, R. & Schroeder, J. (1982). Principle of partial participation and individual adaptations in educational programs for severely handicapped students. *Journal of the Association for Severely Handicapped,* 1, 17–27.
Brigance, A. (1978). *Brigance diagnostic inventories.* Billerica, Mass: Curriculum Associates.

Brown, L., Nietupski, J. & Hamre-Nietupski, S. (1976). Criterion of ultimate functioning. In M.A. Thomas (ed.) *Hey, don't forget me!* Reston, VA: C.E.C. pp. 2–15.
Campbell, R. F., Bridges, E. M. & Nystrand, R. O. (1977). *Introduction to educational administration.* (5th ed.). Boston: Allyn & Bacon, pp. 210–231.
Christian, W. P., Hannan, G. T.; & Glahn, T. J. (Eds.) (1984). *Programming effective human services.* New York; Plenum Press
Churchman, C. W. (1968). *The systems approach.* New York: Dell.
Donnellan, A. (1976). *Teaching makes a difference: A teacher's manual.* Santa Barbara, Calif.: Santa Barbara County Autism Program.
Edmark Associates (1977). *The Edmark reading program.* Bellevue, Wash.
Englemann, S. & Bruner, E. (1974). *The DISTAR reading series.* Chicago: Science Research Associates.
Foster, R.W. (1978). *The use of systems technology in developing education and therapy systems.* Manuscript copyright, Ray W. Foster.
Fredericks, H. D. (1976). *The teaching research curriculum for moderately and severely handicapped.* Springfield, Ill.: Charles C. Thomas.
Frederiksen, L. W. (Ed.) (1982). *Handbook of organizational behavioral management.* New York: John Wiley and sons.
Goldstein, H. (1972). Construction of a social learning curriculum. In E. L. Meyen, G. A. Vergason, and R. J. Whelan (Eds.), *Strategies for teaching exceptional children.* Denver, Colo.: Love Publishing, pp. 94–114.
Groden, J., Groden, G., Baron, G. & Stevenson, S. E. (1984). Day treatment services for children with severe behavior disorders. In W. P. Christian, G. T. Hannah, & T. J. Glahn, (Eds.) *Programming effective human services: Strategies for institutional change and client transition.* New York: Plenum Press.
Koegel, R. L., Rincover, A. & Egel, A. L. (1982). *Educating and understanding autistic children.* San Diego, Calif.: College Hill.
Liao, T. T. & Miller, D. C. (Eds.) (1977). *Systems approach to instructional design.* Technology of Learning Systems Series. New York: Baywood Publishing Company.
Lindsley, O. R. (1971). Precision teaching in perspective: An interview with Ogden R. Lindsley. *Teaching Exceptional Children,* 3, 114–119.
Lovaas, O. I. (1981). *Teaching developmentally disabled children: The me book.* Baltimore: University Park Press.
Lynch, K. P., Kiernan, W. E. & Stard, K. A. (Eds.) 1982. *Prevocational and vocational education for special needs youth. A blueprint for the 1980s.* Baltimore: Paul H. Brookes Publishers.
Meals, D. W. (1977). A process approach to educational systems design. In T. T. Liao, and D. C. Miller, (Eds.) *Systems approach to instructional design.* Technology of learning systems series. New York: Baywood Publishing Company.
Nirje, B. (1969). The normalization principle and its human management implications. In R. Koegel and W. Wolfensberger (Eds.), *Changing patterns in residential services for the mentally retarded.* Washington: President's Committee on Mental Retardation, pp. 179–195 (B).
Paine, S. C., Bellamy, G. T. & Wilcox, B. (Eds.) (1984). *Human services that work. From innovation to standard practice.* Baltimore: Paul H. Brookes Publishers.
Ragland, E., Kerr, M. & Strain, P. (1978). Behavior of withdrawn children, effects of peer social initiations. *Behavior Modification,* 2, pp. 565–578.

Sulzer-Azaroff, B. & Mayer, G.R. (1977). *Applying behavior-analysis procedures with children and youth.* New York: Holt, Rinehart and Winston.

Slosson Educational Publications, Inc. (1963). *Slosson Oral Reading Test.* East Aurora, N.Y.

Thompson, R. Paul. (1980). "Afterword" in critical issues in educating autistic children and youth. In B. Wilcox, and A. Thompson, (Eds.) *U.S. Department of Education,* 336–340.

Wehman, P. (1981). *Competitive employment. New horizons for severely disabled individuals.* Baltimore: Paul H. Brookes Publishers.

White, G.D. (1977). The effects of observer presence on the activity level of families. *Journal of Applied Behavior Analysis, 10,* 734.

Zuckerman, R.A. (1978). A comprehensive curriculum model for the education of moderately, severely, and profoundly handicapped persons. Unpublished manuscript: Kent State University.

Zais, R.S. (1976). *Curriculum principles and foundations.* New York: Harper and Row Publishers, Inc.

INDEX

Adaptation,
   to physical limitations/disease, 27, 43
"adult model of language", 102
Affective contact, 4, 5–6
Age-equivalents (mental ages/test ages), 84, 85, 87
Age-limited services, 8–9
American Psychiatric Association (APA), 4
   Diagnostic and statistical manual of mental disorders, 4
Anoxia,
   as cause of retardation, 22
   and development of autism, 137
Antecedent events (see also Consequent events), 29–32
Anticonvulsive therapy, 142, 145
Anxiety, 25, 90
   -eliciting events, 25
   verification, 25
Aphasia, 81
Assessment, 22–48, 206–210
   behavioral approach, 23–48, 208
   criterion-referenced measures, 105, 209
   by etiology, 22
   functional, 206–207
   of imagery, 64
   initial, 208–209
   interviews and family systems analysis, 210
   procedures, 22, 117–118
   reassessment, 210
   screening, 208
   standardized tests, 209
   by symptomology/classification, 22–23
   of teacher characteristics, 183
   traditional, 206–207
Attention, 5–6
   span, 3, 221–222
Attentional difficulties, 16
Autism,
   and behavior therapy, 6–9
   birth trauma and, 137
   definition of, 3–4, 100
   as developmental problem, 2, 4
   etiology, 2–3, 4–6, 136, 139
   genetic factors, 136
   multiaxial approach to classification, 3
   neurological basis for, 5
   as organic dysfunction, 160
   rubella and, 136
   symptoms of, 3
   vaginal bleeding during pregnancy and, 136–137
Aversive procedures, 55–56
Avoidance,
   and punishment, 61–62
Awareness,
   parental, 153
Aylon, T., 154

Baer, D. M., 7, 53
Bailey, J. S., 160
Bartak, L., 81
Baseline assessment/present performance level, 29–32
   duration, 29, 30
   frequency, 29.
   intensity, 29, 30
   latency, 29,
Bashir, A. S., 106, 118
Bayley Scales of Infant Development,

84, 85, 86–87
Bean, A. W., 156
Behavior,
  abnormal/maladaptive, 6
  aggressive, 23
  compulsive, 3, 4
  covert, 25
  deceleration, 56
  language, 106
  life-threatening, 28
  negative, 91, 144
  non-psychotic, 5–6
  normal/adaptive, 6
  ritualistic, 3, 4, 76
Behavior modification, 153
  and the natural environment, 153
behavior therapy/behavior modification, 6–8
Behavioral assessment procedures, 15–16, 23–48
  assessment and intervention, 24
Behavioral domains,
  establishing priorities among, 28–29
  performance level in, 29
Behavioral evaluation, 15, 24–48
  format, 24–25, 40
Behavioral observation, 32–34, 109–110
  frequency measures, 33–34
  in functioning environments, 52, 109
  interval recordings, 33, 34
  response rate, 33
Behavioral patterns,
  determining strength of, 24
  repetitive, 27, 44–45
Behavioral programming, 16, 50–53
  choice of intervention, 53–58
Behavioral response,
  range of, 25
Behavioral syndrome,
  autism as, 3–4
Berlin, I., 138
Bettelheim, B., 5, 160
Birth trauma,
  and development of autism, 137
Blass, J., 143
Bleuler, E., 3
Bloom, L., 101, 102, 116
Brain-damaged,
  children labelled as, 23,
Breger, L., 79

Brigance Diagnostic Inventories, 209
Britten, K., 161
Brown, L., 213
Brown's rules, 116

Campbell, A., 144, 145
Carr, E., 56, 57
Casey, L., 160
Categorization,
  as classification system, 22
Cathect, 5
Cautela, J., ix, 57, 59, 64, 170
"cherchez la mère", 5
Childhood psychopathology, 2
Childhood psychosis, 2, 77
Client participation, 10
"clinical creativity", 48
Cognitive ability,
  on global measure, 77
Cognitive deficits, 79–82
  inability to extract similarities or rules, 79, 80, 82
  inability to generalize/discriminate, 79–82
  language deviance and delay, 80–81
  stimulus overselectivity, 81
Cognitive functioning, 16, 24, 79
Coleman, M., 143
Communication (see also Language, Interaction)
  as appropriate behavior, 56
  cognitive deficits in autism, 80–81
  in daily routines, 128
  and imagery procedures, 67
  methods of, 44
  nonverbal, 118
  in play, 124–128
  therapy, 15
Communication disorder, 100–107, 160
  as inherent to definition of autism, 100
Competency Area Plan (CAP), 194, 198–199
Condon, W., 101
"conference chart", 122–124
Consequent events (see also Antecedent events), 6, 29–32
  aversive/punishing events, 31–32
  extinguishing/neutral events, 31–32
  negative reinforcement, 31
  positive reinforcement, 31

Index

Contracting, 44
Core competencies, 188
Covert conditioning, imagery-based, 10, 16, 62–70, 169–170
  or imaginal procedures, 7
  procedures, 62–64
  and "trainable retarded" students, 64–67
Covert modeling, 63, 64, 65–67
Covert negative reinforcement, 63
Covert reinforcement, 63, 64, 65–67, 68
Covert response cost, 63
Covert sensitization, 63, 68
Curriculum domains, 27–28, 29, 42–47
  idiosyncratic problem behaviors, 27, 44–47
  independent living skills, 27, 42–43
  social interaction, 27, 43–44
Cutler, B., 162, 171

Darley, F., 117
Data analysis,
  ongoing, 15, 226–234
Data collection, 35–36, 105, 122–124
Day-to-day functioning, 8
  use of imagery abilities, 67
DeMyer, M., 6–7, 50, 77, 94
Desensitization, 90–91, 146
  and relaxation therapy, 61
Developmental-ecological-behavioral model (DEB), 100, 106–107
Developmental Science Analysis, 116
Developmental Test of Visual-Motor Integration, 89
Direct Instruction Program, 218
Directed readings, 122
DISTAR curriculum, 226
Documentation procedures, 223–226
Donnellan, A., ix, 4, 9, 51, 56, 58, 162
Drucker, W., 66
Drug treatments, 144–145

Early Intervention Program, 14
Echolalia, 3, 94, 139
Edmark Reading Program, 218
Eisenberg, L., 3, 4
Electroencephalogram (EEG), 142–143, 145
Emerick L., 105
Environment,
  altering variables, 57
  and assessment, 208–209
  and behavioral differences, 30
  design, 221
  educational, 35
  and language use, 101–102, 121
Events
  antecedent, 29–32
  aversive, 31–32, 41–42
  consequent, 29–32
  extinguishing, 31–32
  reinforcing, 41
Extinction, 7, 32, 51, 52, 154
Eyeburg, S., 159

Family competence, 164
  day program participation, 168
  home/community programs, 165–167
  individual and family counseling, 168–170
  introductory workshops, 163–165
  maximizing, 162
  model, 162–171
  parent-family library, 170–171
  respite, 170
  sibling programs, 167–168
Family factors, 4
  dysfunction, 9
Family history, 136–137
Family services, 15, 171
Fear, 22
Feedback Loop System (FLS), 204, 205–234
  assessment phase, 205–210
  documentation procedures, 223–226
  environmental design, 221
  implementation, 219
  intervention strategies, 222–223
  ongoing data analysis, 226–234
  plan development, 211–219
  program analysis, 230
  program change, 230–233
  scheduling concerns, 221–222
Fein, D., 80
Fenfluramine,
  effect on children with autism, 14, 144–145
Ferster, C. B., 6–7, 50, 160
Field/service setting, 181, 182–183, 198
Fish, B., 145
Fluency problems, 117, 118
Folstein, S., 136

Forehand, R., 156, 158
Foxx, R. M., 183
Fragile X chromosome,
  role in autism, 14
  and infantile autism, 143
Freeman, B., 77
French Pictorial Test of Intelligence, 89
Functional Imagery Checklist, 64, 67

Generalization of treatment effects, 53, 58
Goldman-Fristoe Articulation Test, 117
Goldstein, S., 160
Goodenough-Harris Drawing Test, 89
Gottesman, I., 136
Groden Center, vii, viii, ix, 13–15, 64

Hand movements,
  stereotypic, 22
Hansen, D., 158
Hanson, D., 136
Harris, D., 160, 170
Hatten, J., 105
Head Start program/Department of Education, 13
Hearing problems, 118
Helm, D., 161
Helmsley, R., 161
Hermelin, B., 79, 95
Hiskey-Nebraska Test of Learning Aptitude, 89
Home environment, 152–153
  assessment in, 16
Home visit, 36–37, 165, 166
  team approach, 37
Hudson, A. M. 155
Hutt, C., 142
Hyperactive, 24

Idiosyncratic problem behaviors, 44–47
  sexual touching of others, 46
Illinois Test of Psycholinguistic Abilities, 89
Imagery-based operant procedures, 62
  and special-needs children, 63
  as standard intervention strategy, 63
Imagery skills development, 69
Independent living skills, 6
"Indiscriminable contingencies", 53
Individual Education Plan (IEP), 188–204
Individual Program Plan (IPP), 37, 47, 120–121, 205

instructional arrangements, 218
method of evaluation, 219
program materials, 218–223
schedule, 218–219
Individualized program,
  evaluation, 94–95
  planning, 9–10, 93–95
  vocational planning, 94
"infantile autism", 2, 136
  genetic factors and, 136, 143
Information gathering, 24
Ingram, D.,
  methods for analyzing phonological processes, 117
Intellectual assessment, 15, 16, 83–91
  as basis for discussion with parents, 92–93
  results of, 91–95
  tests/instruments, 84–91
Intellectual deficits, 76
Intellectual functioning, 16, 76–79
  level of, 76–77
  pattern of, 77–79
  variability of, 85
Interaction (see also Communication, Language)
  with family, 40
  methods of, 27
  parent, 157
  parent-child, 36–37, 157
  pattern of, 24
  with peers, 44, 66
  process of, 7
  sibling, 36–37, 53
  social, 27
  tactile, 37
  variable styles of, 184
Interpretation of events, 164, 169
Intervention, 37
  and assessment, 24
  behavior therapy as, 7
  models, 10–13
  procedures, 9
  strategies, 222–223
  surgical, 22
Interventions, behavioral, 50–58
  choice of, 53–58
  positive, 55–56
  repertoire of, 53–58
Intervention strategies, 23, 222–223
  imagery based procedures, 63
  positive, 61
IQ measures, 83, 87, 88, 94

Index

as predictors, 77
of "psychotic children", 77

Johns Hopkins University, 2
Johnson, S., 159, 160

Kanner, L., 2–3, 4–5, 80, 160
Kaufman, K., 155, 158, 161
Kearney, A., 170
Key Math Diagnostic Arithmetic Test, 209
Klebanoff, L., 152
Koegel, R., 82, 155, 164
Kolvin, I., 142
Kozloff, M., 161, 162

Labels, 22–23, 24
  diagnostic, 101
  indiscriminate use of, 23
  pessimistic, 26
  as self-description, 23
  used for secondary gain, 23
Lahey, M., 101, 102, 116
Language comprehension, 114–115
Language development/learning, 100, 107, 139
  cognitive basis for learning, 101–102
  through play, 124–128
  use of language in, 101–102, 116–118
Language disorders/impairment, 100–120
  diagnosis, 101–102
  evaluating, 107–120
Language facilitators, 104, 116, 122
Language samples, 105
  spontaneous, 116
Language therapy, 100–107, 120–124, 129
  assessment of, 100
  clinician as "third party", 103–104, 121, 129
  therapy strategies, 100, 103–104, 106–107
Lanyon, R., 160
LaVigna, G., ix, 51
Learning,
  of behaviors, 6
  imagery as central mediating role in, 69
  incidental, 9
  laboratory-based psychological studies, 6
  molar or molecular, 31
  systematic, 6–7
Lee, L., 116
Leiter International Performance Scale, 78, 87–88
  Arthur adaptation, 110
Liberman, R., 154, 155–156, 158
Liebergott, J., 110
Lindsley, O. 155, 226, 228
Lockyer, L., 3, 77
Lovaas, O., 5, 7, 50, 57, 77, 81–82, 161, 164
Lowe, T., 143

Marcus, L., 161
McCarthy Scales of Children's Abilities, 85, 86, 88
  General Cognitive Index (GCI), 88
McMahon, R., 155
Meals, D., 205
Mean length of utterance (MLU), 116
"mediating generalization", 53
Medical evaluation, 15, 16, 146–147
Medical history, 136–138
  early development, 138–139
  family, 136
  gestation, 136, 137
  neonatal period, 137–138
  perinatal period, 137
  preconception, 136
Mental retardation,
  autism as distinguished from, 78–79
  due to anoxia, 22
Michael, J., 154
Milan, M., 159
Milch, R., 160
Mira, M., 156, 159
Mirenda, P., 162
Mobility training, 42
Modeling, 43
  negative, 62
Moore, B., 160
Motor control,
  poor, 22
Motor development, 138, 141
Motor feedback, 142
Muir, K., 159
Muscle tension, 59–60

National Institute of Neurological Diseases and Stroke Collaborative Perinatal Study, 136–137

Index

National Society for Children and Adults with Autism, 3
"natural maintaining contingencies", 53
Neurochemistry, 143
Newsom, C., 146
Nordquist, V., 160

O'Connor, N., 79, 95
O'Dell, S., 153, 155, 156, 158
Olley, J. Gregory, ix
On-site employment, 15
Operant learning/operant conditioning, 6, 7–8, 50
 methods, 7, 52, 62
 techniques and hospitalized psychotic adults, 6
Ornitz, E., 3, 4, 142
Orthogenic School, 5

Parent cooperation, 159, 162
Parent interaction, 156
Parent training, 152, 153–161
 behavioral, 153–154
 general behavioral principles, 155
 individual versus group format, 156–157
 manipulation of reinforcement contingencies, 154
 problem-solving strategies, 156
 reflective, 153
 self-management procedures, 156
 setting for, 157
 techniques, 158
Parental/family involvement, 16, 152, 164
 effectiveness of, 154
 as preventive aspect, 152
Parental psychopathology, 5
 as root of child's autism, 152
Parental tension, 90
Parenting Self-Efficacy Scale, 159
Patterson, G., 155, 156, 157, 158, 159
Pavlov, I., 6, 7
Peabody Individual Achievement Test (PIAT), 209
Peabody Picture Vocabulary Test-Revised (PPVT-R), 89, 114–115
Pediatric evaluation, 139–141
 anthropometric data, 140
 detecting self-abusive behavior, 141
 neurologic examination 141–142
Perceptual disturbances, 3
Personalization, 52–53

Personnel Instruction Program (PIP), 187–191, 199–200
 application of, 191–199
 Staff Orientation Sequence (SOS), 191–198
Personnel preparation, 16, 180, 198–200
 ecological perspective, 186
 identification of training targets, 186
 model, 181–187
 program, 181
Phonemes, 117
Piaget, J., 110
Plan development (see also Individualized Program Plan), 211, 215–219
 content, 232
 process, 232
Play,
 environments, 125
 exploratory, 124, 128
 functional, 124, 128
 language in, 124–128
 practice, 124, 128
 symbolic/pretend, 124–125, 128
Play progress charts, 124–128
Potentiating variables, 30
Precision, 52
"precision teaching" model, 209–210
Preoperational processes, 110, 111–112, 114–115
 attending, 111, 114
 classification, 111–112, 115
 numeration, 113, 115
 representational skills, 111, 114
 seriation, 112, 115
Prescriptive programming, 69
Prizang, T., 57
Problem definition, 24–25
 operational, 25
Progressive relaxation, 7
Pronomial reversal, 3
Public Law 94:142, 12
Pueschel, S., 143
Punishment, 7, 51, 52, 61–62
 and deprivation, 155–156
 as treatment of choice, 155–156

Ragland, E., 208–209
Rapid eye movement (REM), 142
Real-life, full service approach, vii, 8–9, 54
 circumstances, 69, 125

continuum of services, 13
environments/settings, 10
Reassessment, 210
Reese, E., ix, 34
Reevaluation, 120–121
Reinforcement, 28, 37, 156
  clinician as source of, 51
  concrete, 60
  contingencies, 28, 37, 156
  effectiveness of, 30
  evaluator as source of, 34–35
  positive, 7, 31, 35, 51, 52, 60, 156
  negative, 7, 31, 51, 52
  social, 60, 90
Relaxation response, 59–62
Relaxation training, 10, 16, 42–43, 47, 59–62, 69–70, 169–170
  procedures, 91, 164
  as treatment goal, 25–26
Remedial programs, 91
Rendle-Short, J., 3
repertoire, behavioral, 35, 52, 67
  expanded, 58–70
  and imaging behavior, 63–64
  maintaining desired behavior in, 56
  maximizing flexibility of 28
Repetitive movements, 3–4, 44–45
Respite program, 14, 170
Respondent learning principles, 7
Responsiveness,
  hyper-, 3
  hypo-, 3
  pathological, 4
Reynolds, B., 82
Ricks, D., 80
Rimland, B., 5, 79
Ritvo, E. R., 3, 4, 136
Roberts, M., 156
Rote memory, 2, 4, 78, 79–80, 88
Rutter, M., 2–3, 4, 77, 136

Sameness,
  preservation of, 3–5
Sattler, J., 86
Schizophrenia,
  childhood, 2–3
  adult, 3
Schreibman, L., 82, 161
Self-abusive activities, 28, 141
Self-awareness, 40
Self-care, 42
Self-control, 6, 16, 42–43, 53, 57–58
  ability, 27
  procedures, 58–70, 164
  therapies, 7, 10
Self-controlling response, 59, 68
Self-destructive behaviors, 5
Self-efficacy, 159
Self-injury, 3
Self-injurious behavior, 4, 59, 67
Self-instruction, 58–59
Self-monitoring, 58
Self-regulation, 58
Self-reinforcement, 59
Semantic/syntactic analysis, 116
Sensorimotor processes, 110–111, 112–113
  attending, 111, 112
  imitation processes, 111, 112–113
  means-ends relationships, 111, 113
  object permanence, 111, 113, 119
Sensory-motor behavior, 142
"sequential modification", 53
Services provision, 10–15
  education model, 11–12
  medical model, 11–12
  national model, 11–12
  whole-child model, 11, 12–13
"setting events", 220–221
  multiagency cooperative approach, 220
  multiagency nonparticipatory approach, 220
  single-agency team approach, 220, 221
Shane, H., 106, 118
Shaping, 7, 53,
  and fading, 51, 60
Sherman, J., 7
Simon, S., 146, 160
Sindelar, P., 83
Singer, J., 164
Skills,
  age-appropriate, 54
  functional, 54
  job-related, 27
  leisure, 44
  readiness, 60
  recreation and play, 27
  self-care, 27, 42
  sequencing, 27
  verbal, 44
Skinner, B. F., 6
Slosson Oral Reading Test, 209
Social stimulus values, 27, 28, 43, 184

Special Needs Reinforcement Survey, 41
Spectrum model, 211–215
   as framework for personalized plan, 213
   functionality, 212, 213–214
   integration, 215
   normalization, 212, 214
   partial participation, 214–215
   prioritization, 213
Speech, delayed, 22
Speech-language problem, 100
   determining extent of, 107
Spreistersback, D., 117
Staff Orientation Sequence (SOS), 191–192
Standard Celeration Charts, 228
Stanford-Binet Intelligence Scale, 77, 84, 85–86, 87, 89
Stimuli,
   discriminative, 29–30
   facilitating, 30–31
   instructional, 29
Stimulus overselectivity, 81–82
Stokes, T., 53
Structured environments, 6, 37, 109
   for play, 125
   treatment center as, 24, 34–37
Sulzer-Azaroff, B., ix, 34
Swope, S., 110
Systematic desensitization, 7, 22
Systems, theory and analysis, 408
Szurek, I., 138

Tantrums, 68–69, 155
   as idiosyncratic Problem behavior, 27, 46–47
   provoking of, 30
Task Objective Sheet, 223, 232
Teaching for performance, 181, 187, 199
Teaching Research Curriculum, 218
Teaching Research Infant and Child Curriculum, 209
Team performance, 182
Test of Auditory Comprehension of Language, 115
Tharp, R., 165
Therapy model, 26
Thompson, R., 204
Thought stopping, 7
Torrey, E., 137
"train and hope" method, 53

"training sufficient exemplars", 53
Treatment, 25–28
   child's role as passive in, 9–10
   environment changes, 56–57
   integrated behavioral, 28
   realistic, 26
Treatment goals,
   establishment of 25–28
   relevance, 27–28
   specificity, 26
   workability, 26
Tunnel vision, 82
Tymchuk, A., 152, 170

University of California, Los Angeles, Neuropsychiatric Institute, 14
"untestable", 83, 86
Uzgriz, I., 110

Valett, R., 86
Vestibular dysfunction, 142
Vineland Social Maturity Scale, 84
Violent/destructive behaviors, 27, 28, 45–46
Visuo-spatial understanding, 78, 85
Vitamin/metabolic therapies, 145–146
Vocational programs, 26, 232–233
Vocational services, 15

Wahler, R., 159, 160
Watson, J., 6
Weathers, 154, 155–156, 158
Webster-Stratton, C., 158
Wechsler Intelligence Scale for Children-Revised (WISC-R), 77, 78, 84, 86, 88–89, 110
Wechsler Preschool and Primary Scale of Intelligence (WPPSI), 84, 110
Weekly Program Cover Sheet, 228
Wetzel, R., 160, 165
White, O., 209
"Whole Child" model, 37
Wildman, R., 160
Wilhelm, H., 82
Williams, C., 154
Wing, L., 79, 80
Withdrawal,
   into fantasy, 3
Wolf, M. M., 7, 161
Wolpe, J., 7
Woodcock Reading Mastery Test, 209

Zigler, E., 13